HOW TO FIND OUT IN HISTORY

HOW TO FIND OUT IN HISTORY

by

PHILIP HEPWORTH, M.A., F.L.A.

A Guide to Sources of Information for All

PERGAMON PRESS

OXFORD · LONDON · EDINBURGH · NEW YORK
TORONTO · PARIS · BRAUNSCHWEIG

Pergamon Press Ltd., Headington Hill Hall, Oxford
4 & 5 Fitzroy Square, London W.1
Pergamon Press (Scotland) Ltd., 2 & 3 Teviot Place, Edinburgh 1
Pergamon Press Inc., 44–01 21st Street, Long Island City, New York 11101
Pergamon of Canada, Ltd., 6 Adelaide Street East, Toronto, Ontario
Pergamon Press S.A.R.L., 24 rue des Ecoles, Paris 5e
Friedr. Vieweg & Sohn Verlag, Postfach 185, 33 Braunschweig, West
Germany

Printed in Great Britain by Billing & Sons Limited, Guildford and London

JOHN LESLIE HOBBS 1916–1964

*who spent his life
furthering local history in libraries*

Contents

List of Illustrations

Specimen Entries from Important Sources of Information reproduced by kind permission of the publishers and authors named. (All these works are fully described, dated and evaluated in the text.)

Preface

THIS book aims at describing sources of information on history and its allied subject biography, and methods of approach to them. It is designed to meet the needs of students at schools, colleges and universities, apprentices seeking historical background to their callings, and, in particular, staff employed or considering employment in bookshops and libraries, as well as the general public interested in the history of all ages.

Those who use this book would be well advised to read first the key volume in the Libraries and Technical Information Division of the Commonwealth and International Library of which it forms a unit, Dr. G. Chandler's *How to Find Out* (Pergamon Press, 1963). A valuable feature of all the books in this series, unique to books at present in print, is the large number of reproductions of sample pages from works referred to, this being designed especially to help those without continuous access to large libraries or bookshops. Permission to include so many reproductions from other books is gratefully acknowledged to all the publishers concerned, but the reproductions should not be used invariably as substitutes for the complete books. If possible, readers are advised to make a series of expeditions to the nearest large town, armed with this book, to handle at least some of the originals. By this means they should find it possible to distinguish, perhaps for life, the typography, abbreviations, inclusiveness, editorial additions and binding styles of seemingly similar works, and attach an individuality to what would otherwise be a mere list of names of reference books. Wherever possible, publisher and place of publication have been given for all books noted, but "London" is to be understood where no place is given.

I am greatly indebted to two of my colleagues, Elisabeth Kilby, A.L.A., for much help and criticism, and Georgina Yallop for retyping a most difficult manuscript.

CHAPTER 1

General Considerations

INTRODUCTION

Every department of knowledge has its own history. This book deals mainly with history in its own right, ignoring for the most part the histories of philosophy, religion, language, literature, technology and the rest, which form part of the detailed study of those sciences. It would be logical to go straight on to consider those learned and detailed books which tell you what to read next—logical but perhaps unrewarding. You will be a better student of history if you can decide before commencing to read why it is you want to find out about history, and indeed conjure up not merely a wish but an impelling urge to do so. Perhaps the choice is not really your own—you find yourself enjoying higher education and choose to concentrate on history, a pleasant humane subject, because you have no stronger bent. Possibly history is only one of several subjects you require to study for an examination, general (G.C.E., degree) or vocational (law, librarianship).

Goethe declared that you cannot understand history without having lived through it yourself—a difficult attainment. Man's primal need for history is proved by the memorials and traditions that even the newest nationalities quickly create. Monuments a mere century old are in the New World accorded the adulation of an Indian Taj Mahal or a British Norman cathedral; even the modern inheritors of the age-old Pharaonic civilization of Egypt did not hesitate to set up a military museum to celebrate their first achievement of modern nationalism in 1956. Let us examine the Suez crisis a little closer in the light of certain great men's

1

reflections on history. The British anti-nationalistic contemporary view might well have reflected Voltaire, "the history of the great events of this world is little more than the history of crimes", or Charles Kingsley, "history is a pack of lies"; but once more, as after the great world wars of this century, the Emersonian view is beginning to prevail, "the first lesson of history is the good of evil" for "our ignorance of history makes us libel our own times. People have always been like this" (Flaubert). "That certain kings reigned and certain battles were fought we can depend upon as true, but all the colouring, all the philosophy of history is conjecture" (Dr. Johnson).

If history is not bunk, as Henry Ford held, neither is it fact—"it would be an excellent thing if only it were true" (Tolstoy). It represents a mellowing and sifting of evidence, "philosophy teaching by examples" (Bolinbroke); sometimes, if evidence be lacking, it can be no more than a "distillation of rumour" (Carlyle). As men not animals nor generally earth movements have shaped history, we may properly separate it from prehistory at the date of the emergence of mankind; "there is properly no history only biography" (Emerson). To us, of course, as we go about our daily lives, history is the changing landscape and buildings we see around us; the background to the recorded happenings in our newspapers. You have only to pick up any newspaper or journal to be convinced of the pervasive force of history. "We regret to record the death of John Smith"—the news is not here but in the next historical statement—"the celebrated banker who reformed the currency of the Lebanon." "Coal exchange pulled down", "pit to close", "Lord Samuel ill", "cathedral consecrated". What value have these statements without accompanying comment on the spread of new buildings in the City of London, the decline in coal-mining, a retrospect of former parliaments, an account of diocesan organization, all predominantly historical?

Closer to us even than the record in our daily newspaper is our own local history—our firm, school, college, or church, our town or family. Much has been written recently on local history—introductory books on this and on the study of general history are listed below. One final word of warning. Many of the guides with which this book is mainly concerned do not assess quality, for that is a matter of opinion. Others do. Many, however, record the minutiae by which quality may be evaluated—footnotes, indexes, bibliographies, references to sources, historical introductions. In describing individual titles we shall draw attention to these points. In the general plan of the book we shall deal first with secondary, later with primary sources, the latter being used by more advanced students.

It is clear that history must be split up in order to make it manageable, into ancient (to about A.D. 395), mediaeval (A.D. 395–1450) and modern (A.D. 1450 to present day), but ancient history has close links with archaeology and prehistory, and modern history with politics and contemporary biography. For the vast ramifications of the subject the student may consult any good library classification (e.g. *Dewey Decimal Classification*, 17th edition, **1**, pp. 1158–1254, 1965), or the section "Classification of Articles" at the end of volume 32 of the thirteenth edition of the *Encyclopaedia Britannica* where he will discover such subjects as heraldry, arbitration, archives, diplomacy, serfdom, slavery, sovereignty, suzerainty and war, as well as the name of every conceivable country in the world in 1911. We have already indicated that we cannot treat fully of the history that every other branch of knowledge has, but we cannot fail altogether to take account of the fact that travel, discovery and topography cover much the same territory as history. This prompts another thought—should we divide our subject by period or by place?

Fortunately, the method of learning history has been settled traditionally in the universities of the British Commonwealth for close on a century. Students do, in fact, have a general acquaintance with universal history, then select one or two main periods, and within those periods specialize on a country and perhaps a continent and one or two special topics. The newer universities are varying this a little by studying whole civilizations or combinations of them. But where even the history specialist is completely ignorant of vast tracts of time and continents, not within his chosen programme, the author of a textbook such as this can scarcely hope to do more than indicate from personal knowledge some outstanding general or special works and point to the bibliographical sources for any aspect of history in a somewhat uncritical way. The following titles are excellent appetizers for the more detailed studies to come.

ROWSE, A. L., *The Use of History*, E.U.P., revised edition, 1963.
HOSKINS, W. G., *Local History in England*, Longmans, 1959.

THE ATMOSPHERE OF HISTORY

This section may be omitted by those who are so intent on a particular topic that they may wish straight away to get to know those books—mainly librarians' and booksellers' reference books—that are not particularly interesting in themselves, but merely useful as guides to other books. The danger with such works is that they do not help students to form independent judgements. They either confuse the novice by their very comprehensiveness or, if they attempt evaluative selections, they impose a second-hand opinion. Let us, then, read a little history before reading about history books. It has been said that "the writing of history at its highest level is a combination of scientific and artistic genius. The greatest history in English, *The Decline and Fall of the Roman Empire*, is a supreme example of the results of painstaking research and artistic understanding which time has corrected only in minor detail. Carlyle's *French Revolution*, on the other hand, may not now be regarded as an adequate treatment of its subject, yet the exhilaration gained by reading it more than compensates for its subjective distortion. It is probable that the whole impression left in the reader's mind of that great upheaval is emotionally as near to reality as any history can give, although more modern studies are required for detailed reference."[1]

If you read *in* these books you will find out what history is, not

[1] Seymour Smith, F., *An English Library*, National Book Council, 1st edition, 1943, p. 47. The latest edition (Deutsch, 1963) does not include this judgement.

merely what facts it records. Or you may prefer part of the famous third chapter of Macaulay which reflects the height of Britain's greatness "the reign of Queen Victoria . . . the time when England was truly merry England, when all classes were bound together by brotherly sympathy, when the rich did not grind the faces of the poor, and when the poor did not envy the splendour of the rich".[1] Lord Acton's immensely scholarly Cambridge inaugural lecture proclaimed pathetically that (his religion had excluded him from university as a young man) "liberty is the palm, and the prize, and the crown" and even more significantly that "it is by solidity of criticism more than by the plenitude of erudition, that the study of history strengthens, and straightens, and extends the mind".[2] Many other historians such as Francis Parkman, A. F. Pollard and, nearer our own times, G. M. Trevelyan and Arnold Toynbee have expressed universal historic truths through memorable aphorisms. The process continues still for J. H. Plumb criticizes contemporary pessimistic views of a situation in which "fewer and fewer historians believe that their art has any social purpose: any function as a co-ordinator of human endeavour or human thought".[3] The subject is immaterial—if perusing any of the master historians can stimulate and convince you into following, albeit critically, his theme, this interlude will not have been wasted.

ACTON, F. D. (1st baron), Lectures on Modern History, Macmillan, 1906.

POLLARD, A. F., Factors in Modern History, 3rd edition, Constable, 1932.

TOYNBEE, A. J., A Study of History, Abridgement by D. C. Somervell, Oxford Univ. Press, 1960.

TREVELYAN, G. M., Clio a Muse, and Other Essays, new edition, Longmans, 1930.

[1] History of England (edited by Firth), Vol. 1, p. 421.
[2] Lectures on Modern History, pp. 12, 15.
[3] Crisis in the Humanities (edited by J. H. Plumb), pp. 25–6.

SOME GENERAL BIBLIOGRAPHIES

Clearly information about history is given in the numerous general works covered by Dr. Chandler's "key" book to this series, *How to Find Out*.[1] Such works as Besterman's *World Bibliography of Bibliographies*,[2] Collison's shorter but recent *Bibliographies Subject and National*, or Malclès' *Manuel de bibliographie*; national bibliographies like *Biblio*, the *Bolletino delle pubblicazioni italiane*, not to mention the *British National Bibliography* or the full range of H. W. Wilson Company publications, though relevant to our subject, do not properly fall within the scope of this book, and only brief reference will be made to general encyclopaedias and dictionaries. Catalogues based on great libraries such as the *Library of Congress Subject Catalog* or the great *British Museum Subject Index* are not appropriately treated here. Before going on to works dealing solely with history, however, it would seem desirable to look at certain other comprehensive works from the point of view of history, for the following reasons:

(a) The size, importance, and reliability of these works, mostly frequently revised, ensure that they are as valuable for the study of history and allied topics as many monographs.

(b) It is an extremely valuable exercise to compare different treatments of the same subject by different editors, particularly those of different nationalities.

(c) The comprehensive works selected are nearly all likely to be found in most large reference libraries. The same cannot be said of many individual bibliographical monographs.

The works we propose to examine from the viewpoint of the student of history are:

(Fig. 1), H. R. Hoffman (editor), *The Reader's Adviser* (10th edition, Bowker, New York, 1964). This standard American book (best known from the older editions as Bessie Graham's *Bookman's*

[1] Pergamon Press, 1963.

[2] For sample page reproduction see Chandler, *How to Find Out*, Pergamon Press, 1963, p. 10, Fig. 1.

based their writings on scientifically conducted investigations. With the dawn of the nineteenth century, history became a science for specialists, the methods of the older historians being discredited. In England, we have the statement of George Peabody Gooch for the fact, "all eighteenth century historians are condemned except Gibbon."

The English Historical Documents Series (*q. v.*) is invaluable. Two sources of histori-cal information are no longer in print: "The Fugger News Letters" (ed. by Victor von Klarwill, trans. by L. R. Byrne 1926), written by correspondents of the Bavarian banking house of Fugger (1568–1605) and including contemporary reports of the defeat of the Spanish Armada, the execution of Mary Queen of Scots, the Essex conspiracy and new light on Queen Elizabeth; and "The Greville Memoirs" (ed. by Lytton Strachey and Roger Fulford 1938 8 vols.), the unexpurgated memoirs of Charles Cavendish Greville (1794–1865), which covers the reigns of George IV, William IV and Queen Victoria, although another edition is now in the Historical Memoirs Series (*q. v.*) and Louis Kronenberger's "The Great World" (*Doubleday* 1963 $4.95) covers portraits and scenes from the Memoirs, 1814–1860. Since autobiographies, letters, diaries and memoirs form the raw material of history, *see the following in the Autobiography Section of the Chapter on Biography and Autobiography*: John Evelyn (1620–1706); Samuel Pepys (1633–1703); Horatio or Horace Walpole, 4th Earl of Orford (1717–1797); James Boswell (1740–1795); William Maxwell Aitken Beaverbrook, 1st Baron (1879–   ); and Sir Anthony (Robert) Eden, Earl of Avon (1897–   ).

Some of the older well-known English histories are now no longer in print: "History of My Own Times" (1723) by Gilbert Burnet, Bishop of Salisbury (1643–1715), who was royal chaplain to William III and whose history was biased especially against James II; the eminently readable but unreliable "History of England from the Fall of Wolsey to the Defeat of the Spanish Armada, 1529–1588" (1856–70) by James Anthony Froude (1818–1894), who has been called England's National Historian; Henry Thomas Buckle's (1821–1862) brilliant but unfinished "Introduction to the History of Civilization in England, 1857–1861"; and the scholarly but "dryasdust" "Constitutional History of England" (1874–78 3 vols.) by William Stubbs, Bishop of Oxford.

No one who is interested in English history should miss Sellar and Yeatman's hilarious satire, "1066 and All That: A Memorable History of England, Comprising all the Parts You Can Remember, Including 103 Good Things, 5 Bad Kings and 2 Genuine Dates" (1931 *Dutton* 1950 $2.95 pap. $.95)

Ashley, Maurice. GREAT BRITAIN TO 1688; and Smellie, K. B. GREAT BRITAIN SINCE 1688. An up-to-date, interestingly written, well-digested English history. *Univ. of Michigan Press* History of the Modern World Series 1961–62 each $7.50

BIBLIOGRAPHY OF BRITISH HISTORY: Tudor Period 1485–1603. Ed. by Conyers Read. *Oxford* 1933 2nd ed. 1959 $10.10; Stuart Period 1603–1714. Ed. by Godfrey Davies. *Oxford* 1928 $4.00

THE CAMBRIDGE HISTORY OF THE BRITISH EMPIRE. J. Holland Rose, A. P. Newton and E. A. Benians, General Eds. *Cambridge* 1929—8 vols. each $14.50–$19.50

Vol. 1. The Old Empire, from the Beginnings to 1783 $15.50; Vol. 2. The Growth of the New Empire, 1783–1870 $15.50; Vol. 3. The Empire Commonwealth, 1870–1919 $19.50; Vol. 4. British India, 1479–1858 reprinting; Vol. 5. Indian Empire, 1858–1918 reprinting; Vol. 6. Canada and Newfoundland, $14.50; Vol. 7. (Part I) Australia, reprinting; Vol. 7. (Part II) New Zealand, reprinting; Vol. 8. South Africa new ed. $17.50.

Costain, Thomas B. THE PAGEANT OF ENGLAND SERIES. *Doubleday* 1951—Vol. 1 The Conquering Family. England from the Norman Conquest Through the Crusades. 1949; Vol. 2 The Magnificent Century. Story of the 13th Century. 1951; Vol. 3 The Three Edwards. 1958; Vol. 4 The Last Plantagenets. History of England during the reign of the Plantagenet kings. 1962 4 vols. each $5.75

ENGLISH HISTORICAL DOCUMENTS SERIES. D. C. Douglas, Gen. Ed. 12 vols. *Oxford* 1953–59 each $15.20

The basic material of English history in the form of documents rendered in full. Vol. I c. 500–1042. Ed. by Dorothy Whitelock 1955; Vol. II 1042–1189. Ed. by D. C. Douglas and G. W. Greenaway 1953; Vol. VIII 1660–1714. Ed. by Andrew Browning 1953; Vol. IX American Colonial Documents to 1776.

Fig. 1. HOFFMAN, H. R., *The Reader's Adviser*. (Copyright: Bowker.)

Manual, a title for the first time abandoned in the ninth edition) has always been compiled by and primarily intended for booksellers. The present edition generally lists only books in print in the United States in 1963; "out of print editions, now obtainable in second-hand stores, have been omitted in the main text, often with much regret. Important out of print editions, a few authoritative subscription editions, not handled in bookshops, and out of print titles of modern authors significant to their development have been mentioned in the discussion paragraphs" (preface). This is a particularly serious limitation to the student of history, a large part of whose required material is normally out of print. Section 21 (pp. 561–606) deals with biography and autobiography, section 38 (pp. 1143–1243) with history, these totalling about a tenth of the book. The sections may be further summarized as follows:

BIOGRAPHY

"Emphasis . . . on great *biographers* rather than upon lives of great men" (p. 561). Such a definition, though original, greatly limits the usefulness of this section which begins with general definitions, how to write biography (1 p.), reference books on collected biography ($\frac{1}{2}$ p.), selected collected biographies and biographies in series (4 pp.). The longest entry under biography (14 pp.) is on Boswell and Johnsoniana (3 pp.). This and the surprisingly longer section autobiography (31 pp., including 1 p. collected autobiography) are arranged by the author's date of birth.

The judgements are of great interest, e.g. "the question: 'which is the greatest autobiography in literature?' is not answered with the same agreement as is the question 'which is the greatest biography?' Although the English are supreme in biography the place of honour in autobiography belongs either to the Italians, because of the Cellini and Goldoni autobiographies, or to the French for the *Confessions* of Rousseau" (pp. 580–1). There is little American bias in the biography section though more in the autobiographies. Lincoln (1$\frac{1}{2}$ pp.) and Franklin (1$\frac{1}{2}$ pp.) have longer entries than Churchill (1 p.), Pepys ($\frac{3}{4}$ p.) or Gibbon ($\frac{1}{4}$ p.), but this mainly reflects the number of works *available* in the United States.

HISTORY

Introduction (1 p.), philosophical books (1 p.), reference books ($\frac{3}{4}$ p.—also refers to another section), ancient history (2 pp.), Greek historians, including collected works (3 pp.), Roman history (2 pp.), ancient history by modern writers (2 pp.), English history general (2 pp.), individuals ($4\frac{1}{2}$ pp.), American history—general including series, reference and background books, civil war, constitution (8 pp.), individuals (12 pp.). Finally, there is a very general section, Continental, European and world history (19 pp.). Limited as it is to books in print in America, this section is far more of a hotch-potch than the corresponding sections in other works, but the descriptions and criticisms of writers are of great value, e.g. comparisons of the merits of different translations of the classics and assessments of recent writers (Churchill, Toynbee).

(Fig. 2), L. N. Malclès, *Cours de bibliographie* (Droz, Geneva, 1954). This work by the Librarian of the Sorbonne University, Paris, is a shortened version of the same author's *Les Sources du travail bibliographique* (3 vols. in 4, 1950–8), and is specifically directed to university students and candidates for examinations in librarianship. Chapter XII (pp. 139–44) deals with biography and chapters XV–XVII (pp. 161–93) with the historical sciences (prehistory is included but archaeology is dealt with later under the arts). The sections of interest to us total once more about a tenth of the book.

BIOGRAPHY

Introduction (1 p.) pointing out the relationship to general encyclopaedia, and the different types of biography—universal, national, special to a nation, region, occupation, etc. The next $3\frac{1}{2}$ pp. are divided into bibliographies of biographies, universal biographies (all periods), universal biographies (contemporary), universal specialized biographies and national biographies; within the major countries there is a division between the retrospective and contemporary biographies. France is dealt with most fully, of course, but Germany, Austria, Belgium, Canada, Spain, the

GARNEAU (François-Xavier). *Histoire du Canada*. 5e éd. rev., annotée et publ. avec une introd. et des appendices par Hector GARNEAU. Paris, Alcan, 1913-1920, 2 vol. 8°. (Bibliothèque France-Amérique.)
Les appendices sont les sources bibliographiques : pp. 499-593.
Ed. canadienne. Montréal, Ed. de l'Arbre, 1944, 9 vol.

BIBLIOGRAPHIE COURANTE

Canadian historical review. Toronto, 1920-
Contient : *Recent publications relating to Canada, graduate theses in Canadian history.*

* * *

BIBLIOGRAPHIES DE L'HISTOIRE DE LA GRANDE-BRETAGNE

Plusieurs grandes synthèses servent de sources bibliographiques pour l'histoire de Grande-Bretagne. *The political history of England*, dir. par W. HUNT et R. L. POOLE, commence en 1905 et compte 12 vol. ; *A history of England*, dir. par W. C. OMAN, souvent rééditée depuis 1907, a 8 vol. La dernière en date où les références sont copieuses, commence en 1936 et doit avoir 14 volumes dont 12 ont paru en 1953 : *Oxford history of England*, dir. par G. N. CLARK.
Les répertoires bibliographiques de l'histoire de Grande-Bretagne s'enchaînent de la façon suivante :

De l'origine à 1485

* GROSS (Charles). *The sources and literature of English history from the earliest times to about 1485*. 2nd ed. rev. and enl. London, Longmans, 1915, 8°, xxiii-820 p.

1485-1603

* READ (Conyers). *Bibliography of British history. Tudor period, 1485-1603*. Oxford, Clarendon Pr., 1933, 8°, xxiii-467 p.

1603-1714

* DAVIES (Godfrey). *Bibliography of British history. Stuart period, 1603-1714*. Oxford, Clarendon Pr., 1928, 8°, x-549 p.

1714-1789

* PARGELLIS (Stanley) and MEDLEY (Dudley Julius). *Bibliography of British history: the 18th century, 1714-1789: issued under the dir. of the American historical assoc. and the Royal historical soc. of Great Britain*. Oxford, Clarendon Pr., 1951, 4°, xxvi-642 p. 1558 n[os].

BIBLIOGRAPHIE COURANTE

Annual bulletin of historical literature. London, 1911- . Voir p. 166.

* *Writings on British history. 1934- . A bibliography of books and articles on the history of Great Britain from about 450 A.D. to 1914 published during the year 1934-.* Compiled by Alex. Taylor MILNE. London, Cape, 1937- , 8°. (Royal historical Society.)
Année 1939 (1953), 310 p.

Writings on Irish history. 1936- . Ds : *Irish historical studies*. 1936.

Fig. 2. MALCLÈS, L. N., *Cours de bibliographie*. (Copyright: Droz.)

U.S.A., U.K. and Switzerland also receive separate treatment. There are no comments, the main virtue of the treatment being its lucidity and logicality. Exercises follow.

HISTORY

XVI: "Mediaeval and modern history." Introduction (3 pp.) pointing out how the long single-author history has been superseded by the planned series of volumes or articles. Especially valuable on the various French series. General section (6 pp.) listing not only bibliographies but long general works which include bibliographies. French, German, British and American titles are treated with reasonable fullness. Especially valuable for details of the French "synthèses collectives" and current French international bibliographies.

XV: "Greece and Rome" (placed out of order). Introduction (1 p.) with the usual summary of leading treatises (French bias). Language and literature are covered as well as history. Bibliographies, encyclopaedias and dictionaries on the whole field (2 pp.) followed by separate sections (French works only) on Greek history and Roman history ($\frac{1}{2}$ p. each). Two pages mainly on literature are followed by bibliographies on the whole of the ancient civilizations ($2\frac{1}{2}$ pp., including exercises). Collections of texts record the *Loeb Classical Library* and periodicals, e.g. *Speculum* (U.S.A.). It is useful to have some periodicals listed in this brief general bibliography.

XVII: "History of the nations." There is no introduction. Some titles included under the general sections XV and XVI are listed again. Very full on France ($5\frac{1}{2}$ pp.)—collected works, retrospective bibliographies with a separate treatment for Paris and French regions. Germany (1 p.), Belgium and Holland ($\frac{3}{4}$ p.), separate treatment for Spain, U.S.A., and Canada, Great Britain, Italy and Switzerland. There is passing reference to the importance of collections of documents (French examples only cited) followed by 2 pp. on the French Empire.

(Fig. 3), R. W. Murphey, *How and Where to Look it up* (McGraw-

Annals of European Civilization, 1501–1900.
Alfred Mayer. London: Cassell & Co., Ltd.
1949. 457 pp.

Essentially a cultural chronology, this work
is divided into two parts: first, general chronology of cultural events in European history
for the period covered; second, the same field
by classified subjects, such as literature, architecture, and religion. Index to personal and
geographical names.

Atlas of European History. Edward Whiting
Foss and H. S. Deighton, eds. New York:
Oxford University Press. 1956. 87 pp.

A collection of maps depicting European
history arranged for detailed study. Maps of
physical geography are shown in photographic
relief.

Dictionary of European History. William E.
Roeder. New York: Philosophical Library,
Inc. 1954. 316 pp.

An alphabetical dictionary of entries under
personal names, place names, and other subjects of European history from about A.D. 500
to modern times.

Europe since 1815. Henry W. Littlefield. 17th
ed. New York: Barnes & Noble, Inc. 1953.
321 pp.

One of the "College Outline Series," this
surveys modern European history. Many
maps.

History of Europe, 1500–1848. Henry W.
Littlefield. 5th ed. New York: Barnes &
Noble, Inc. 1951. 181 pp.

A companion volume to the above.

A Select List of Books on European History,
1815–1914. Allan Bullock and A. J. P.
Taylor, eds. 2d ed. New York: Oxford University Press. 1957. 79 pp.

A well-selected bibliography, prepared for
the Oxford Recent History Group.

A Survey of European Civilization. Wallace
Klipper Ferguson and Geoffrey Bruhn. 2d
ed. Boston. Houghton Mifflin Company.
1952. 998 pp.

A most complete textbook-style study of
European history from ancient times to the
present, useful for reference because of its
excellent index, use of much specific fact, and
appendixes. These include chronologies, genealogical tables, tables of rulers, and a bibliography. More than 100 maps and many charts
and illustrations.

g. FAR EASTERN HISTORY

A Select List of Books on the Civilizations
of the Orient [15·3] is an annotated bibliography citing numerous works on the history
of the Far East.

Short History of the Far East. Kenneth Scott
Latourette. 3d ed. New York: The Macmillan Company. 1957. 768 pp.

An excellent standard history of the Orient,
with an index detailed enough to permit locating most desired information rapidly. Numerous maps.

h. GREAT BRITAIN, HISTORY OF

Bibliography of British History. Stanley Pargellis and D. J. Medley, eds. Oxford: Clarendon Press. 1928– .

A projected comprehensive bibliography of
British history carried out under the direction
of the American Historical Association and
the Royal Historical Society. The starting date
is 1485. Vol. 1 covers the Tudor period
(1485–1603); Vol. 2, the Stuart period (1603–
1714); Vol. 3, the eighteenth century (1714–
1789). Subsequent volumes have been planned
to cover later eras. Each volume is arranged
by subjects, with selected listings including
books, pamphlets, documents, and some periodical material. Author indexes.

Dictionary of National Biography [14·3] is
a major source of information on British history when desired facts can be linked to
specific persons. It is especially valuable because of its great authority and detailed bibliographies of additional source material.

Guide to Sources of English History. E. S.
Upton. New Brunswick, N.J.: Scarecrow
Press. 1952. 151 pp.

A rather elementary bibliography of source
materials useful primarily to the not too advanced student.

History of England. Charles Oman, ed. New
York: G. P. Putnam's Sons. 1904–1948.
8 vols.

A standard comprehensive history of England, arranged chronologically. Various authors, all of high standing, wrote the different
volumes. Of special reference value are the
maps and diagrams, genealogical charts, and
bibliographies. Revised editions of different
volumes have appeared from time to time.

Oxford History of England. Oxford: Clarendon Press. 1934– . 14 vols.

451

Fig. 3. MURPHEY, R. W., *How and Where to Look it up.* (Copyright:
McGraw-Hill.)

Hill, New York, 1958). This is the only general guide to reading sources designed for laymen. The author is editor for a publishing house. "It has seemed to me preferable rather to limit the number of books listed and to use space thus made available to exploit fully the value of the books cited by detailed analysis of their contents. In selecting books for listing, I have chosen ones that are commonly available, that cover subjects of sufficient interest to meet the needs of a fair number of readers, and that are reasonably up-to-date" (preface).

As it is mainly confined to American books of the period 1945–57, it has similar limitations to the *Reader's Adviser*, but is more cautious in its assessments. Biography has a section to itself (section 14: "How to Find Out About People") but history is only a small subdivision of section 16: "How to Find Out About Things". Biography and history occupy 61 (of 649) main sequence pages.

BIOGRAPHY

Section 14. Interesting introduction ($1\frac{1}{2}$ pp.) pointing out that biography occupies the largest part of most reference books. There are useful hints on titles and pseudonyms. The pitfalls of reference information, such as doubtful sources, are mentioned. Types of biography include book-length biographies, chapter-length biographies, general encyclopaedias, encyclopaedic yearbooks, dictionaries, almanacs, Who's Whos, bound newspapers (indexed), textbooks, directories.

14.1 General guides. Refers to general guides to all knowledge and six American guides.

14.2 General biographical sources. Refers to encyclopaedias (a few foreign examples) and a wide range of biographical dictionaries, including indexes to newspapers.

14.3 General biographical sources limited geographically. Section on the main countries, arranged under continents, mainly dealing with English language material. The very useful cross-referencing of this work is shown by its section on the Middle East which refers to the *Encyclopedia of Islam* and the Europa publication *Middle East*, as well as to two Who's Whos.

14.4 Specialized biographical sources. Comprehensive and original, e.g. the headings under A are actors; advertising, figures in; allergists; anthropologists; architects; artists; authors; aviation, figures in, with numerous cross-references.

14.5 Sources of biographical pictures—entirely American.

There is strong American bias throughout the whole work—to an English reader the heading "Women, see also first ladies", when neither kings nor queens get a heading is somewhat laughable. The heading "librarians" omits reference to the English specialized Who's Who on the subject.

HISTORY

16.216. Introduction ($\frac{3}{4}$ p.) commences with valuable cross-references to such subjects as documents, municipalities, etc., then refers to general encyclopaedias but surprisingly not to the fact that every subject has its own history. Section a, general sources, does not make the usual distinction between bibliographies and comprehensive works, though both are listed. The sections on the different countries are somewhat shorter than those in the other general bibliographies, but the sections g, Far eastern history; i, Japanese history; j, Jewish history; k, Korean history; m, Middle eastern history and n, Russian history give a modern approach. U.S. history is, of course, by far the largest section (3 pp.).

(Fig. 4.), W. S. Sonnenschein, *The Best Books; a Reader's Guide and Literary Reference Book* (3rd edition, 6 vols., Routledge, London, 1910–35). It is safe to say that in the unlikely event of any future compiler engaging on a work such as this, no compositor would set it up. It records some 150,000 British and American works mainly on the "title a line" principle of nineteenth-century printed library catalogues. Its compiler, W. S. Sonnenschein, worked on its successive editions for fifty years, and personally completed the five text volumes of this final edition. Members of his family completed the valuable sixth volume (index, summary of classification, memoir, etc.). Sonnenschein grew tired of his work as the years passed: "the task [he wrote] was possible in 1887 when I

VON BOTHMER, C'ess A. [ed.] The Sovn. Ladies of Eur. ; 153 ill. $4 (16/) m 8° Lippincott oo
" ENGLISH OFFICER, (AN) " Soc. Recollns. in Paris & Vienna : 1879-1904 ; ill.
                 [$3 Appleton] 12/ 8° Long 98
    ,,   More Society Recollections ; ports.   12/ 8° Long o8
Former, worthless gossip ab. unkn. attachés, actors, grisettes, etc. ; latter, ord. tourg. experces. on Cont.—and Lhasa.

F., A.M.   Foreign Courts and Foreign Homes   6/ c 8° Longman 98
    Hanoverian and Fch. Society under Kg. ERNEST and NAP. III. Stories, anecdotes, etc.

FRYE, Maj. W. E. After Waterloo : reminisces. of Eur. travel : 1815-19 10/6 8° Heinemann o8
    Diary of a commonpl. Brit. officer, converted into bk. of value by learned notes of Edr., Salomon REINACH

HEGERMANN-LINDENCRONE, Anna L. In the Cts. of Memory ; ill. [1858-75] $2 (12/6) Harper 12
    ,,   The Sunny Side of Diplomatic Life ; ill. $2 (12/6) 8° Harper 14
    Reminces. of diplom. world in Paris, Rome, Berl., Copenh., by wife of Dan. ex-Ambas.r.

LOFTUS, L'd Aug. [1817-1904] —in his Diplomatic Reminiscences —ut F § 27
MACDONELL, L'y Reminiscences of Diplom. Life ; 16 pl. [Eur.; S. Am.; $3 Macm.] 7/6 8° Black 13
MAYNE, Jno. [1791-1829] Jl. dur. Tour of Cont. 1814, ed. J. M. Collins   12/6 ($4) 8° Lane 09
    Faithful (but not excitg.) descr. of tour aft. reopeng. of Cont. on abdic. of NAP. and bet. the 100 Days.

METTERNICH [-WINNEBURG], Pr'ce [1773-1859] Memoirs—v. F § 50
PAGET, Walpurga, L'y Scenes & Memories ; ill.   [$2.25 Scribner] 7/6 8° Smith & Elder 13
RADZIWILL, P'cess Luise [1770-1836] Forty-five years of my Life [tr.] ; ports.
                 [1770-1815] $4.25 8° McBride, N.Y. 12
RADZIWILL, P'cess Cath. Memoirs of Forty Years ; ill.   [$3.75 Funk] 16/ 8° Cassell 14
    ,,   The Royal Marriage Market of Europe ; ill. [$2 Funk] 7/6 8° Cassell 15
    ,,   Sovereigns & Statesmen of Europe ; ill. [$2.50 Funk] 10/6 r 8° Cassell 15
V. STOCKMAR, Bar. C. F. [1787-1863] Memoirs —v. F § 27
DE TALLEYRAND, Pr'ce [1776-1839] Correspondence with Louis XVIII [tr.], 2 vols. —ut F § 50
WADDINGTON, Mme. L'rs of a Diplomat's Wife [1883-1900 ; $2.50 Scrib.] 10/6 8° Smith & Elder o3
" WIDOW OF A DIPLOMAT (THE) " Intimacies of Ct. & Soc. ; ill. [$2.50 Dodd] 10/6 8° Hurst 12
    Deals with five European capitals : Government House, Canada, and Washington, U.S.A.

16 : HISTORY OF ENGLAND : GENERAL AND COMPREHENSIVE WORKS

Bibliography ; Guides to Sources —v. also F § 13
BEARD, Prf. C. A.   Introduction to the English Historians $1.60 (7/) c 8° Macm. o6
Bibliography of Modern British History, 3 vols. in prep.
    To continue the wk. of GROSS [ut inf.]. In prep. by a joint comm. R. Hist. Soc. and Amer. Hist. Assocn.
BIBLIOTHECA LINDESIANA : Bibliography of Roy. Proclamations, 3 vols. —ut K § 4
    ,, Handlist of Proclamations, 3 vols. & Suppl. [1509-1901] f° Aberd. Univ. Pr. 93-01
BODLEIAN LIB. (Oxon.) : Calendar of Charters & Rolls, by W. H. Turner 31/6 ($9.75) 8° Cl. Pr. 78
BRITISH MUSEUM : Index to Charters & Rolls in MSS. Dep., by Ellis + Bickley, 2 v.
                 ea. 35/ 8° Brit. Mus. oo-12
COBHAM, Visc. Descr. Catal. of Charters in possn. of ; ed. I. H. Jeayes 15/ r 8° C. J. Clark 93
COOPER, C. P. Acc. of Most Imp. Pub. Recds. & Pubns. of Rec. Comm., etc., 2 v. o.p. 8° London 32
EARLE, Prf. Jno. Hdbk. to Land Charters & O'r Sax. Documts. 16/ ($4) c 8° Clar. Pr. 88
    For use w. KEMBLE'S Codex Diplom., repub. by BIRCH in his Cartul. Sax. [ut F § 18].
EWALD, A. C.   The Public Records   o.p. [pb. 9/] 8° Pickering 73
FITZHARDINGE, L'd Descr. Catal. of Charters in Possn. of, ed. I. H. Jeayes 8° priv. prin. 92
    Descrns. of ab. 1000 deeds, commencing in middle 12 cent. ; royal grants, eccles. charters, geneal. docums., &c.
GAIRDNER, Dr Jas. Early Chroniclers of Europe : England   4/ c 8° S.P.C.K. 79
GRANT, A. J.   English Historians —ut F § 1 [a historiography]
*GROSS, Prf. Chas. Sources & Literature of English History [to 1485] $6 (24/) 8° Longman [oo] 15
    System. surv. of prtd. matls. (3234 entries) rel. to pol., const., leg., soc., and econ. hist. of Eng., Wales, Irel. Chief wks. and
    authorities comp. in gen. annotns. Pt. i : Gen. and introd. subjs. ; ii : authorities to close of Rom. Occn. ; iii : A.-S.
    times ; iv : 1066-1485. Good auth. and Subjs. Indexes.
*   ,,   Bibliography of English Municipal History —ut D § 124

                 1141 ·

Fig. 4. SONNENSCHEIN, W. S., *The Best Books; a Reader's Guide and
Literary Reference Book.* (Copyright: Routledge.)

published the first edition. Each edition has become more impossible. Now it is almost absurd to attempt it." "He endeavoured to compromise between the wants of the general reader who desires to make some detailed research, the scholar, and the bookseller, and was fearful lest his efforts to make the book very useful for booksellers might have spoiled it for the specialist, e.g. by the too lavish introduction of entries of school-books" (preface).

HISTORY (class F), with archaeology and historical collaterals (class G), occupies pp. 1067–1679. BIOGRAPHY is included. These sections occupy nearly a fifth of the whole work—a striking comment in a book of the 1930's on the comparative decline of the humanities in our own time, due to the emphasis paid to science and technology. Sonnenschein has no general introductions and plunges straight into his divisions and subdivisions, which are too numerous to note here. As an example, within class F are nine main headings; I, universal history; II, primitive society; III, antiquity; IV, the middle ages; V–IX, a class for each of the five continents. Europe occupies subdivisions 15–60 of the 76 subdivisions in class F. Subjects thought of too late for inclusion in the main scheme are either given asterisks (46* Balkan peninsula —46 is Austria) or simply added out of order (76, gypsies is placed in IX, America). Apart from the classified heads Sonnenschein's work is noteworthy for its interpolated subdivisions. Section F 20, a typical example, dealing with the history of England, A.D. 1199–1327, has some 150 entries subdivided mainly into sources and modern writers, but with a final hotch-potch of special heads such as Bannockburn, battle of; crusades (fifth to eighth); Falkirk, battle of; friars (coming of the); gilds; Jews; Lewes, battle of; Magna Carta; Rochester, sieges of; taxation; treaties; trials; Welsh wars; biography. One has heard of most of the titles listed; those selected for brief appraisement are in many cases still standard books. Nothing so comprehensive has ever been prepared that was not a library catalogue (it includes out-of-print material), and the whole is crowned by an enormous index of authors, titles and subjects. Little of value thirty to fifty years ago escaped Sonnenschein; today, only a computer could attempt the compiler's mammoth task. Where so much is garnered in one may distrust standards, but Sonnenschein will always retain its place, along with the *London Library Catalogues*, as an exhaustive record of all that was best in our literature when costs of production were not a vital deterrent to leisurely, even pedantic authorship. Sonnenschein "intentionally retained a large selection of books edited by the older editors—'they are so often more scholarly and more lovingly edited than those by moderns' ". For example he has five editions of Macaulay's *History*, three of them annotated, and all these three bearing his star of distinction. Three other editions are referred to, and yet the total entry on Macaulay is only $1\frac{1}{2}$ inches deep. For librarians, Sonnenschein records the books no longer on their open shelves, which still find an honoured place in the stack rooms, unless they have foolishly discarded them.

(Fig. 5), W. Totok and R. Weitzel, *Handbuch der bibliographischen Nachschlagewerke*, Klostermann, Frankfurt (2nd edition, 1959). A systematically arranged bibliography giving nearly equal treatment to general bibliographies (part I) and subject bibliographies (part II).

BIOGRAPHY is covered in part I, pp. 133–45; HISTORY in part II, pp. 225–40. The history section seems remarkably comprehensive when it is realized that the whole work covers only some 2500 titles, compared with 150,000 in Sonnenschein; actually with 28 pp. it has a comparatively low proportion of the 304 pp. of text. The typography and arrangement are remarkably clear, and the large number of German titles recorded is a very useful feature. Even so, the international biography section has good entries on the two great nineteenth-century French works by Michaud and Hoefer as well as on Hyamson (British) and Arnim (German). Ten German national biographies are listed. Both the biography and history national sections list works under Germany, Austria, Switzerland, Holland, Denmark, Sweden, Norway, Great Britain, U.S.A., France, Belgium, Italy and Spain, and under history there are additional headings for Latin America, eastern Europe, Hungary, U.S.S.R., and Asia—an interesting arrangement. The work distinguishes merely by small side notes, bibliographies proper

Historisk Tidskrift. Stockholm 1881ff.

Bringt eine jährliche Bibliographie von Büchern und Zeitschriftenaufsätzen über schwedische Geschichte.

Setterwall, K. (1921–1935: P. Sjögren): Svensk historisk bibliografi 1771–1874, 1875 bis 1900, 1901–1920, 1921–1935. Uppsala [später] Stockholm 1907–56.

Verzeichnet die Literatur mit großer Vollständigkeit. Systematisch geordnet, innerhalb jeder Abteilung chronologisch nach geschichtlichen Epochen.

Norwegen

Norges Historie. Bibliografi for 1916ff.

Bibliographische Beilage der Zeitschrift Historisk Tidsskrift. Oslo 1871ff. Erscheint jährlich. Verfasserreg. für 1916–25, 1926–35, 1936–45.

Schweigaard, J.: Norges topografi. [Nebst] Anh. Kra, Oslo 1918–30.

Bibliographisches Verzeichnis der Norwegen betreffenden topographischen und lokalgeschichtlichen Literatur. Bücher und Aufsätze.

Großbritannien

Annual Bulletin of historical literature. London 1911ff.
Vgl. S. 229.

Cannon, H. L.: Reading References for English history. Boston [usw.] 1910. 559 S.

Bibliographisches Handbuch zur englischen Geschichte. Chronologisch und systematisch geordnet.

Milne, A. T.: Writings on British history. A bibliography of books and articles on the history of Great Britain from about 450 A. D. to 1914, published during the year . . . Vol. 1–6: 1934–1939. London 1937–53.

Hrsg. von der Royal Historical Society. T. 1. systematisch und topographisch, T. 2. chronologisch geordnet.

Gross, C.: The Sources and Literature of English history from the earliest times to about 1485. 2. ed. London 1915. 820 S.

Verzeichnis der primären und sekundären Quellen zur englischen Geschichte. Mit Erläuterungen. Neudr. 1951.

Bibliography of British history. Tudor period, 1485–1603. Ed. by C. Read. Oxford 1933. 467 S.

Setzt Gross fort. Nach Sachgebieten gegliedert. Innerhalb dieser alphabetisch nach Verfassern.

Bibliography of British history. Stuart period, 1603–1714. Ed. by G. Davies. Oxford 1928. 459 S.

Bibliographien, Quellen, Sekundärliteratur. Nach Sachgebieten geordnet. Innerhalb dieser alphabetisch nach Schlagwörtern.

. . . aphy of British history. The eighteenth century, 1714–1789. Ed. by S. Pargellis and D. J. Medley. Oxford 1951. 642 S.

Systematisch gegliedert. Mit Verfasser- und Sachreg.

Fig. 5. Totok and Weitzel, *Handbuch der bibliographischen Nachschlagewerke.* (Copyright: Klostermann.)

and general treatises, but this distinction, is, except for librarians, an academic one. Students in search of material might well not realize from certain other bibliographies that these two types of work often serve the same purpose, as the general treatises more often than not include valuable bibliographies. Preceding the history national lists are 6½ pp. of general references—"aids" (place names, chronologies, palaeography, inscriptions, diplomatic, heraldry, genealogy, numismatics, portraits, lists of officials, prehistory, universal history, and different periods of history). Folklore, law, politics and economics are comprehended within the historical sciences. The great merits of Totok and Weitzel are the clarity of the page, and the quality and balance of the selection within a fairly narrow compass. It probably packs more evaluated information into the square inch than all its competitors.

(Fig. 6), A. J. Walford, *Guide to Reference Material* (Library Association, London, 1959. *Supplement*, 1963). (A new edition in 3 vols. is planned for 1966.) Among British librarians, Walford is now the best-known general guide, as it is the most recent. The main work contains some 3000 main entries, the supplement 2000, with some repetition. In the original work BIOGRAPHY and HISTORY occupy pp. 408–78, about a sixth of the book. There are no general introductions to sections. Under biography there are entries for Jersey, Wales, Portugal, Malaya, Egypt, Nigeria, Mauritius, British West Indies and some South American states, as well as the countries more frequently included in such a context. The evaluations are particularly valuable, covering such points as previous editions, further parts to come and annotations usually quoted from reviews. There are numerous cross-references. On the other hand, as sections of the work necessarily had to be farmed out, there is some unevenness. The editor has sometimes, in default of better works, included textbooks which would be more appropriate to such a work as Sonnenschein. A good number of sets and series are included, and these are analysed, though individual works seldom are. Walford usefully expresses an opinion as between similar works, e.g. Burke's and Debrett's

German foreign policy, 1918-45 (H.M.S.O., 1949-. In progress); *Documenti diplomatici italiani*, nona serie 1939-43 (Rome, Libreria dello Stato, 1954-. In progress); and *Foreign relations of the United States*. Diplomatic papers: The Soviet Union, 1933-39. (Washington, Government Printing Office, 1952).

A general guide to printed materials for the history of the Second World War is badly needed, the only bibliographies being those published from time to time in 'The military library', in *Military affairs* (Washington, American Military Institute), from v. 13, 1949.

Slavic Europe

940-11:016

KERNER, R. J. Slavic Europe: a selected bibliography in the Western European languages, comprising history, languages and literature. Oxford, Univ. Press, 1918. [ii], xxiv, 402p. (Harvard Bibliographies. Library series, v. 1).

Select list of fundamental works on various aspects of Slavonic life, in Western languages. The few bibliographies with Slavonic titles listed contain references to bibliographies and sources in western languages. Arrangement is ethnological rather than by country.

British Commonwealth

941-44

The Cambridge history of the British Empire. General editors, J. H. Rose, A. P. Newton, E. A. Benians. Cambridge, Univ. Press, 1929-. v. 1-2, 4-8. (In progress)

v. 1 : *The old Empire, from the beginning to 1783.* 75s.

v. 2 : *Growth of the new empire, 1783-1870.* 84s.

v. 3 : *The Empire-Commonwealth, 1870-1919.* Announced for January 1959.

v. 4 : *British India, 1497-1858.* 40s.

v. 5 : *Indian Empire, 1858-1918*, with chapters on the development of administration, 1818-58. 35s.

v. 6 : *Canada and Newfoundland.* 70s.

v. 7 : pt. 1: *Australia.* 50s.; v. 7, pt. 2: *New Zealand.* 20s.

v. 8 : *South Africa, Rhodesia and the Protectorates.* 63s.

On similar lines to the *Cambridge modern history*, each volume containing some 20-30 chapters by specialists. Social, economic and cultural aspects are touched upon. The lengthy bibliography appended to each volume is divided into pt. 1, Collections of MSS. in public and private archives and official papers and publications, and pt. 2, Other works.

941-44:016

ROYAL EMPIRE SOCIETY. Subject catalogue of the library of the Royal Empire Society, formerly the Royal Colonial Institute, by E. Lewin. London, the Society, 1930-37. 4v. o.p.

v. 1 : *British Empire generally, and Africa.*

v. 2 : *Australia, New Zealand, South Africa, general voyages and travels, Arctic and Antarctic.*

v. 3 : *Canada, Newfoundland, West Indies, colonial America.*

v. 4 : *Mediterranean dependencies, Middle East, India, Burma, Ceylon, Malaya, East Indies, Far East.*

Arranged geographically under subjects and in chronological order. Indicates pamphlets and periodical articles as well as books. The fine library of the Royal Empire Society was damaged in the bombing of London and the catalogue no longer strictly applies to it. It remains an indispensable bibliography. V. 5, covering biography, was not published.

941-44:016

HEWITT, A. R. Guide to resources for Commonwealth studies in London, Oxford and Cambridge; with bibliographical and other information. London, Athlone Press, for Institute of Commonwealth Studies, Univ. of London, 1957. viii, 219p. 21s.

Includes a concise survey of library resources by subjects (p. 50-68), bibliographies and works of reference (p. 72-90), and notes on individual collections (p. 93-179).

* Great Britain

Bibliography

941:016

ANDERSON, J. P. The book of British topography: a classified catalogue of the topographical works in the library of the British Museum relating to Great Britain and Ireland. London, Satchell, 1881. xvi, 472p. 25s.

Nearly 14,000 items, with full titles of works, but no annotation or pagination.
Contents: Catalogues.—General topography (including England and English counties, A-Z).—Wales (general; regional; counties, A-Z).—Scotland (general; counties, A-Z).—Ireland (general; counties, A-Z).—Addenda.—Index of places and subjects. The "General topography" section includes such topics as antiquities, directories, islands, railways and views.

941:016

Bibliography of British history. Tudor period, 1485-1603; edited by C. Read. Issued under the direction of the American Historical Association and the Royal Historical Society of Great Britain. Oxford, Clarendon Press, 1933. xiv, 467p. 35s.

———— **Stuart period, 1603-1714;** edited by G. Davies . . . Oxford, Clarendon Press, 1928. x, 459p. 25s.

———— **The eighteenth century, 1714-1789;** edited by S. Pargellis and D. J. Medley. Oxford, Clarendon Press, 1951. xxvi, 642p. 45s.

These 3v. provide a continuation of Gross's *Sources and literature of English history . . . to about 1485* (see at 942:016). The Tudor volume has been criticized for inaccuracies and the third volume for lack of balance. New editions are planned, with further volumes for 1789-1914.

The starting point for advanced work. As selected, annotated bibliographies, they cover

---

* The material on local history which follows is highly selective. For details of the older local histories see such lists as The National Book League exhibition catalogue, *Mirror of Britain* (1957, p. 15-36) and J. Minto's *Reference books* (1929), p. 249-76.

Fig. 6. WALFORD, A. J., *Guide to Reference Material.* (Copyright: A. J. Walford.)

peerages. Out-of-print material is included. The value of the work
for British history is illustrated by the long section on the English
counties (11 pp.) which I have laid under contribution in Chapter 3,
below. Naturally enough, other countries are very scantily treated,
and Walford's emphasis on British material is quite justifiable, as
no similar guide has been produced in Great Britain since Minto's
Reference Books (1929; *Supplement* 1931). The sections on biography
and history have no special merits; indeed, the unevenness referred
to above is somewhat manifest in them. Whereas all the county
entries refer to the relevant volumes of the *Victoria County History*,
if published (and even the county that made its own plans for such
a history—Northumberland—is not forgotten), the older county
histories are somewhat unevenly recorded. Hasted's *Kent* is there,
but not Morant's *Essex*, for example.

(Fig. 7), C. M. Winchell, *Guide to Reference Books* (7th edition,
American Library Association, Chicago, 1951, and supplements,
1950–62). (An eighth edition is under active preparation.) Founded
in 1902, this work is still, perhaps, best known to the older generation by the name of its editor from 1910 to 1936, Isadore Gilbert
Mudge. The best-known guide to reference books, and the only
one with a regular plan for supplements (four have appeared up to
1963, taking coverage up to 1962). Much fuller than the other
post-war works discussed, with its four supplements it lists nearly
9000 books (excluding items referred to in the notes).

In the main volume, BIOGRAPHY (section S) includes 221 main
entries, and there is a brief introduction. Annotations are similar
to those in Walford, but fuller, and typographically Winchell is
superior. There is heavy emphasis on the Americas—U.S.A. has
double the British entries. However, where regional treatment is
not possible (e.g. for such countries as France and Germany),
reference is made in a small paragraph to where details can be found.

GENEALOGY (T) has a section to itself (85 titles). HISTORY (V) has
469 titles; these and associated sections comprise about a seventh
of the main work. The subheadings relating to history are not so
clearly demarcated as in some other guides, nor is the general

Hubert Hall. Lond., King, 1914. 350p. (Studies in economics and political science, ed. by the director of the London School of Economics and Political Science)   **V272**

A well-selected list of sources and secondary works.

Gross, Charles. Sources and literature of English history from the earliest times to about 1485. 2d ed., rev. and enl. Lond. and N.Y., Longmans, 1915. 820p.   **V273**

The best bibliography of English history for the period before 1485, valuable both for its selection of material and for the annotations. Includes more than 3234 closely classified titles (numbered to 3234, but actually more because of insertions) with general index.

Appendices: A. Reports of the deputy-keeper of the public records; B. The Historical Manuscripts Commission; C. Rolls series; D. Chronological tables of the principal sources.

Continued in period by the following:

16th and 17th centuries

Bibliography of British history: Tudor period 1485–1603, Stuart period 1603–1714. Issued under the direction of the American Historical Association and the Royal Historical Society of Great Britain. Ox., Univ. Pr., 1928–33. 2v. Tudor period, 30s.; $10. Stuart period, 21s.; $7.   **V274**

Tudor period, 1485–1603, ed. by Conyers Read. 1933. 467p.; Stuart period, 1603–1714, ed. by Godfrey Davies. 1928. 459p.

In 1909 the Royal Historical Society and the American Historical Association undertook the compilation of a bibliography of British history from 1485. A joint committee of the two societies had the bibliography in hand for many years and the Tudor and Stuart volumes listed above are the results of their long intensive work. The original plan called for two more sections: (1) a bibliography of the modern period, 1715– ; and (2) a bibliography of general and allied material introductory to the whole. With Gross (V273), the two volumes already completed give a continuous bibliography from the earliest period to 1714.

The Tudor and Stuart volumes are alike in general plan, i.e., a select classified-subject list, with author indexes, of book, pamphlet and document material in the field, with a liberal inclusion of articles in periodicals and society transactions. They are useful as the most satisfactory bibliography of the periods yet produced but are, on the whole, less well done than Gross's monumental work, and the Tudor volume especially must be used with some caution as it shows many inaccuracies in titles; some of the inaccuracies are minor misprints, others are serious enough to cause real difficulty in finding the material or to be actually misleading.

For a list of some corrections *see* London, University Institute of Historical Research, *Bulletin* 11:80–84, 1933.

Abbott, Wilbur Cortez. A bibliography of Oliver Cromwell; a list of printed materials relating to Oliver Cromwell, together with a list of portraits and caricatures. Camb., Harv. Univ. Pr., 1929. 551p. $12.50.   **V275**

Material on the Cromwell period published from 1597 to 1928.

New York (City). Union Theological Seminary. Library. Catalogue of the McAlpin collection of British history and theology; comp. and ed. by C. R. Gillett. N.Y., 1927–30. 5v.   **V276**

Valuable for historical material published from 1500–1700. Arranged chronologically with alphabetical index.

18th and 19th centuries

Grose, Clyde Leclare. A select bibliography of British history, 1660–1760. Chic., Univ. of Chic. Pr., 1939. 507p. $9.   **V277**

Divided by periods: General, 1660–1760; 1660–88; 1689–1714; 1715–60. Classified arrangement, detailed table of contents shows scheme. Includes some major collections of manuscripts as well as printed works. Annotated. Works considered exceptionally useful are starred.

Morgan, William Thomas and Morgan, Chloe Siner. Bibliography of British history (1700–1715) with special reference to the reign of Queen Anne. Bloomington, Ind. 1934–42. 5v. (Indiana Univ. studies nos. 94, 95, 114-116, 119-124)   **V278**

Contents: v.1-2, Pamphlets and memoirs, 1700–1715; v.3, Source materials published in 1717 and later; Correspondence, autobiographies, diaries, and journals; Periodicals, including newspapers and annuals (1700–1715); Plays and other dramatic works; Secondary materials (to about June 1938); v.4, Unpublished manuscripts with index; v.5, Addenda and corrigenda; Supplements to v.1-3; Appendices; Comprehensive index to v.1,2,3, and 5.

Williams, Judith Blow. A guide to the printed materials for English social and economic history, 1750–1850. N.Y., Columbia Univ. Pr., 1926. 2v. (Records of civilization: Sources and studies, ed. by J. T. Shotwell)   **V279**

A classed work, including sections on biography and local history. Alphabetical index.

Current

Guide to the historical publications of the societies of England and Wales; Suppl. 1, 1929– . Lond., Longmans, 1930- . pts. 1- . (Bulletin of the Institute of Historical Research, Suppl., Nov. 1930-) 2s. 6d. ea.   **V280**

Prepared by a committee of the Institute and of the Congress of Archaeological Societies, the supplements appearing before the basic work which is still in preparation. Planned to do for the societies of England and Wales what Terry (V320) and Matheson (V321) do for those of Scotland and also to take the place of the discontinued *Index of archaeological papers* (V270). The supplements merely record issues for the years covered, leaving the historical information about the societies and the records of publication, index, etc., to be given in the basic volume.

Fig. 7.   WINCHELL, C. M., *Guide to Reference Books*. (Copyright: American Library Association.)

arrangement so useful, at least for British users. The section "general works" has subsections guides; bibliography; historiography; dictionaries, etc.; illustrations; annuals and atlases. The next main sections—archaeology; classical antiquities; mediaeval and modern history—are short, but the "countries" section is extensive, Great Britain running to 5 pp. and U.S.A. to 4 pp. The supplements to Winchell are identical typographically with the main work and, so far as history is concerned, seem to give an improved coverage of Continental works. Descriptions are so full as to enable librarians or booksellers to advise their clients without seeing the work in question. As an example the entry for the important new abstracting periodical *Historical Abstracts* lists the title very fully and even gives alternative prices which are available to institutions with different resources. The U.S. publishing address is followed by a note of the number of abstracts in Vol. 1, and the period covered; there is also a full note of indexes and supplementary features—information which would even take a reader who had this Viennese publication in front of him a considerable time to procure, and which is, of course, even more valuable if he does not know whether to try to acquire it or not.

COMPARISONS

We have dealt fully from the standpoint of biography and history with the seven works listed above. Few readers of this book will fail to have access to at least two of them, Winchell and the *Reader's Adviser*. Some may be able to substitute other titles, though most of these would be a century old such as Watt's *Bibliotheca Britannica*, Lowndes' *Bibliographer's Manual*, Graesse's *Trésor des livres rares et précieux*, Brunet's *Manuel du libraire*, or other titles already mentioned. Even in the largest library or bookshop, however, no one student could monopolize continually all seven titles, and it has therefore been thought useful to reproduce a page from each of them—in each case, for comparison, the page referring to volumes of the standard retrospective British historical bibliography. Is there any value for those of us connected with books in knowing what a sample page looks like? Much can be learned from type, and the national characteristics of American, British, French and German styles can be discerned from the examples before us. It is not unfair to say that an American work will probably be more flamboyant than the others, with somewhat gay and showy presentation, and informality. Standard British typography is somewhat dull, and though there has been some improvement in the years since the appearance of Sonnenschein no present-day list could match that work for detail. Nowadays there is less spidery type, fewer uses of bold type, and much less mixing of founts—compare the workmanlike though undistinguished appearance of Walford.

French typography has changed little in the last century and is generally as unremarkable as the paper of French books. On the whole the Germans, perhaps the finest printers in the world, give the cleanest appearance to the page, and, certainly of the examples before us, adopt the most systematic methods. The type area of a page has a definite mnemonic quality, greater even, or more lasting, than the jacket or the binding. When he said "due attention to the inside of books, and due contempt for the outside is the proper relation between a man of sense and his books", Lord Chesterfield was writing before edition binding prevented the private owner giving an individuality to his own favourite books. Even so the advent of the ephemeral paper back, and the continual rebinding of books in libraries used by the public, gives modern point to his dictum.

Turning now to the treatment accorded similar works by the different contributors, as shown in Figs. 1–7, note that Hoffman refers only to the two in-print volumes of the *Bibliography of British History*—and those not very fully. On the other hand, she has some useful general background for the novice; no one on either side of the Atlantic would question her judgements or selection of English historians, but the serious student must realize it *is* only a selection. In her main sequence the *Pageant of England Series* entry would not be acceptable to all scholarly tastes. Within its space limits Malclès' entry is more useful. Longmans', Methuen's, the Oxford histories and the four period bibliographies listed are absolutely authoritative, and current bibliographies find a place. Malclès' titles alone (and she is not writing about her own country) would set the student well on the way to finding out about history—but he would acquire no background material. Hoffman is, of course, limited to books in print in America; Murphey is restricted by his own set limits (1945 onwards). Even so his entries are fuller than both Hoffman's and Malclès'. Note the cross-reference to the main entry for the *Dictionary of National Biography*, and that only American and British material is included. Murphey considers the informal arrangement of his book an improvement; personally I doubt whether the average historical user of it would prefer his material interspersed amongst such topics as high fidelity, hobbies and hockey.

Sonnenschein is, of course, like nothing else. He highlights with an asterisk the material (Gross*: *Sources and Literature of English History to 1485*) we are looking for, saying nearly as much in $\frac{1}{4}$ inch as does Winchell in 2 inches. Personally I doubt whether today's students are prepared to cope with his particular brand of shorthand. As a guide to what to read, his work is confusing as well as outdated. Noting only the lower half of the reproduced page 1141, he first makes a general reference elsewhere. I doubt whether his second title (Beard) merited placing in a list of best books as late as the thirties though it could well find a place in such works as Munford's *Books for Basic Stock*, or in the representative books section of the McColvin's *Library Stock and Assistance to Readers*, so long as it were made clear that other excluded titles were equally worthy. Nevertheless, he tells us the English and American price, format, publisher and date of first publication. He then refers quite adequately for his date (*Bibliography of Modern British History*, 3 vols., In preparation) to Conyers Read and the rest. What is the value of the other material he lists which the others omit? I doubt whether his methods would send students straight to read it, standard though most of it is, or was. How many would extend his cryptic entry under Earle to "Professor John, *Handbook to the Land Charters and Other Saxonic Documents*. 16s. ($4) crown octavo, Clarendon Press, 1888. For use with Kemble's *Codex Diplomaticus*, republished by Birch in his *Cartularium Saxonicum* (see group F, section 18)"? I suppose the fault is not with Sonnenschein but with our own laziness. Although we now have others to advise us more conveniently what to read, he does help us, as librarians or booksellers, to answer the difficult question "Shall I throw away this last copy I know of, or shall I keep it?" Sonnenschein is still a very present help to stack-room custodians.

The great merit of Totok and Weitzel, apart from the clarity already referred to, is its coverage of Nordic material—Norway and Sweden happen to be represented on the page reproduced. General series, as distinct from bibliographies, are excluded, as is the Irish material listed by the rather similar Malclès. Comparing these two (our non-Anglo-Saxon examples), the superior typography of Totok and Weitzel is obvious, and the German work has brief annotations.

Walford and Winchell naturally invite comparisons, and it is fair to say that Walford would never have appeared had Winchell been completely satisfactory for English users. A comparison has recently been made in *College and Research Libraries* between Walford, Winchell and the large version of Malclès (*Les Sources du travail bibliographique*) which shows that Walford's annotations are best, but Winchell has superior indexing. Walford lacks Winchell's introductions, but Malclès' comments are often a model of precision. Winchell covers technology worst; Malclès best. As might be expected Walford lists 230 books of British origin compared with Winchell's 163, but only 60 of United States origin compared with Winchell's 400. Each of the three works fails to represent the reference books of certain countries; Walford has nothing from Latin America, Holland, Spain or Scandinavia; Winchell nothing from Belgium, Spain or Scandinavia, Malclès nothing from Latin America, Holland or the British Commonwealth as a whole. However, Malclès has by far the most entries on the U.S.S.R., Italy and Germany. "Walford's greatest drawback is the number of titles he includes. The work cannot really stand alone and should be used in connection with Winchell." As a critique of the *Bibliography of British History* (in which Walford and Winchell are supreme over the others), Winchell is slightly superior. Typographically also it is clearer and the index is more comprehensive. This is, however, exceptional, and Walford's entries for British material are usually better. Apart from Gross, the other material on p. 501 of Winchell is not of much practical value in Great Britain; p. 446 of Walford includes only one item (Kerner) that a British history student at undergraduate level might not readily know. Excellent as both Walford and Winchell are, the fact that there is room for both clearly shows that no scholar can be truly international, and that history cannot fail to be looked at nationally, however bad this may be in theory. Let us then be tolerant, and not scathingly amused, at the extravagant monuments to forgotten minor wars and their heroes that we may find in Corsica, the Middle West, the Tyrol, or Liechtenstein. Our own examination of general historical bibliography from only four national viewpoints has revealed wide, undoubtedly sincere, divergence of viewpoint—how then can we expect an African, a Malayan, or a Russian to accept what we declare to be history, or the means of learning it, as accurate? If our study of these seven sample pages, and the very reputable bibliographies from which they are reproduced, has done no more than impress us with the inevitable bias of history, and teach us how humbly we must approach the search for truth, particularly in studying our own national history, it will have been well worth while. It is a useful prelude to the study of international sources with which we begin the next chapter.

CHAPTER 2

Universal Biographical and Historical Works

INTRODUCTION

Having discovered some six or seven books which list a large number of other books, what should we consult next for our specific problem? Dr. Chandler's opening five chapters[1] set out his particular methodology, but we cannot emphasize too strongly that the ultimate decision on approach must be our own. Above (pp. 6–27) we could have plunged straight into our study of general bibliographies without concerning ourselves with the atmosphere of history (pp. 4–5), but at some loss of appreciation and pleasure. Similarly, if we know our inquiry relates to a recent election, or sixteenth-century Peru, we could go straight to an issue of a fact finding service (no book would as yet have been written about the subject of the first example), or to Prescott's *History of the Conquest of Peru* for the second example. Although this method might well be rewarded and indeed be the best for the experienced researcher, it would not be the most helpful way of learning how to answer future queries. A good rule is to work from the general to the particular. A universal historical bibliography would give not only Prescott's but several other histories of Peru in various languages. A universal historical abstracting service would give not only a British but many other nationalistic views of the 1964 election. Of course, our approach must be dictated by circumstances. Dr. Chandler lists nine common sources of inquiries: books, articles, yearbooks, periodicals, newspapers, documents, local,

[1] Chandler, *How to Find Out*, Pergamon Press, 1963, pp. 1–60.

Hager, Hermann ⟨Apotheker; Chemiker⟩ † 1897
Poggendorff: Handwörterb. IV.

Hager, Hermann ⟨Goetheforscher⟩ † 1895
Börsenbl. Deutsch. Buchhandel LXIV, 1897
S. 1201 f.

Hager, P. Karl ⟨Forstbotaniker⟩ † 1918
Verhandl. Schweiz. Naturf. Ges. 1919 Nekr.
S. 23 f. — Carl Schröter: P. K. Hager. 1918
⟨= Bündner Monatsbl. Nr. 11, 1918⟩.

Hagerup, Andreas ⟨Ornithologe⟩ † 1919
Dansk ornitol. foren. tidsskr. 1919/20 S. 85.

Hagerup, George Francis ⟨Jurist⟩
Inbjudn. juris doktorsprom. Lund. 1918 S. VIII f.
— Halvorsen: Norsk Forf.-Lex. II, 1888 S. 471 f.

Hagerup, Olaf ⟨Botaniker⟩
Christensen: Danske botan. litter. 1912/1939.
1940 S. 180.

Haggard, Henry Rider ⟨Schriftsteller⟩ † 1925
English Illustrated Magazine XXXI, 1904 S. 298 f.
— G. L. Mackay: A Bibliogr. writings of Sir R.
Haggard. 1931 (= Bookman's Journ. XVIII,
1930 Nr. 12 S. 1-22; Nr. 13 S. 23-67).

Hagge, Karl ⟨Mathematiker⟩
Poggendorff: Handwörterb. VI.

Haggerty, Melvin Everett ⟨Psychologie⟩
Psychological Register. 1929 S. 96 u. 1932 S. 308 f.

Hagić, Jovan ⟨Schriftsteller⟩
M. Kićović: J. Hagić. 1930 S. 227-236 ⟨Diss.⟩.

Hagihara, Yusuke ⟨Astronom⟩
Poggendorff: Handwörterb. VI.

Haglund, Erik Emil ⟨Botaniker⟩
Krok: Biblioth. botan. suec. 1925 S. 253 f.

Hagmeier, Arthur ⟨Meeresbiologe⟩
Kürschner's Gel. Kal. IV, 1931.

Hagströmer, Anders Johan ⟨Chirurg⟩ † 1830
Callisen: Medic. Schriftst.-Lex. VIII, 1831 S. 29 ff.

Hagströmer, Johan ⟨Jurist⟩ † 1910
Uppsala Universitets Matrikel 1896 S. 56-58;
1906 S. 62 f.

Hague, Arnold ⟨Geologe⟩ † 1917
Bull. Geolog. Soc. America XXIX, 1917 S. 46-48.
— Biogr. Memoirs National Acad. Sciences IX,
1919 S. 36-38. — Bull. U.S. Geolog. Surv. 746,
1923 S. 437. — Poggendorff: Hdwb. III. IV.

Hague, Bernard ⟨Elektrizität⟩
Poggendorff: Handwörterb. VI.

Haguenau, Jacques ⟨Mediziner⟩
Titres et travaux scientif. du Dr. J. Haguenau.
1929.

Hahl, Carl ⟨Mediziner⟩
Bergholm: Finlands Läkare. 1927 S. 158. — Carpelan u. Tudeer: Helsingfors Univers. Lärare.
1925 S. 311 f.

Hahl, Filip Hjalmar ⟨Literarhistoriker⟩
Carpelan u. Tudeer: Helsingfors Univers. Lärare.
1925 S. 312 f.

Hahmann, Kurt ⟨Angew. Botanik⟩
Verzeichnis kolonialwiss. Schriften Hamburg.
1939 S. 13 f.

Hahn, Alfred ⟨Gynäkologe⟩
Gynäkologen-Verzeichnis. 1939 S. 156.

Hahn, Amandus ⟨Biologe⟩
Poggendorff: Handwörterb. VI.

Hahn, August ⟨Theologe⟩ † 1863
F. Haase: Bresl. Theol. Fakult. 1911 S. 189.

Hahn, Dorothy ⟨Chemie⟩
Poggendorff: Handwörterb. VI.

Hahn, Eduard ⟨Ethnologe⟩ † 1928
· Studien u. Forschungen z. Menschen- u. Völker-
kunde XIV, 1917 S. VII-XI.

Hahn, Eugen ⟨Chirurg⟩ † 1902
Deutsche Zeitschr. f. Chirurgie LXVIII, 1903
H. 3/4 S. I. — Revue de chirurgie XXVI, 1902
S. 894-896.

Hahn, François Louis ⟨Mediziner⟩
Dictionnaire biogr. membres soc. sav. I, 1899
S. 120 f.

Hahn, Friedrich ⟨Chemiker⟩
Poggendorff: Handwörterb. V. VI.

Hahn, Friedrich Felix ⟨Geologe⟩ † 1914
Mitteil. Geogr. Ges. München X, 1915 S. 71. —
Zentralbl. f. Mineralogie 1915 S. 215-223.

Hahn, Friedrich Gustav ⟨Geograph⟩ † 1917
Geographische Zeitschrift XXIII, 1917 S. 340 f.

Hahn, Friedrich-Vinzenz von ⟨Kolloidforscher⟩
Poggendorff: Handwörterb. VI.

Hahn, Fritz ⟨Serologe⟩
Kürschner's Gel. Kal. VI, 1940/41.

Hahn, Georg ⟨Chemiker⟩
Poggendorff: Handwörterb. VI.

Hahn, Guillaume ⟨Naturforscher⟩
A. Weber: Bibliogr. Verviétoise. II, 1901 S. 120 ff.

Hahn, Heinrich ⟨Mediziner⟩ † 1882
F. Baeumker: Dr. med. H. Hahn. 1932 S. 693-695.

Hahn, Helmut ⟨Sinnesphysiologie⟩
Kürschner's Gel. Kal. VI, 1940/41.

Hahn, Hermann ⟨Anatom⟩
Chronik Univ. München 1895/96 S. 32 u. ff. Jgg.
bis 1910/11.

Hahn, Ida ⟨Volkskunde⟩
Mannus XXXI, 1939 S. 322 f. — Zeitschr. f.
Ethnologie LXXI, 1939 S. 144 f.

Hahn, Otto ⟨Chemiker⟩
. Poggendorff: Handwörterb. V. VI.

Hahn, Otto ⟨Chirurg⟩
Chirurgen-Verzeichnis. 1938 S. 241 f.

Fig. 8. ARNIM, M., *Internationale Personalbibliographie*. (Copyright: Hiersemann.)

national and international experts. We may not currently have access to all of them; we may think it wise to quit our library and accost instead the Professor of Peruvian history who will be addressing the local branch of the Historical Association this afternoon. Even so we should know, though we may not this time require, the full range of bibliographies and other sources that would be at our disposal in the British Museum, or Library of Congress.

BIOGRAPHY: INDEXES

Let us start not with a universal biography but with the fullest recent guide to bibliographies of individuals (Fig. 8), Max Arnim's *Internationale Personalbibliographie 1800–1943* (2nd edition, 2 vols., Hiersemann, Leipzig and Stuttgart, 1944–52). (A supplementary Vol. III, 1944–59, is in progress.) It indexes bibliographies contained in books, periodicals, biographical dictionaries and *Festschriften* (essays "presented to" famous literary figures usually on their retirement, birthday or even written in their honour after their death). There are some 60,000 entries with a strong German emphasis; on an average each entry receives two or three references. The first edition of this work published in 1936 has 25,000 entries relating to the years 1850–1935, but it has some material that has been dropped from the current edition for political reasons. One or other of the editions of this work would be a natural starting point for someone tracing information on a person whose nationality was not known, or on a series of persons of different nationalities, though the entries are so brief as to make identification difficult and prominent persons will not be traced unless a *bibliography* of their works has been published. Compare the entry for Sir Henry Rider Haggard on the page reproduced. The second edition includes occupations and dates of death. From Arnim research might continue to (Fig. 9), *Biography Index; a Cumulative Index to Biographical Material in Books and Magazines* (H. W. Wilson, New York, vols. 1–, 1946–, In progress). This is a quarterly with annual and triennial cumulations; "it includes current books in the English language wherever published; biographical material

Biography Index

AUGUST 1962

All biographees are American unless otherwise indicated

A.E. pseud. See Russell, G. W.
ABD-el-Krim, 1880?- Moroccan chieftain
Return of the lion. Newsweek 59:48 My 28
'62
ABIGAIL, biblical character
Ockenga, Harold John. Women who made
Bible history. Zondervan '62 p 101-9
ABRAHAM, patriarch

Fiction

Keyes, Nelson Beecher. Abraham, the friend
of God. Vantage '61 239p
ABRAHAM ben David de Posquières, 1125?-
1198, French biblical scholar
Twersky, Isadore. Rabad of Posquières, a
twelfth-century Talmudist. (Harvard univ.
Semitic ser, v 18) Harvard univ. press '62
336p bibliog
ACCIOLY, Hildebrando Pompeu Pinto, 1888-
1962, Brazilian lawyer and diplomat
Obituary
N Y Times p25 Ap 7 '62
ADAMS, Abigail (Smith) 1744-1818, president's
wife
Hurd, Charles, and Hurd. E. B. Treasury
of great American letters. Hawthorn bks.
'61 p75-7
Logan, Logna B. Ladies of the White House.
Vantage '62 p 15-21
ADAMS, John, 1735-1826, president
Bailyn, B. Butterfield's Adams; notes for
a sketch. William & Mary Q 19:238-56 Ap
'62
Bruce, David Kirkpatrick Este. Sixteen
American presidents. Bobbs '62 p35-58 por
New York university. Hall of fame for great
Americans. Hall of fame for great Ameri-
cans at New York university; official hand-
book. N.Y. univ. press '62 p 115 por
Servant of the young Republic. il por Life
52:56-66+ My 25 '62

Pictorial works

Durant, John, and Durant, A. K. R. Pictorial
history of American presidents. Barnes '62
p26-31, 314
ADAMS, John Quincy, 1767-1848, president
Bruce, David Kirkpatrick Este. Sixteen
American presidents. Bobbs '62 p 137-72
por
New York university. Hall of fame for great
Americans. Hall of fame for great Americans at New York university; official handbook. N.Y. univ. press '62 p 116 por

Pictorial works

Durant, John, and Durant, A. K. R. Pictorial
history of American presidents. Barnes '62
p50-7, 315
ADAMS, Junius Greene, 1884-1962, judge and
cattle breeder
Obituary
Jersey J por 9:26+ F 5 '62
ADAMS, Louisa Catherine (Johnson) 1775-1852,
president's wife
Logan, Logna B. Ladies of the White House.

AGASSIZ, Louis, 1807-1873, Swiss naturalist
New York university. Hall of fame for great
Americans. Hall of fame for great Ameri-
cans at New York university: official hand-
book. N.Y. univ. press '62 p67 por
AGEE, James, 1909-1955, author and poet
Agee, James. Letters of James Agee to
Father Flye. Braziller '62 235p por
AGNES, Saint, 292-305
André-Delastre, Louise. Saint Agnes; tr. by
Rosemary Sheed. (Your name—your saint
ser) Macmillan '62 102p biblog
AGOSTINI, Peter, 1913- sculptor
Navaretta, E. A. Agostini makes a sculp-
ture. il pors autograph Art N 61:27-30+
My '62
AILRED, Saint. See Aelred
AITKEN, Beekman, 1905-1962, lawyer
Obituary
N Y Times p37 My 17 '62
AKAKA, Abraham K. 1916- clergyman
Ukuleles are not enough. por Newsweek 59:
106 Ap 16 '62
ALBERS, Josef, 1888- German-American
painter
Biography
Cur Biog por 23:3-4 Je '62
ALBERT the Great, Saint, 1206-1280
Marie Stephen, Sister. Albert the Great—
new mathematician of the middle ages?
Math Teach 55:291-5 Ap. '62
ALCOTT, Amos Bronson, 1799-1888, educator
and philosopher
Cooke, George Willis. Historical and bi-
ographical introduction to accompany the
Dial. Russell '61 v2 p40-50, 148-60
ALCOTT, Louisa May, 1832-1888, author

Juvenile literature

Wagoner, Jean (Brown). Louisa Alcott, girl
of old Boston; il. by Claudine Nankivel.
(Childhood of famous Americans) Bobbs
'62 200p
ALEICHEM, Shalom, pseud. See Rabinowitz,
S.
ALEXANDER, Harold Rupert Leofric George,
1st earl Alexander of Tunis. See Alexander
of Tunis, H. R. L. G. A. 1st earl
ALEXANDER, Will Winton, 1884-1956, govern-
ment official
Dykeman, Wilma, and Stokely, James. Seeds
of southern change; the life of Will Alex-
ander. Univ. of Chicago press '62 343p bib-
liog il pors
ALEXANDER of Tunis, Harold Rupert Leofric
George Alexander, 1st earl, 1891- British
field marshal
Where are they now? por Newsweek 59:16
Je 11 '62
ALEXANDRA, princess of Great Britain, 1936-

Pictorial works

Princess in Oxford and Sweden. Illus Lond N
240:904 Je 2 '62
ALLEN, Bernard Keith, 1939- baseball player
Bingham, W. Pair of twins named Pie and
Tv. por Sports Illus 16:86+ My 21 '62
ALLEN, George Venable, 1903- diplomat
Logsdon, J. D. Introduction of George V.

Fig. 9. *Biography Index.* (Copyright: H. W. Wilson Co.)

from the 1500 periodicals now regularly indexed in the Wilson indexes, plus a selected list of professional journals in the fields of law and medicine; obituaries of national and international interest from the *New York Times*. All types of biographical material are covered: pure biography, critical material of biographical significance, autobiography, letters, diaries, memoirs, journals, genealogies, fiction, drama, poetry, bibliographies, obituaries, pictorial works and juvenile literature. Works of collective biography are fully analysed. Incidental biographical material such as prefaces and chapters in otherwise non-biographical books is included. Portraits are included when they appear in conjunction with indexed material" (preface). This long extract has been included to show the extent to which conscientious indexing can go; the *Biography Index* has lists of occupations following the main sequence. The companion *Essay and General Literature Index* (1934–, In progress[1]) also includes much biographical material as, in practice, it is often impossible to separate the biography from the criticism of individuals. The illustrated catalogue *Wilson Publications* (free on request) has many helpful mnemonic pictures of spines of Wilson publications.

There is an English biographical index, universal so far as English language material is concerned (Fig. 10), P. M. Riches (comp.), *An Analytical Bibliography of Universal Collected Biography* (Library Association, 1934). This, however, as it states, deals only with information in collected biographies, not in the wide number of types of publication covered by Arnim and the *Biography Index*. Riches, in its main section—alphabetically arranged by biographee—has more entries (56,000) than the first edition of Arnim; a three-year cumulation of the *Biography Index* has about 40,000 entries. The 3000 works indexed and listed in Riches include the widest list of biographical sources available at the publication date, and they are of the type normally accessible in the larger reference libraries. It is unfortunate that a supplementary volume has never been brought out. A useful older work is E. M. Oettinger's *Bibliographie biographique universelle* (2 vols., Stienon, Brussels,

[1] For sample page reproduction, see Chandler, *op. cit.*, Fig. 12.

Fig. 10. RICHES, P. M., *An Analytical Bibliography of Universal Collected Biography.* (Copyright: Library Association.)

1854), a list of 45,000 separately published works. See also C. U. Chevalier's work (below, p. 53).

BIOGRAPHY: COMPREHENSIVE WORKS

Biographical inquiries of an international character can often be answered from comprehensive works. This is no place to describe the great encyclopaedias[1], but all of them contain biographical information, mostly in their straightforward sequences, sometimes extracted from non-biographical articles by use of the index. The larger encyclopaedias give good though not always up-to-date bibliographies, though these should normally be used with more caution than those in the universal biographical indexes. Countries of origin and latest issue dates of the following encyclopaedias are noted; although they aim at being universal in scope all show nationalistic bias.

Great Britain

Chambers's Encyclopaedia,[2] 3rd edition, 15 vols., Newnes, 1959.
    Supplement: *Chambers's Encyclopaedic World Survey* (annual).
Children's Britannica, Encyclopaedia Britannica, 12 vols., 1960.
Everyman's Encyclopaedia, 4th revised edition, 12 vols., Dent, 1958.
Oxford Junior Encyclopaedia, 2nd edition, 13 vols., Oxford Univ.
    Press, 1964.

U.S.A.

Collier's Encyclopaedia, 24 vols., Collier, New York, 1964.
Columbia Encyclopaedia, 3rd edition, Columbia Univ. Press, New York, 1963.
Compton's Pictured Encyclopaedia, 15 vols., Compton, Chicago, 1965.
    Supplement: *Compton Year Book*.
Encyclopaedia Americana,[3] 30 vols., Grolier Inc., New York, 1964.

---

[1] See R. L. Collison, *Encyclopaedias: their history throughout the ages*, Hafner, 1964.

[2] For sample page reproductions see Chandler, *op. cit.*, Fig. 10.

[3] For sample page reproduction see Chandler, *op. cit.*, Fig. 9.

Encyclopaedia Britannica[1], 25 vols., Encyclopaedia Britannica, Chicago and London. Annual printings. Supplement: *Britannica Book of the Year* (annual).

Canada

Encyclopaedia Canadiana, 10 vols., Grolier, Ottawa, 1964.

Australia

Australian Encyclopaedia[2], 10 vols., Angus & Robertson, Sydney, 1958.

France

Encyclopédie française, Comité de l'Encyclopédie Française, Paris, 1937–, In progress.
Grande Larousse encyclopédie, 10 vols., Larousse, Paris, 1960–4.
La grande encyclopédie, 31 vols., Lamirault, Paris, 1886–1902.

Germany

Der Grosse Brockhaus, 13 vols. and atlas, Brockhaus, Wiesbaden, 1952–60. Note also *Der Kleine Brockhaus* (2 vols.) and *Der Neue Brockhaus* (6 vols.).
Der Grosse Herder, 10 vols., Herder, Freiburg, 1953–6. Supplement, 2 vols., 1962.

Switzerland

Schweizer Lexicon, 7 vols., Encyclios-Verlag, Zurich, 1945–8.

Belgium

Grande encyclopédie de la Belgique et du Congo, Wauthoz de Grand, Brussels, 1938–, In progress.

[1] Chandler, *op. cit.*, Fig. 8.   [2] Below, Fig. 53, p. 171.

Holland

E.N.S.I.E., 12 vols., E.N.S.I.E., Amsterdam, 1946–60.
Winkler Prins Encyclopaedie, 20 vols., Elsevier, Amsterdam, 1947–60.

Sweden

Svensk uppslagsbok, 32 vols., Forlagshuset Norder, Malmo, 1947–57.

Italy

Enciclopedia italiana di scienze, lettere ed arti, 36 vols., Istituto della Enciclopedia Italiana, Rome, 1929–39. Three *Appendices* (to 1960) have now appeared.

Spain

Enciclopedia universal illustrada europeo-americana, 80 (81) vols., Espasa, Barcelona, 1905–33. *Suplemento anual* since 1934 (first year covers 1930–3).

Russia

Bol'shaya sovetskaya entsiklopediya, 50 vols., Gosudarstvennoe Nauchnoe Izdatel'stvo, Moscow, 1949–57. Supplementary vols. (51, etc.) are appearing.

Walford and/or Winchell and their supplements (above, pp. 19–23) refer to numerous other encyclopaedias based on Norway, Denmark, Portugal, Yugoslavia, Hungary, Czechoslovakia, Brazil, Greece, Israel, Japan, Latvia, Poland, Rumania, Turkey and Indonesia, as well as to others relating to the countries mentioned above. Perhaps more significant than the existence of all these is the absence of traceable general encyclopaedias produced in Africa or in large parts of Asia. All that Walford, Winchell and Collison say about the scope and use of general encyclopaedias should be carefully noted.

oraison funèbre de Thomas Erpenius, prononcée à Leyde, en 1624, parle avec éloge d'Aartsbergen.

Ferwerda, *Nederlandsch Geslacht-Stam-en-Wapen-Boek*, article VAN DER CAPELLEN. — Wagenaar, *Vaderlandsche Historie*, XII, 74, etc. — Van der Aa, *Biographisch Woordenbœk*.

AARTSEN ou **AERTSEN** (*Pierre*), peintre hollandais, surnommé *Lange Peter* (Long Pierre), né à Amsterdam en 1507, mort en 1573. Élève d'Aert Claesson, de Leyde, il fut admis, en 1533, dans la maîtrise des peintres anversois. On a de lui des tableaux estimés, représentant l'intérieur d'une cuisine, des mets, des fruits, des animaux, etc. Il peignit aussi quelques sujets religieux pour les églises d'Amsterdam, de Louvain, etc.

Vanmander, *Het leven der Nederlandsche Schilders* (*Vie des peintres hollandais*). — Descamps, *Vie des peintres flamands*.

AASCOW (*Urbain-Bruan*), médecin danois, vivait dans la seconde moitié du dix-huitième siècle. Il fut médecin des armées navales, et attaché au service de la marine royale du Danemark. Il a publié à Copenhague, en 1774, un *Journal d'observations* sur les maladies qui régnèrent sur la flotte danoise que l'on avait équipée pour bombarder Alger en 1770.

Erslew, *Forfatter-Lexicon*.

AASSIM ou **ASSIM** (*Ben-Abderrahman effendi*), écrivain turc, mort en 1086 de l'hégire (1675 de J.-C.). Il continua jusqu'à son époque l'anthologie turque (*Subdetol-esshaar*) du célèbre Kafsade.

Hammer, dans *Allgemeine Encyclopædie*, t. I, 21.

AASSIM (*Ismael effendi*), mufti, mort en 1172 de l'hégire (1758 de J.-C.). Il laissa quelques livres d'histoire et un recueil de lettres, dont Wassif fait un très-grand cas. Sa bibliothèque se montait à plus de mille volumes.

Hammer, dans *Allgemeine Encyclopædie*.

ABA ou **OWON** (*Samuel*), roi de Hongrie, né le 5 février 1010, mort en 1044. Il fut le beau-frère de saint Étienne et le premier roi chrétien de la Hongrie, élu en 1041, après avoir été chassé du pays. Il vainquit Pierre, surnommé *l'Allemand*, neveu de saint Étienne, et détesté des grands du royaume. Il ravagea l'Autriche et la Bavière, où Pierre s'était retiré. Mais il fut défait par l'empereur Henri III, dit *le Noir*, et massacré le 4 juillet 1044, par ses propres sujets.

Bonfin, *Rerum Hungar Decad.*, lib. II. — Schwarz, *Tractatus de Samuele rege Hungariæ, qui vulgo Aba audit*; Lempo, 1761, in-4°. — Thwrocz, *Chron. Hungarorum*. . Ranzanus *Epitome Rerum Hungaricarum.* — Mailath, *Geschichte der Magyaren*.

ABACA-KAN. Voy. ABAGAKAN.

ABACCO ou **L'ABACCO** (*Antonio*), architecte et graveur italien, vivait à Rome dans la seconde moitié du seizième siècle. Il était élève d'Antonio di San-Gallo. Il a gravé les planches de son ouvrage intitulé *Libro d'Antonio Abacco, appartenente all' architectura, nel quale si figurano alcune nobili antichita di Roma*; Venise, 1558; *ibid.*, 1576. Abbaco grava aussi les plans de l'église de Saint-Pierre de Rome,

d'après les dessins de San-Gallo. On ignore l'époque de sa mort.

Heineken, *Dictionnaire des artistes*.

ABACO (*Paolo DALL'*), mathématicien et poëte florentin, mort en 1365. Son véritable nom était *Paul Dagomari*. On a de lui quelques écrits (inédits) sur l'arithmétique et l'algèbre. Selon Villani, il publia en Italie le premier almanach.

Libri, *Histoire des sciences mathématiques en Italie*, t. II, p. 295.

ABACUC. Voy. HABACUC.

ABAD Ier (*Abou'l-Cacem-Mohammed*), premier roi maure de Séville, fondateur de la dynastie des Abadytes, mort le 24 janvier 1042, (le 29 djoumadi 1er, an 433 de l'hégire). Son père, Ismael ben-Abad, était originaire d'Émèse, en Syrie. Un de ses ancêtres vint en Espagne au deuxième siècle de l'hégire, et se fixa dans les environs de Séville, à Tocina, près du Guadalquivir. Par son opulence et son habileté, Ismael acquit beaucoup de considération et d'autorité à Séville : sa maison devint l'asile des bannis de Cordoue pendant les dissensions civiles : son fils Abou'l-Cacem-Mohammed marcha sur ses traces, gagna la confiance du roi de Cordoue Al-Cacem-Al-Mamoun, et obtint la charge de grand-cadi de Séville, avec le gouvernement de la province. Lorsque ce dernier perdit pour la seconde fois le trône de Cordoue, Abad se rendit indépendant, l'an 413 de l'hégire (1023 de J.-C.), par le secours des cheiks et des vizirs, que ses largesses avaient gagnés. La défaite et la mort d'Yahia-Al-Motaly, prince de Cordoue, l'an 417 (1026 de J.-C.), déterminèrent le premier acte de révolte d'Abad, et consolidèrent sa souveraineté. Après l'extinction des Omeyades, il prit le titre de roi, et ne laissa échapper aucune occasion d'agrandir sa puissance. Il tourna ses armes contre Mohammed ben-Abdallah Al-Boracely (*Barzeli* ou *Barozila* de quelques historiens), maître absolu de Carmone et d'Ecija, lui enleva plusieurs places, et l'assiégea dans sa capitale. Serré de près et manquant de provisions, Al-Boracely s'évada de Carmone, envoya son fils solliciter les secours du roi de Grenade, et alla lui-même implorer l'assistance du roi de Malaga. Ismael, fils d'Abad, surprit d'abord isolément les troupes de ces souverains, et les défit; mais, après leur jonction, il succomba, et perdit la vie, dans une bataille sanglante. Le roi de Séville, craignant d'être accablé si le roi de Cordoue se déclarait contre lui, eut recours à un stratagème. Il fit annoncer que le kalife Hescham II Al-Môwaïad, dont on ignorait depuis longtemps le sort, avait reparu à Calatrava, et était venu se mettre sous sa protection. Afin d'accréditer le bruit de l'existence de ce prince, il voulut que le nom de Hescham fût proclamé dans la Khothbah et gravé sur les monnaies, au mois de moharrem 427 (novembre 1035); en même temps il an-

Fig. 11. HOEFER, *Nouvelle biographie générale*. (Copyright: Rosenkilde & Bagger.)

Turning now to universal biographies, pride of place must be given to (Fig. 11) the *Nouvelle biographie générale* (46 vols., Firmin Didot, Paris, 1853–66), which is currently being reissued (1963–8) by Rosenkilde and Bagger, Copenhagen. This work made a bad start in 1852 when its editor, Dr. Hoefer (by whose name the work is usually cited), and his publisher were successfully sued for plagiarism from the longer work by Michaud (described below). Even so the work continued, and was planned to be at the same time more concise and more comprehensive than Michaud. It includes more names than Michaud under A–M; fewer under N–Z, and is handier to use than the second edition of this work. However, although it may be somewhat inferior to Michaud, its value can be no better illustrated than in a recent tribute by a Norwegian national, Harald Tveteras, Librarian of the University Library, Oslo; his remarks, indeed, are a significant comment on nineteenth-century scholarship in general: "it is still a living and comprehensive reference work for scientists and students within all fields of the history of the human race. In great libraries and research institutions not one day passes without its being used. Even if more recent investigations may often supplement the picture of the persons dealt with, the exact information given by the work will nevertheless, in most cases, prove to be sufficient, and at any rate the work is an excellent starting point. A work like the *Nouvelle biographie générale*, with its wealth of information and its great accuracy, it will hardly be possible to compile quite from the beginning in our days. It would be far too costly and take too much time. It is practically incomprehensible that it was then published within fourteen years".

(Fig. 12), J. F. Michaud, *Biographie universelle, ancienne et moderne* (2nd edition, 45 vols., Paris, 1843–65), though not being reprinted, is generally considered superior to Hoefer. Winchell says it is "the most important of the large dictionaries of universal biography, still very useful. . . . In spite of various inaccuracies, Michaud is more carefully edited [than Hoefer], its articles, which are signed with initials, are longer and often better". The first edition of Michaud comprehended 52 vols. (1811–28), but many of the

2   A A G

rendit en 1737 à l'université d'Iéna, fut nommé en 1739 président de la communion luthérienne à Alcmaer, et en 1742 à Harlem où il prêcha pendant 51 ans avec tant de succès, que son église était toujours remplie d'auditeurs de toutes les religions. Il fut un des fondateurs et le secrétaire de la société hollandaise des sciences, érigée à Harlem en 1752. On a de lui des sermons, et des mémoires sur l'histoire naturelle lus dans cette société. Un an avant sa mort, en 1792, il eut le rare plaisir de célébrer, pour la cinquantième fois, l'anniversaire de son entrée dans le ministère à Harlem. Un des meilleurs artistes de la Hollande, J. G. Holtrey, a consacré cet événement par une médaille dont la description se trouve dans le 10ᵉ. vol. du *Koust-en Letterbode*.   D—G.

AAGARD (CHRISTIAN), poète danois, né à Vibourg au commencement du 17ᵉ. siècle, fut professeur de poésie à Soroë et à Copenhague. Il mourut en 1664, à l'âge de 68 ans. On a de lui quelques poésies latines qui étaient estimées de son temps ; elles ont été recueillies dans le tom. Iᵉʳ. des *Deliciæ quorumdam poetarum danorum Frederici Rostgaard*, pag. 339. *Lugduni Batav.* 1693, 2 vol. in-12. Sa vie écrite par son fils, se trouve également dans le même recueil. — Nicolas AAGARD, son frère, bibliothécaire de l'académie de Soroë, a publié des ouvrages de philosophie et de physique, dont on trouve le catalogue dans *Bartholini bibliotheca septentrionis eruditi*, pag. 102 et 103.   M—B—N.

AAGESEN (SVEND, connu aussi sous le nom latin *Sueno Agonis* F.), historien danois, florissait en 1186, du temps de l'archevêque Absalon, dont il paraît avoir été le secrétaire. Il écrivit, par ordre d'Absalon, une his-

A A R

toire du Danemarck, sous ce titre : *Compendiosa historia regum Daniæ à Skioldo ad Canutum VI*. Cet ouvrage est très inférieur pour le style à celui de *Saxo Grammaticus;* mais sur quelques points de critique historique, Svend Aagesen a eu des opinions plus conformes à la tradition des Islandais, adoptée aujourd'hui par les savants du Nord. Il ne remonte pas jusqu'à *Dan I*, roi fabuleux de Saxo. On a encore de lui un ouvrage intitulé : *Historia legum castrensium Regis Canuti magni ;* c'est une traduction latine de la loi dite de *Witherlag*, donnée par Canut - le - Grand et publiée de nouveau par Absalon, sous le roi Canut VI. Aagesen l'a mise en tête d'une notice historique sur l'origine de cette loi. On trouve l'un et l'autre ouvrage dans le recueil intitulé : SUENONIS AGONIS FILII, *Christierni nepotis, primi Daniæ gentis historici, quæ extant* OPUSCULA. STEPHANUS JOHANNIS STEPHANIUS *ex vetustissimo codice membraneo MS. regiæ bibliothecæ Hafniensis primus publici juris fecit. Soræ, typis Henrici Crusii.* 1642. 222 p. in-8°. Dans cet intitulé, il faut, par *regiæ bibliothecæ*, entendre la bibliothèque de l'université de Copenhague. On trouve encore l'Histoire de Danemarck de Svend Aagesen insérée avec des notes excellentes, dans les *Scriptores* de Langebek, tom. I. p. 42. sqq. La traduction des *Leges castrenses regis Canuti Magni* est également imprimée dans les *Scriptores*, tom. III. p. 139, sqq.   M—B—N.

AALST. *Voyez* AELST.

AARE (DIRK VAN DER), évêque et seigneur d'Utrecht dans le 13ᵉ. siècle, avait été prévôt à Maëstricht. Parvenu à l'épiscopat, il eut bientôt à soutenir une guerre périlleuse contre Guillaume, comte de Hollande, qui le bat-

Fig. 12. MICHAUD, J. F., *Biographie universelle*.

articles in it had a strong Catholic and Royalist bias which was corrected in the second edition and in the supplement to the first edition; this was of 30 vols. (1834–62) and 3 vols. on mythological figures (1832–3) separate it from the original set. Largely owing to the defects in Michaud's early volumes noted above, which were not entirely removed from the second edition, Hoefer is superior in some respects in the A–M section; it has more articles, particularly minor ones, and some of its longer ones are more balanced. Throughout, moreover, Hoefer's bibliographies are cited in the language of the original; Michaud translates his references into French.

It must not be thought that works so old as this have no present-day value. A manuscript of association value to the author's library, but by a very obscure Spanish writer, was recently auctioned at Sotheby's, and Michaud gave by far the best available account of the man's background. A similar English work of this type, though not comparable for scholarship, is (Fig. 13) A. Chalmers, *The General Biographical Dictionary* (32 vols., Nichols, 1812–17). It seeks to stand comparison with the first edition of the *Biographie universelle* which had started to appear a year earlier. However, without its supplement, the French work ran to 52 vols. compared with the 32 of Chalmers. Chalmers said "a preference will be given to the Worthies of our own country; a preference, however, not of selfish partiality, but of absolute necessity, as all foreign collections are notoriously deficient in the English series. For this it would be unfair to account either from want of learning or research. A more obvious reason is that most of the foreign biographical collections have been made by Catholics, and in Catholic countries, where it would have been unsafe to enter into the merits of Englishmen of renown, either in Church or State". This is a point of view that would never occur to a contemporary bibliographer. Whether the complaint in the preface to Vol. 52 in the first edition of Michaud of "l'insuffisance des lois contre les vols ou plagiats litteraires" is justified may be seen by a comparison (Figs. 12 and 13) of similar entries in Michaud (1811) and Chalmers (1812). An even older German work of this type still valuable is

2   A A.

chief hand in establishing the Haerlem Society of Sciences,
and in 1778 formed a separate branch for the study of
Œconomics. In both he acted as secretary for many
years; and, besides some Sermons, published, in the
Transactions of that Society, a variety of scientific papers.
He died at Haerlem in 1795[1].

AAGARD (CHRISTIAN), a Danish poet, born at Wi-
bourg in 1616, was professor of poetry at Sora, and afterwards lecturer in theology at Ripen, in Jutland. Among
his poems are : 1. " De hommagio Frederici III. Daniæ et
Norw. Regis," Hafniæ, 1660, fol. ; and 2. " Threni Hy-
perborei" on the death of Christian IV. All his pieces are
inserted in the " Deliciæ quorundam Poetarum Danorum,
Frederici Rostgaard," Leyden, 1695, 2 vols. 12mo. He
died in February 1664, leaving a son, Severin Aagard,
who wrote his life in the above collection[2].

AAGARD (NICHOLAS), brother of the above, was librarian and professor in the University of Sora, in Denmark,
where he died Jan. 22, 1657, aged forty-five years, and
left several critical and philosophical works, written in
Latin. The principal are : 1. "A treatise on Subterra-
neous Fires." 2. "Dissertation on Tacitus." 3. "Observations on Ammianus Marcellinus." And 4. "A disputation on the Style of the New Testament," Sora, 4to,
1655. He and his brother were both of the Lutheran
Church[3].

AAGESEN (SUEND, in Latin SUENO AGONIS), a Danish
historian, flourished about the year 1186, and appears to
have been secretary to the archbishop Absalon, by whose
orders he wrote a history of Denmark, intituled, " Compendiosa historia regum Daniæ à Skioldo ad Canutum VI."
This work is thought inferior in style to that of Saxo Grammaticus; but, on some points, his opinions are in more
strict conformity to what are now entertained by the lite-
rati of the North. He was also author of " Historia legum
castrensium Regis Canuti magni," which is a translation
into Latin of the law called the law of Witherlag, enacted
by Canute the Great, and re-published by Absalon in
the reign of Canute VI. with an introduction by Aagesen
on the origin of that law. Both works are included in
" Suenonis Agonis filii, Christierni nepotis, primi Daniæ
gentis historici, quæ extant opuscula. Stephanus Johannis

[1] Dict. Hist. edit. 1810.   [2] Moreri.—Dict. Hist. 1810.   [3] Ibid.

Fig. 13. CHALMERS, A., *The General Biographical Dictionary*.

DICTIONARY OF UNIVERSAL
BIOGRAPHY

(*An asterisk * affixed to a date intimates that the year is approximate*)

AA   **A**   **ABBEY**

Aa, Abr. Jac van der: Dutch miscell. wr. and official, 1792–1857. P
Aa, Christ, Chas. Hy. van der: Dutch schol., 1718–1793. O: P
Aa, Christ. Pet. Eliza Robidé van der: Dutch official and poet, 1791–1851. P
Aa, Corn. van der: Dutch wr., 1749–1815. P
Aa, Mart. Wilh. van der: Dutch journ., 1831–1905. P
Aa, Peter van der: Dutch jurist, 1530–1594. O: K: R
Aa, Pet. van der: Dutch publisher,   –1730*. O
Aa, Philips van der: Dutch burgomaster, fl. 1564–1586. P
Aa, Pierre Jean Bapt. Chas. van der: Dutch class. schol., 1766–1812. P
Aachen (Aach), Joh. von: Germ. pntr., 1552–1615. M: O: R
Aagard, Christ.: Dan. Latin poet, 1616–1664. O
Aagard, Niels: Dan. philos. 1612–1657. O
Aagesen, And.: Dan. jurist, 1826–1879. V
Aagesen, Sweyn: Dan. hist., 12th and 13th cents. O
Aall, Mehemet: Turk. statesm., 1815–1871. V
Aali: See Mustafa Ben Achmed ben A.M.
Aalst: See Aelst.
Aalstius (van Aalst), Johannes: Dutch Carthusian, 1660–1712. P
Aara, Dirk van der: Bp. and Ld. of Utrecht, –1212. O
Aaron, St.: fdr. of 1st monastery in Bretagne, –528*. J
Aaron, the Levite: Span. rabbinical wr., 13th and 14th cents. T
Aaron Abiob: rabbi and comment. of Salonica, fl. 1540. O
Aaron ben Abr. ibn Hayyim: Moroccan bibl. and Talmudic comment.,   –1632. T
Aaron-Acharon, Caraïte rabbi of Nicomedia: See Aaron ben Elijah.
Aaron Ariscon (Hariechon): Caraïte rabbi and physn. of Constantinople, 13th cent. T
Aaron of Baghdad: Jew. Talmudist and mystic, 9th cent. T
Aaron ben Elijah, the Caraïte: Caraïte schol., philos. and poet, 1300*–1369*. O: T
Aaron ben Jacob ben David ben Isaac, Ha Kohen: Fr. Talmudist, 13th and 14th cents. O: T
Aaron ben Joseph: Caraïte schol., Hebraist and poet, 1250(60)–1320*. T
Aaron ben Joseph Hakohen Sargado: Jew. schol. and teacher of Pumbedita (Baghdad), fl. 942–960. T
Aaron ben Joseph Ha Levi, of Barcelona: Span. Jew. schol. and rabbi,   –post 1300. T
Aaron ben Joseph Sason: Jew. rabbi and wr. of Salonica,   –1608. O
Aaron of Lincoln: Anglo-Jew. financ., 1125*–1182. T
Aaron ben Moses ben Asher: Palestinian bibl. schol., 10th cent. O: T
Aaron of Starosselye: Jew. cabbalist and wr., 1766–1828. T
Aaron Worms: Chief Rabbi of Metz, 1754–1836. J
Aaron of Zhitomir: Pol. Jew. rabbi and preacher,   –1817*. T
Aaron, Pietro: Ital. monk and wr. on music, 1480*–ante 1541. O: Q
Aarschot, Phil. von Croy, Duke of: Flemish diplomat   –1595. O
Aarsens, Pieter: See Aertsen.
Aerssens, Frans. van: Dutch diplom. and statesm., 1572–1641. O: V.
Aartjen van Leiden: See Claessen, Aartjen.
Aartsbergen, Alex. van der Capellen, Seigneur d': Dutch statesm.,   –1656. O
Aartsen (Aarsens), Pieter: (Lange Peer).: See Aertszen.
Aartsz, Rijkaert: Dutch pntr., 1482–1577. M
Aasen, Ivar: Norw. philol. and lexicog., 1813–1896. V
Abacco, Ant. d': Ital. archt. and engrav., fl. 1558. M: O
Abaco, Evaristo Felice Dall': Ital. viol. and mus. comp., 1675–1742. Q
Abaco, Gius. Clemens Ferd., Bar dall': Ital. cellist, 1700*– . Q
Abad I. (Aboul Cacem Mohammed): 1st Moorish king of Seville,   –1042. O
Abad II.: Moorish king of Seville, 1012–1069. O
Abad III.: King of Seville, 1039–1095. O
Abad y Queipo, Man.: Span. bp., 1775–1824. O

Abadie, Arnaud d': Fr. bp.,   –1438. J
Abadie, Jean Marie: Fr. friar and philanth., 1822–1884. J
Abadie, Jean Melchior d': Fr. sold., 1748–1820. J
Abadie, Jos. Bern.: Fr. publisher, 1824–1876. J
Abadie, Michel: Fr. poet, 1866–1922. J
Abafli (Apafi), Michel: Prince of Transylvania,   –1690. O
Abain or Abin, Louis Chasteigner de la Roche-Posay: Fr. schol. and amb., 1535–1595. J
Abamonti, Gius.: Ital. patriot, 1759–1818. L: V
Abancourt, Chas. Franç-Frérot d': Fr engin. and surv., 1756–1801. J
Abancourt, Chas. Xav. Jos. Franqueville d': Fr. statesm., 1758–1792. J: O: V
Abano (Apono), Pietro d': Ital. philos., astrol. and physn., 1250–1316. O: V
Abarbanel, Isaac: See Abrabanel.
Abarca, Maria de: Span. min. and port. pntr.,   –1656*. M
Abarca, Gius. Cesare: Ital. patriot, poet and senator, 1838–1910. L3
Abba-Cornaglia, Pietro: Ital. mus. comp. and hist., 1854–1894. Q
Abba Mari: Fr. rabbi, poet and jurist, fl. 1250–1310. J: T: V
Abbadie, Anselme d': Fr. sold. and colonist,   –1728. J
Abbadie, Ant. Thomson d': Irish-Fr. astron. and wr. on Brazil and Abyssinia, 1810–1897. J: V
Abbadie, Arnaud Michel d': Irish-Fr. trav. and expl., 1815–1893. J: V
Abbadie, D.: Gov. of Louisiana, 1726–1765. J
Abbadie, Jacques: Dean of Killaloe, Fr.-Eng. rel. and pol. wr., 1654*–1727. A: J: O: V
Abbas: uncle of Mohammed, 565–652. O
Abbas, Pierre Basile Jos.: Swiss-Fr. pol. and div., 1799–1890. J
Abbas I.: Shah of Persia ('The Great'), 1557–1628. O: T: V
Abbas II.: Shah of Persia, 1629–1666. O: T
Abbas III.: Shah of Persia, 1732–1736. O
Abbas Mirza: Prince of Persia, 1785–1833. O: V
Abbas Pacha: Vic. of Egypt., 1813–1854. O: S: V
Abbas II.: Khedive of Egypt, 1874–1944. V: V8
Abbas, Sir Abdul Baha: The Bahai, 1844–1921. S
Abbas, Sam. abu Nasr ibn: North Afr. Jew. apostate, physn., math. and opponent of Judaism, 12th cent. T
Abbassi, Abu Moses Ibn: Fr. Jew. Talmudist, philos. and trans., 13th cent. T
Abbate (Abbati), Niccolo (Niccolino): Mod. fresco pntr., 1512–1571. J: O
Abbati, Gius.: Neap. pntr., 1886–1868. M
Abbatini, Ant. Maria: Ital. music. and wr. on music, 1597*–1679. O: Q
Abbatucci, Chas.: Fr. gen., 1771–1796. O
Abbatucci, Jacques Pierre: Fr. gen., 1726–1812. O
Abbatucci, Jacques Pierre Chas.: Corsican pol., 1792–1857. J
Abbe, Cleveland: Amer. astron. and meteorol., 1838–1916. B
Abbé, Hend.: Flem. engrav., pntr. and archt., 1639–post 1670. K: M
Abbe, Jos. Barnabe St. Sevin l': Fr. music. and comp., 1727–1803. Q
Abbé, Pierre de St. Sevin l': Fr. music.,   –1777. Q
Abbé, Pierre Phil. St. Sevin l': Fr. music.,   –1768. Q
Abbema, Ealth. Elias: Dutch patriot and banker, 1739–1805. P
Abbett, Leon: Gov. of New Jersey, 1836–1894. B
Abbey, Edwin Austin: Amer.-Eng. pntr., 1852–1911. A2: B: S:
Abbey, Hy.: Amer. poet, 1842–1911. B

D.U.B.—1   1

Fig. 14. HYAMSON, A. M., *Dictionary of Universal Biography.*
(Copyright: Routledge.)

G. C. Jöcher's *Allgemeines Gelehrten-Lexicon* (4 vols., Gleditsch, Leipzig, 1750–1), and its continuation *Fortsetzung und Ergänzungen* (7 vols., to letter R only, 1784–7). This was reprinted in 1960–1.

For length of entry at the international level, the above works have never been surpassed. The virtue of inclusiveness, however, is almost as valuable as length of entry and in respect of that (Fig. 14) A. M. Hyamson's *Dictionary of Universal Biography* (2nd edition, Routledge, 1951) is supreme. A "title-a-line" work generally, it gives nationality, dates, profession and "not only includes far more names than does any other [work] in existence, but may claim without hesitation to deal with more individuals than the aggregate of any score of other works" (preface).

Hyamson could be regarded as an index as well as a comprehensive work, for every entry refers to a source giving a full biography. Hoefer is indexed, but not Michaud, probably because it is later. Twenty-four comprehensive works have been used in the compilation of Hyamson, but only the *Dictionaries of National Biography* and of *American Biography* have been completely indexed. Other works used include the *Annual Register*, and the eleventh edition of the *Encyclopaedia Britannica*. Entries, though brief, are full enough for some purposes. On the page illustrated, for example, we can discover that Ivar Aasen (1813–96) was a Norwegian philologist and lexicographer (the list of abbreviations might have to be employed here). The letter V signifies that a fuller account of Aasen is to be found in the 1911 edition of the *Encyclopaedia Britannica*.

Hyamson even has twenty-two names under letter X! However (Fig. 15), *Webster's Biographical Dictionary* (Merriam, Springfield, 1963) has seventeen, though many of its entries run to ten lines or more. It includes over 40,000 names; "American and British names have been . . . accorded fuller treatment than names of other persons of similar eminence . . ." (preface). Thomas J. Lippincott's *Universal Pronouncing Dictionary of Biography and Mythology* (5th edition, Lippincott, Philadelphia, 1930) is even longer than Webster's, having 2550 pp. (Webster's 1698 smaller pp.), but is by no means so up to date, corrections after 1901 having been made in the stereos

sionary to Mohammedans of north African regions, and was finally stoned to death outside the walls of Bougie. Among his writings are *Blanquerna* (a novel describing a new Utopia), *Libre de Maravelles, Lo Cant de Ramon.*

Lum'holtz (lōōm'hŏlts), **Carl Sofus.** 1851–1922. Norwegian explorer and ethnologist.

Lu·mière' (lü'myâr'), **Louis Jean.** 1864–1948. French chemist and industrialist, b. in Besançon. With his brother **Auguste Marie Louis Nicolas** (1862–1954), also a chemist, founded in Lyons a factory for producing photographic plates, paper, and chemicals. They invented the Lumière process of color photography and an early motion-picture camera (1893); also, originated a theory attributing to the properties of colloidal substances the principal part in the various phenomena of life.

Lum'mer (lōōm'ēr), **Otto.** 1860–1925. German physicist; known for investigations in the fields of optics and radiations; discovered interference in a plane-parallel glass plate, which developed into the Lummer-Gehrcke plate (a type of interferometer); with Brodhun devised an improved photometer which uses a combination of prisms in place of greased paper. See also Ernst PRINGSHEIM.

Lum'mis (lŭm'ĭs), **Charles Fletcher.** 1859–1928. American author and editor, b. Lynn, Mass. Lived among Pueblo Indians in New Mexico. On ethnological expedition to Peru and Bolivia (1892–94). Interested himself in preserving Spanish missions and other historical relics in California. Author of *Birch Bark Poems* (1879), *A New Mexico David* (1891), *A Tramp Across the Continent* (1892), *The Land of Poco Tiempo* (1893), *The Spanish Pioneers* (1893), *The Awakening of a Nation: Mexico of Today* (1898), *Mesa, Cañon and Pueblo* (1925), *A Bronco Pegasus* (1928), and volumes of Pueblo folk tales and old California Spanish songs.

Lu'na (lōō'nä), **Álvaro de.** 1388?–1453. Spanish statesman; minister of John II of Castile; appointed constable of Castile (1423). Grand master of the Military Order of Santiago (1445) and commander in chief of the army. Created duke of Trujillo, count of Gormaz, of San Esteban, and of Ledesma, and lord of many cities and castles; raised his brother to archbishop of Toledo and primate of Spain; married his daughter into the royal family.

Luna, Pedro de. 1328?–?1423. Antipope as Benedict XIII, at Avignon (1394–1423); b. in Aragon, Spain. A cardinal deacon, joined French cardinals in election (1378) of Antipope Clement VII; legate of Avignon in various countries; deposed at Council of Pisa (1409) but refused to accept decision; again deposed (1417) at Council of Constance; died unsubmissive.

Lu·na·char'ski (lōō-nü-chär'skŭ-ĭ; *Angl.* -skĭ), **Anatoli Vasilievich.** 1875–1933. Russian Communist leader and writer; joined Social Democratic party (1898); arrested and deported (1899). Escaped to Paris; at schism in Socialist party (1903), joined Bolsheviks under Lenin. Soon after outbreak of Russian Revolution (1917), joined Lenin and Trotsky in Russia and aided in Bolshevik coup d'état (Nov., 1917). Commissar for education (1917–29); introduced widespread reforms in public education in Russia. Author of *Religion and Socialism* (2 vols., 1911), *Culture and the Working Class* (1919).

Lu'na·li'lo (lōō'nä-lē'lō), **William C.** 1832–1874. King of Hawaiian Islands (1873–74). Elected king to succeed Kamehameha V, last of the direct Kamehameha line; had liberal ideas; worked for improvements in constitution; favored reciprocity treaty with U.S.

Lu'na y A'rel·la'no (lōō'nä ē ä'rä-lyä'nō), **Tristán de.** fl. 1530–1561. Spanish explorer in America; served under Coronado in New Mexico expedition. Named governor and captain general of Florida; sailed for Florida (1559); landed at Pensacola Bay; ships and provisions lost in storm; relieved of command (1561).

Lund, Troels Frederik. *Known as* **Troels'–Lund'** (trŏls'lŏōn'). 1840–1921. Danish writer and educator, chief work, a history of Danish and Norwegian culture in the 16th century. Appointed historiographer-royal to the king of Denmark.

Lun'de·gård (lün'dĕ-gōrd), **Axel.** 1861–1930. Swedish novelist; author of *At Daybreak* (1885), *Titania. A Love Saga* (1892), *Struensee* (1898–1900), *Queen Margaret* (1905–06), etc.

Lun·dell' (lün-dĕl'), **Johan August.** 1851–1940. Swedish philologist; best known for his study of Swedish dialects.

Lund'gren (lünd'grän), **Egron Sellif.** 1815–1875. Swedish water-color painter.

Lun'dy (lŭn'dĭ), **Benjamin.** 1789–1839. American abolitionist; organized The Union Humane Society, in St. Clairsville, Ohio (1815), one of the first antislavery societies. Traveled, wrote, and spoke in various states agitating against slavery. Assaulted by Baltimore slave dealer (1827) and his property destroyed by Philadelphia mob (1838).

Lü'ne·burg (lü'nĕ-bōōrk), Dukes of. See HANOVER.

Lung'e (lŏōng'ĕ), **Georg.** 1839–1923. German chemist; contributed to development of processes for commercial production of soda and inorganic acids.

Lunt (lŭnt), **Alfred.** 1893– . American actor, b. Milwaukee, Wis.; m. Lynn Fontanne (*q.v.*). Among plays in which he has appeared are: *Sweet Nell of Old Drury, The Guardsman, Elizabeth the Queen, Design for Living, Taming of the Shrew.*

Lu·pe'scu (lōō-pĕ'skōō), **Magda.** *Orig. name said to be* **Wolff.** 1904?– . Rumanian adventuress, b. in Iaşi, of a Jewish father and Viennese Catholic mother. Educ. in a convent; m. an army officer; met Prince Carol (1921?); divorced her husband; left Rumania (1925) to live with Carol in Paris; lived in Neuilly (1925–30); returned to Rumania (1930) soon after Carol seized throne; during Carol's reign (1930–40) exerted great influence over political events of kingdom; made many political enemies; forced to flee with Carol to Spain (1940) and Cuba (1941).

Lu·pi'no (lōō-pē'nō). Name of a family of actors including: **George** (1853–1932), English comedian of Italian descent; his son **Stanley** (1895–1942), b. in London, actor, playwright, and producer of stage and screen plays; Stanley's daughter **Ida** (1916–), b. in London, actress on English stage and in motion pictures in Hollywood.

Lu'pot' (lü'pō'), **Nicolas.** 1758–1824. French violin-maker, b. Stuttgart; especially skillful in imitating the instruments made by Stradivarius.

Lup'ton (lŭp'tŭn), **Thomas Goff.** 1791–1873. English mezzotint engraver; one of first to employ steel in his art. Did best work in seascapes and landscapes, esp. in reproductions of J. M. W. Turner's work.

Luqmān. See LOKMAN.

Lu'ria (lōō'ryä), **Isaac ben Solomon Ash'ke·na'zi** (äsh'kĕ-nä'zĭ). 1534–1572. Hebrew mystic and cabalist, b. in Jerusalem of German descent; founder of a school of mystics. His disciple Hayyim Vital collected notes of his lectures and produced numerous works expounding his doctrines, notably *Eẓ Ḥayyim* (6 vols., pub. 1772).

Luria, Ruggiero di. See LAURIA.

Lur'ton (lûr't'n), **Horace Harmon.** 1844–1914. American jurist; served in Confederate army in Civil War. Associate justice, U.S. Supreme Court (1910–14).

Fig. 15. By permission. From *Webster's Biographical Dictionary.* (Copyright 1964 by G. & C. Merriam Co., publishers of the Merriam–Webster Dictionaries.)

by curtailing and inserting. In Webster's (first published 1943) "the names of persons prominent (sometimes only briefly) in sports, in motion pictures, in the contemporary theatre, and in radio are so numerous that the editors were compelled . . . to curtail their representation to the minimum", yet "Babe" Ruth, American baseball player, is here (eight lines), though not in Lippincott. Tommy Handley, English comedian, is not, however, though he gets thirteen lines in (Fig. 16) *Chambers's Biographical Dictionary* (new edition, W. and R. Chambers, Edinburgh, 1961). How came an almost entirely new work of this kind to succeed in 1961, in face of its competitors? It contains only 15,000 entries, less than half the number in Webster's or Lippincott, and its success rests on the completeness of its revision; "Monteverdi, whose great importance in the history of music is today more fully recognized, now receives 59 lines in place of 5 [in the earlier editions], T. S. Eliot has 144 instead of 6, and the meagre allowance formerly given to the great Impressionist painters has been increased to match their current status. Conversely Lord Lytton has less than half the space previously given to him" (preface). Unlike most works of its scale, Chambers's includes criticism as well as facts, so much so that a very well-known author took exception to the article on himself as first published, and a cancel was issued. Yet a detailed comparison of Webster's and Chambers's (Figs. 15 and 16) inclines to favour the former; Chambers's omits the American actor Alfred Lunt, the English comedian Lupino, and Mme Lupescu, though the Chambers's articles are certainly more lively and contemporary in style. *The New Century Cyclopaedia of Names* (3 vols., Appleton–Century Crofts Inc., New York, 1954) includes 100,000 proper names of all kinds, fictional and existing. Two useful French one-volume works of the brief-entry type are G. Vapereau, *Dictionnaire universel des contemporains* (Hachette, Paris, 1893) and P. Grimal (editor), *Dictionnaire des biographies* (2 vols., Presses universitaires de France, Paris, 1958). This gives 6000 adequate entries and 128 photographs.

The works we have so far discussed in this section have comprised either the older, full, retrospective types, or shorter summary works

pastorals. See books by Radet (1891), Prunières (1910).

(2) **Raymond** (sometimes **Lull**) (c. 1232–1315), Spanish theologian and philosopher, 'the enlightened doctor', born at Palma in Majorca, in his youth served as a soldier and led a dissolute life, but from 1266 gave himself up to asceticism and resolved on a spiritual crusade for the conversion of the Mussulmans. To this end, after some years of study, he produced his *Ars Magna*, the 'Lullian method'; a mechanical aid to the acquisition of knowledge and the solution of all possible problems by a systematic manipulation of certain fundamental notions (the Aristotelian categories, &c.). He also wrote a book against the Averroists, and in 1291 went to Tunis to confute and convert the Mohammedans, but was imprisoned and banished. After visiting Naples, Rome, Majorca, Cyprus and Armenia, he again sailed (1305) for Bugia (Bougie) in Algeria, and was again banished; at Paris lectured against the principles of Averroes; and once more at Bugia was stoned so that he died a few days afterwards. The Lullists combined religious mysticism with alchemy, but it has been disproved that Lully himself ever dabbled in alchemy. Apart from his *Ars Magna*, of his works *Llibre de Contemplació* is masterly and he was the first to use a vernacular language for religious or philosophical writings. He also wrote impressive poetry. See *Life* by Allison Peers (1929).

LUMIÈRE, *lüm-yayr*, **Auguste Marie Louis Nicolas** (1862–1954), and **Louis Jean** (1864–1948), French chemists, brothers, manufacturers of photographic materials, invented a cine camera (1893) and a process of colour photography.

LUNARDI, Vincenzo (1759–1806), Italian aeronaut, born at Lucca, made from Moorfields on September 15, 1784, the first hydrogen balloon ascent in England.

LUPTON, Thomas Goff (1791–1873), English mezzotint engraver, was born and died in London. He was one of the first to use steel in engraving. Among his works are Turner's *Ports* and *Rivers*.

LUSIGNAN. See GUY DE LUSIGNAN.

LUTHARDT, Christoph Ernst, *loo-tart* (1823–1902), Lutheran theologian, became professor at Marburg (1854) and at Leipzig (1856). He wrote a Commentary on John's Gospel (1852–53; 2nd ed. 1876), *St John the Author of the Fourth Gospel*, works on ethics, dogmatics, &c. See his *Reminiscences* (2nd ed. 1891).

LUTHER, Martin (1483–1546), German religious reformer, was born at Eisleben, the son of a miner, and went to school at Magdeburg and Eisenach. In 1501 he entered the University of Erfurt, and took his degree in 1505. Before this, however, he was led to the study of the Scriptures, resolved to devote himself to a spiritual life, and spent three years in the Augustinian convent at Erfurt. In 1507 he was ordained a priest, in 1508 lectured on philosophy in the University of Wittenberg, in 1509 on the Scriptures, and as a preacher produced a still more powerful influence. In 1511 he was sent to Rome, and after his return his career as a Reformer

commenced. Money was greatly needed at Rome; and its emissaries sought everywhere to raise funds by the sale of indulgences. Luther's indignation at the shameless traffic carried on by the Dominican John Tetzel (1517) became irrepressible. He drew out ninety-five theses on indulgences, denying to the pope all right to forgive sins; and these on October 31 he nailed on the church door at Wittenberg. Tetzel retreated from Saxony to Frankfurt-on-the-Oder, where he published a set of counter-theses and burnt Luther's. The Wittenberg students retaliated by burning Tetzel's. In 1518 Luther was joined by Melanchthon. The pope, Leo X, at first took little heed of the disturbance, but in 1518 summoned Luther to Rome to answer for his theses. His university and the elector interfered, and ineffective negotiations were undertaken by Cardinal Cajetan and by Miltitz, envoy of the pope to the Saxon court. Eck and Luther held a memorable disputation at Leipzig (1519). Luther meantime attacked the papal system as a whole more boldly. Erasmus and Hutten now joined in the conflict. In 1520 the Reformer published his famous address to the 'Christian Nobles of Germany', followed by a treatise *On the Babylonish Captivity of the Church*, which works attacked also the doctrinal system of the Church of Rome. The papal bull, containing forty-one theses, issued against him he burned before a multitude of doctors, students, and citizens in Wittenberg. Germany was convulsed with excitement. Charles V had convened his first diet at Worms in 1521; an order was issued for the destruction of Luther's books, and he himself was summoned to appear before the diet. His journey thither resembled a triumph; the threats of enemies and the anxieties of friends alike failed to move him; ultimately he was put under the ban of the Empire. On his return from Worms he was seized, at the instigation of the Elector of Saxony, and lodged (really for his protection) in the Wartburg. During the year he spent here he translated the Scriptures and composed various treatises. Disorders recalled Luther to Wittenberg in 1522; he rebuked the unruly spirits, and made a stand against lawlessness on the one hand and tyranny on the other. In this year he published his acrimonious reply to Henry VIII on the seven sacraments. Estrangement had gradually sprung up between Erasmus and Luther, and there was an open breach in 1525, when Erasmus published *De Libero Arbitrio*, and Luther followed with *De Servo Arbitrio*. In that year Luther married Katharina von Bora (q.v.), one of nine nuns who had withdrawn from conventual life. In 1529 he engaged in his famous conference at Marburg with Zwingli and other Swiss divines, obstinately maintaining his views as to the Real (consubstantial) Presence in the Eucharist. The drawing up of the Augsburg Confession, Melanchthon representing Luther, marks the culmination of the German Reformation (1530); henceforward Luther's life was uneventful. He died at Eisleben, and was buried at Wittenberg. Endowed with broad human sympathies, massive energy, manly

Fig. 16. *Chambers's Biographical Dictionary*. (Copyright: W. & R. Chambers.)

which, though they may include some living persons, have devoted most of their space to the dead. There remains a third group—those universal biographies which set out to list contemporaries only of all nations. Probably the best known of these is (Fig. 17) *The International Who's Who*, 28th edition, Europa Publications, 1964. It attempts to include everyone whose name is known outside his own country but its 10,000 entries have a predominantly Anglo-Saxon flavour. The main value of this work is probably the listing of people for whom no national Who's Who exists; the page reproduced does, however, bear out the book's claim to "cover the five continents". *World Biography* (5th edition, Institute for Research in Biography, New York, 1954) ambitiously claims to list the world's notable living personnel. First published in 1940, there are over 18,000 entries, with many portraits (absent from editions earlier than the fifth). A new work in this field is the *Dictionary of International Biography* (2 vols., Monaco and London, 1963–5) arranged by countries. Two volumes in the Wilson series deal with contemporary biography; the *Biography Index* has been covered above (pp. 30–2), *Current Biography* Wilson, New York, 1940) contains articles on the life and work of people in public life, and there are also references to obituaries in the *New York Times*. Monthly issues are published together with an annual cumulated volume; some of these contain cumulated indexes. Portraits are included.

Sir Philip Magnus said recently in the *Sunday Times* "In an age characterised by unprecedented social mobility, television and an obtrusive Press have conditioned public opinion to insist that private faces shall be exposed . . . Reticences imposed by good feeling during the lifetime of a subject's contemporaries will no longer be binding. A biographer must write the history of an individual life. He will fail if he attempts instead to write general history . . . The character-sketch did much, three centuries ago, and could still do something today, to improve the writing of history. In an elaborated form it may have an even greater part to play in aiding the next generation of biographers to carry their art through a challenging period of transition."

Biography is so pervasive that very few published books of non-

S

Saadi, Ali Saleh; Iraqi politician; b. *c.* 30.
General Sec. Baath Party, Iraq; Dep. Prime Minister
and Minister of Interior Feb.-May 63, Dep. Prime
Minister and Minister of Guidance May 63-Nov. 63.
Baath Party, Baghdad, Iraq.

Saari, Eino Armas; Finnish forestry expert and politician; b. 94; ed. Helsinki, Oxford and Yale Univs.
Prof. of Forestry Helsinki Univ. 25-63; mem. of national
and international forestry organisations; cttee. Chair.
Third World Forestry Congress 47-49 (Pres. 49);
Vice-Chair. European Forestry Commission of F.A.O.
50, Chair. 51; Chair. Nat. F.A.O. Comm. of Finland;
Chair. Finnish People's Party 51-58; mem. of Parl. 54-
58; Minister of Social Affairs 56-57; Chancellor School
of Social Sciences 57-.
University Forestry Department, Unioninkatu 40B,
Helsinki, Finland.

Sabah, Sheikh Sir Abdulla as Salim as, K.C.M.G., C.I.E.;
Ruler of Kuwait; b. 95.
Succeeded his cousin, Sheikh Sir Ahmed al Jabir as
Sabah, on Feb. 25th 1950.
Sha'ab Palace, Kuwait, Persian Gulf.

Sabah, Sheikh Sabah al-Ahmad Al-; Kuwaiti politi-
cian; b. 29; ed. Mubarakiyyah National School, Kuwait
and privately.
Member Supreme Exec. Cttee. 55-62; Minister of Public
Information and Guidance, and of Social Affairs 62-63;
Minister of Foreign Affairs 63-.
Ministry of Foreign Affairs, Kuwait, Persian Gulf.

Sabin, Albert B., B.S., M.D.; American virologist;
b. 06; ed. New York Univ.
Research Assoc. in bacteriology, New York Univ. Coll.
of Medicine 26-32; House Physician, Bellevue Hospital,
New York City 32-34; Fellow in Medicine, Nat. Research Council, Lister Inst. (England) 34; Asst., Rocke-
feller Inst., N.Y.C. 35-37, Assoc. 37-39; Assoc. Prof. of
Research Pediatrics, Univ. of Cincinnati Coll. of
Medicine 39-46, Prof. 46-; developer of oral polio
vaccine; Medical Corps. U.S. Army, Second World
War; Hon. Sc.D., L.H.D., Litt.H.D., numerous awards
for work in medical research.
The Children's Hospital Research Foundation, Elland
and Bethesda Avenue, Cincinnati 29, Ohio, U.S.A.

Sabri, Ali; United Arab Republic (Egyptian) politi-
cian.
Fought in Palestine War 48; Minister for Presidential
Affairs, Egypt 57-58, U.A.R. 58-62; Pres. Exec. Council
62-64, Prime Minister 64-.
Office of the Prime Minister of the United Arab Republic,
Cairo, U.A.R.

Saburov, Maxim Zakharovich; Soviet politician;
b. 1900; ed. Communist Univ., Moscow Bauman Engineering Inst.
Engineer, Chief Technologist at the Kramatorsk Engineering Works (Donets Basin) 33-36; Chief Engineer
for the Heavy Machine-Building Admin. of the People's
Commissariat for Machine-Building 37-38; Head of the
Machine-Construction Sector, First Deputy Chair. of
the State Planning Comm. of the U.S.S.R.; Chair. of
the State Planning Comm. of the U.S.S.R., Deputy
Chair. of the Council of People's Commissars of the
U.S.S.R. 41; mem. Cttee. of Defence 44-46; Vice-Chair.
of the Council of Ministers of the U.S.S.R. 47; Chair. of
the State Planning Comm. of the U.S.S.R. 49; mem.
Presidium of the Central Cttee. of the C.P.S.U. 52-57;
Chair. of the State Econ. Comm. of the U.S.S.R.

Council of Ministers for Current Econ. Planning 55-57;
Deputy Chair. of the State Cttee. for Foreign Econ.
Relations 57-59; now Manager of an industrial estab-
lishment.
c/o The Kremlin, Moscow, U.S.S.R.

Sachar, Shri Bhimsin, B.A., LL.B.; Indian politician;
b. 93; ed. Punjab Univ.
Joined Bar 18; joined Non-co-operation Movement 21;
Sec. Punjab Provincial Congress Cttee. 21; Registrar
National Univ., Lahore; Sec. Municipal Cttee., Gujran-
wala 22-24; Municipal Commr. Gujranwala 24-33;
founded Sunlight of India Insurance Co., Ltd.; Dir.
Gujranwala Electric Supply Co. Ltd.; Local Dir.
Punjab Nat. Bank Ltd.; mem. Punjab Legislative
Assembly 36-56; leader Congress Party, Punjab Legis-
lative Assembly 40; Finance Minister, Punjab Govern-
ment 46-47; Dep. Leader Congress Party, Pakistan
Constituent Assembly 47; Leader Congress Legislature
Party, Punjab 49; Chief Minister, Punjab 49, 52-56;
Gov. Orissa 56-57; Gov. Andhra Pradesh 57-62.
Hyderabad, Andhra Pradesh, India.

Sacher, Paul; Swiss musician; b. 06; ed. Univ. and
Conservatoire of Basle.
Founder of Basle Chamber Orchestra 26; founder of
Schola Cantorum Basiliensis 33; conductor of Collegium
Musicum Zürich 41-; has conducted in almost all
European countries since 45; Hon. Pres. Asscn. of
Swiss Musicians; Dr. Phil. h.c. of Basle Univ.; Schön-
berg Medal 53; Mozart Medal 57.
Publs. Articles in reports of Basle Chamber Orchestra,
and book on *Adolf Hamm* (organist).
Schönenberg, Pratteln, Basle, Switzerland.

Sachs, Nelly; German-born Swedish poet and drama-
tist; b. 91; ed. Berlin.
Refugee in Sweden 40; Swedish Lyric Prize, Jahresring
Literature Prize, Annette Droste Prize, Dortmund Prize.
Publs. *Wohnungen des Todes* 47, *Sternverdunkelung* 49,
Und Niemand weiss weiter 57, *Flucht und Verwandlung*
59, *Gesammelte Lyrik* 61, *Gesammelte Dramatik;* translations of Swedish poetry: *Von Welle und Granit* 47, *Aber
auch diese Sonne ist heimatlos* 58, *Ausgewählte Gedichte*
63, *Vom Leiden Israels* 64.
Bergsundstrand 23, Stockholm, Sweden.

Sadat, Col. Anwar es-; United Arab Republic
(Egyptian) officer and politician.
President of Egyptian Nat. Union 57-61; mem. Presi-
dency Council 62-64, Vice-Pres. of U.A.R. 64-; Pres.
Afro-Asian Conf. Cairo 58.
Office of the Vice-Presidents, Cairo, United Arab
Republic.

Sadiq, Issa, PH.D.; Iranian educationist; b. 94; ed.
Univs. of Paris, Cambridge (England), and Columbia
(New York).
Directed various depts. Ministry·of Education 19-30;
mem. Nat. Constituent Assembly 25, 49; Pres. and Prof.
Nat. Teachers' Coll.; Dean of Faculties of Arts and
Science Teheran Univ. 32-41; Chancellor of Univ. 41;
Ministry of Education 41, 43-45, 47, 60-61; Vice-Pres.
Persian Acad. 37-; mem. Board of Governors, Nat. Bank
of Persia 37-52; Senator for Teheran 49-52, 54-60, 63-;
Pres. Persia-America Relations Soc. 49-53; mem. Royal
Cultural Council 62-.
Publs. *Principles of Education, New Methods in Educa-
tion, History of Education, Modern Persia* and *her
Educational System* (in English), *A Year in America,
The March of Education in Persia and the West, A
Brief Course in the History of Education in Iran, A

Fig. 17. *The International Who's Who.* Copyright: Europa
Publications.)

fiction do not cover it to some extent, as do all newspapers, lists of alumni, records of professional associations, transactions of societies in all countries. What we have set down will, however, enable us to make an ordered start to our researches, wherever they may lead us.

HISTORY: BIBLIOGRAPHIES

There are several non-serial bibliographies of historical bibliographies, notably H. Kramm (editor), *Bibliographischer historischer Zeitschriften, 1939–51* (3 vols., Rasch, Marburg, 1952–4) covering Europe and Asia; E. M. Coulter and M. Gerstenfeld, *Historical Bibliographies* (University of California, Berkeley, 1935) arranged by countries, and (a less full list also dealing with periodicals) P. Caron and M. Jaryc, *World List of Historical Periodicals and Bibliographies* (International Committee of Historical Sciences, Oxford, 1939). The most comprehensive guide to all history in the English language is (Fig. 18) *The American Historical Association's Guide to Historical Literature* (Macmillan, New York, 1961).

One might, indeed, wonder what is the need for writing any other books at all, for here are sections on related studies—historiography, the science of writing history, and "auxiliaries" such as philology, archaeology, chronology, diplomatics and numismatics, and even logic, political science, economics, geography, demography and a host of other border-line studies. Section B, general reference resources, of which Constance M. Winchell is a co-editor, reads like an extract from her own publication (pp. 21–3 above). Whereas her work cites several general guides, however, the *Guide* lists only her and the full Malclès. It is easy to spot omissions in any bibliography, but such a comprehensive work "primarily intended to serve those students or teachers who know English" should not have omitted mention of Maunde Thompson or Hilary Jenkinson from the section dealing with palaeography. Perhaps there is no happy mean between the works we are discussing in Chapters 3 and 4 of this book, which concentrate on a more limited field, and a work like Sonnenschein which is almost all-with some notable exceptions, was still primarily a narrator of events to whom the analytical methods and devices of other disciplines were largely unknown. The last quarter century has seen a very great change in this state of affairs; and while the historian has not succumbed entirely to the methodological lures of other fields of knowledge, he has been influenced by them, consciously or unconsciously, to an extent that would have seemed surprising in 1931.

The result of this transformation of outlook is plainly seen in the present compilation. In it are many titles that might scarcely have seemed germane to the study of history when the previous *Guide* appeared. Now it is at least tacitly agreed that they are acceptable, if not to all, certainly to a great many practicing historians. This new breadth of interest does, however, call for a special word of warning, particularly to the student who may be making use of this section as an introduction to British history. Even as historical scholarship is continually expanding and undergoing revision, so too are related fields of study. For that reason the student must remember that this, like every other subject bibliography, can only be a partial guide. If he would stay abreast of current publication, he must not overlook the historical and other learned journals, almost all of which contain book review sections and some of which have lists of current articles appearing elsewhere. Moreover, he will find that the literary supplements of certain newspapers like *The times* of London and *The New York times,* while very general in their coverage, nonetheless notice a number of the most important scholarly works in British history. Finally, it should also be noted that this section of the *Guide* deals only with works covering the history of the British Isles since 1485. For materials on earlier and very recent times, on relations with specific countries, and on British overseas expansion and the Commonwealth, consult the sections pertaining to these periods and areas.

BIBLIOGRAPHIES, LIBRARIES, AND MUSEUMS

Bibliographies

VA1. Gross, Charles. **The sources and literature of English history from the earliest times to about 1485.** See *K4.*

VA2. Read, Conyers. **Bibliography of British history: Tudor period, 1485–1603.** 2nd ed. Oxford, 1959.

VA3. Davies, Godfrey. **Bibliography of British history: Stuart period, 1603–1714.** Oxford, 1928. New edition in preparation. Still useful. Needs to be supplemented by Frewer (*VA9*), Lancaster (*VA10*), and Milne (*VA11*).

VA4. Grose, Clyde L. **A select bibliography of British history, 1660–1760.** Chicago, 1939.

VA5. Pargellis, Stanley, and D. J. Medley. **Bibliography of British history: the eighteenth century, 1714–1789.** Oxford, 1951. A continuation of *VA1–3,* somewhat more detailed than the preceding.

VA6. Williams, Judith B. **A guide to the printed materials for English social and economic history, 1750–1850.** 2 v. N.Y., 1926.

Though out of date, it is still the main bibliographical guide for the early 19th century.

VA7. Pollard, Alfred W., and Gilbert R. Redgrave. **A short-title catalogue of books printed in England, Scotland, and Ireland, and of English books printed abroad, 1475–1640.** See *B29.*

VA8. Wing, Donald G. **Short-title catalogue of books printed in England, Scotland, Ireland, Wales, and British America, and of English books printed in other countries, 1641–1700.** 3 v. N.Y., 1945–51. Continuation of *VA7.*

VA9. Frewer, Louis B. **Bibliography of historical writings published in Great Britain and the empire, 1940–1945.** See *B57.*

VA10. Lancaster, Joan C. **Bibliography of historical works issued in the United Kingdom, 1946–1956.** London, 1957. Chronological listing of materials without annotation.

VA11. Milne, A. Taylor. **Writings on British history.** London, 1934 ff. [Royal Historical Society.] Annual guide to historical writing.

VA12. Historical Association. London.

Fig. 18.   *The American Historical Association's Guide to Historical Literature.* (Copyright: the Macmillan Co.)

inclusive. Yet many individual critical annotations are achieved even in a work of this enormous scope. We are here considering world histories, and such is the scope of the *Guide* that the section entitled "world history and universal treatments" occupies only 11 of 962 pp. Perhaps the most useful section containing material not easily available elsewhere is that named "selected world histories". Here are Orosius, Raleigh, Ranke, Lavisse and Rambaud, Toynbee, Fueter and even the one periodical in the field, *Journal of World History* (see p. 70), but no H. G. Wells. Reference might have been made to the Cambridge histories which are treated sectionally later on.

Perhaps it would have been better if there had been stricter control; an attempt has been made to list universal histories of agriculture (Gras), technology (Singer), architecture (Giedion), etc., though one knows there are more specialized bibliographies to deal with these subjects. If corn mills and gramophone records, why not coal-mines or violins? If there are to be special periods and topics in English and American history, why not areas—the Deep South, the Home Counties? Yet let us not cavil at this enormously thorough and clear work which will no doubt be as supremely useful in Romance and Teutonic countries, in Asia, Africa and Australia, for its coverage of Anglo-American material, as it is in the U.S.A. and Britain for "students of the African, American, Asian, Australasian and Oceanic peoples" (preface). We might have particularized Russia, for what other easily available bibliography lists thirty-two items on libraries, museums and bibliographies, followed by 553 other items on all aspects of Russian civilization, pre- and post-Soviet, by Russians and non-Russians? Here the sections on linguistics, intellectual history, education, folklore, periodicals and society publications do not seem irrelevancies, but indispensable. Our reproduction was selected to compare treatment of some of the works also listed in the general bibliographies (Figs. 1–7). The *Guide* may possibly be cited as Howe (after the Chairman of its board of editors) as the previous edition, fuller on western Europe, was always known as Dutcher. A comprehensive German work is G. Franz, *Bücherkunde zur Weltgeschichte vom Untergang des romischen Weltreiches bis zur*

3

Gegenwart (Oldenbourg, Munich, 1956) with 17,000 references from *c.* A.D. 400 to the present time. An outstanding French work of similar scale to the *American Historical Association's Guide*, though in continuous narrative form, is C. V. Langlois, *Manuel de bibliographie historique* (2 vols., Hachette, Paris, 1902–4). The first volume gives valuable comments on numerous bibliographies, universal, national, of original sources, bibliographies of bibliographies, etc.; the second carries out in a fuller way for Europe (the U.S.A. is touched on) what Gooch's *History and Historians of the Nineteenth Century* has done for a later period for the British part of the field. More critical than enumerative, it discusses the leading historians from the fifteenth to the eighteenth centuries and also the historical publishing programmes of the governments, learned societies, religious and civil corporations.

A work on similar lines to the *American Historical Association's Guide* is C. K. Adams' *Manual of Historical Literature* (3rd edition, 1889) which gives detailed treatment to the best-known nineteenth-century histories, and, like its successors, includes some biographies. A general German work is P. Herre, *Quellenkunde zur Weltgeschichte* (1910). The revised edition of the Historical Association's *Library Catalogue* is a useful, readily available general list (the Association, 1963). What is at once a great library catalogue and the fullest international archaeological bibliography is probably A. Mau, *Katalog der Bibliothek des Deutschen Archäologischen Instituts* (2 vols. in 4, Loscher, Rome, 1913–32). A supplement appeared in 1930. Mau also edited initially the annual *Archäologische Bibliographie* (1913–, In progress). The brief *Readers' Guide to Archaeology* (Library Association, County Libraries Section, 1960) is a useful starting point. Note also R. Montandon, *Bibliographie générale des travaux palethrologiques et archéologiques* (8 vols., Leroux, Paris, 1917–38) now continued in periodical form. Harvard University have published the catalogue of the *Library of the Peabody Museum of Archaeology and Ethnology* (53 vols., Hall, Boston, 1963). Most other general works are limited by period, as: J. S. Van Ooteghem, *Bibliotheca graeca et latina* (2nd edition, Les Études classiques, Namur, 1946), or L. Laurand, *Manuel des études grecques et latines* (13th edition, Picard, Paris, 1956–, In progress), or W. Engelmann, *Bibliotheca scriptorum classicorum* (8th edition, 2 vols., 1880–2), or *L'Annee philologique*, an annual bibliography of antiquity issued in Paris by Belle-lettres. The corresponding English work is the *Year's Work in Classical Studies* and the German work *Jahresbericht über die Fortschritte der Klassischen Altertumswissenschaft.* Both of these have now terminated though *Lustrum* replaces the former.

(Fig. 19), A. Potthast, *Bibliotheca historica medii aevi* (2nd edition, 2 vols., Weber, Berlin, 1896 (reprinted 1954)), is an extremely thorough analysis of the printed sources for mediaeval history in many countries. Part I is arranged by the sources: part II by authors; the arrangement is somewhat difficult to understand. It lists the manuscripts, editions, translations and commentaries on each work.

J. D. Reuss, *Repertorium commentationum a societatibus litterariis*, tomes 8–9, *Historia* (Dieterich, Gottingen, 1810) demonstrates even more forcibly that sound scholarship in the humanities is a long while being superseded; it analyses the productions of the learned societies of various countries up to 1800. L. J. Paetow's *Guide to the Study of Medieval History* (2nd edition, Mediaeval Academy of America, Berkeley, 1931) is a work more in the style of Adams and Howe. Like these works, though not penetrating into the natural and applied sciences, it has valuable annotated sections on palaeography, sphragistics (mentioning the two authorities, Maunde Thompson and Jenkinson, we have criticized Howe for omitting), collections of sources, society publications, periodicals, mediaeval books and libraries, and mediaeval art, etc. The arrangement of Paetow is puzzling until it is seen that it grew out of a series of study-lectures to undergraduates (parts II and III), preceded for publication by what the author modestly calls a book list. *The International Guide to Medieval Studies* (American Bibliographical Service, Darien, 1961–, In progress) indexes periodicals quarterly. A French work on mediaeval studies is C. U. Chevalier, *Répertoire des sources historiques du moyen age* (2nd edition, 2 vols., Picard, Paris, 1894–1903[1]), *bio-bibliographie*, referring to biographies and *topo-bibliographie*. The headings in the *topo-bibliographie* part

[1] Reprinted in 4 vols., 1959–60.

306   CHRONIK — KRONIJK — CRONIJCK — CHRONIJCKE

Chronik, Ronneburger kleine. 1111—1348.   Nach dem Fundorte benannt.

Uebers.: deutsch in Bunges Archiv f. d. Geschichte Liv-, Est- u. Curlands. VIII. Reval 1861. p. 282-285.

polnisch in Math. Strykowskis Litauischer Chronik. Königsberg 1582. p. 323-325 (ed. nova 1846. I. p. 282-284).

Chronik, Rostocker plattdeutsche, von 1310—1329.

Darstellung des Rostocker Aufstandes gegen den Dänenkönig Erich Menved.

Ausg.: hrsgb. von Hans Rud. Schröter *in* Beiträge z. Mecklenburgischen Geschichtskunde. I. 1. Heft. Rostock 1826. 4°.

Erl.-Schr.: Krause, K.E.H., Die Chronistik Rostocks *in* Hansische Geschichtsblätter. Bd. V. Jahrg. 1885. p. 163-165. *Vgl. seinen Aufsatz ibid.* 1872. p. 161 u. *in* Progr. d. Gymnas. Rostock 1873.

Chronik, Sophien-, *vid.* Лѣтописъ Софийскаи.

Chronik, Speierische, v. 1407—1476.

Ungemein reichhaltig, behandelt das ganze Rheinland; durch die aufgenommenen Urkunden und Briefe ist sie ein früher Versuch einer diplomatischen Reichsgeschichte.

Ausg.: ap. Mone, Quellensammlung zur badischen Gesch. I. p. 371-520; *cf.* Einl. p. 367-371.

Erl.-Schr.: Lorenz, Deutschlands Geschichtsquellen. 3. Aufl. I. 1886. p. 134.

Chronik, Stettiner = Gesta priorum S. Jacobi.

Chronik, Stralsunder. 1124—1482.

Ausg.: unt. d. Tit.: Eine alte Stralsunder Chronik hrsgb. von Zober. Stralsund 1842. — Auszüge aus Stralsundischen Chroniken vom J. 1230 —1521 [1] ap. Mohnike und Zober, Stralsundische Chroniken. I. Stralsund 1833. p. 159-224. — [2] *hieraus* Bruchstücke von 1428—1452 ap. Fant, Scr. rer. Svecic. III. sect. 1. 1876. p. 295-299.

Erl.-Schr.: Lorenz, Deutschlands Geschichtsquellen. 3. Aufl. II. 1887. p. 196.
Vgl. Chronicon Sundense.

Chronik, Strasburgische, *vid.* Twinger, Jac., von Königshofen.

Chronik, Stretlinger.

Sie ist im 15. Jahrh. von Eulogius Kiburger, 1446-1456 Pfarrer zu Einigen am Thuner See, geschrieben. Wichtig für Sitten- u. Kulturgeschichte, sowie die Legende des h. Michael.

Ausg.: hrsgb. von Jak. Baechtold. Frauenfeld 1877. gr. 8°. LXXXV. 202 pag. ℳ 5. (*Zugleich von:* Bibliothek aeltorer Schriftwerke der deutschen Schweiz u. ihres Grenzgebiets. Bd. 1.)

Erl.-Schr.: Lorenz, Deutschlands Geschichtsquellen. 3. Aufl. I. 1886. p. 116.

Chronik, Trolzkische, *vid.* Лѣтописъ Троицкая.

Chronik, Ungarisch-polnische Chronicon Hungarorum mixtum et Polonorum.

Chronik, Wendische, *vid.* Chronicon Slavicum parochi Suselensis.

Chronik, Woskresenskische, *vid.* Лѣтописъ по Воскресенскому Списку.

Chronik, Würtembergische, *vid.* Lirer, Thom.

Chronik, Züricher = Chronik, Klingenberger.

Chroniken, Danziger, *vid.*
Aufzeichnungen, Amtliche.
Chronik, Danziger, vom Bunde.
        vom Pfaffenkriege.
Lindau, Joh."
Lubbe, Jac.
Ordenschronik, Danziger.
Weinreich, Casp.

Chronikenfragmente, Lateinische. 1332 —1488.   Betreffen Köln.

Handschr.: Würzburg, Univ.-Bibl. n° 81. chart. sec. XVI. fol.

Ausg.: hrsgb. von H. Cardauns *in* Chroniken der deutschen Städte. XIII. 1876. p. 193-203.

Erl.-Schr.: Lorenz, Deutschlands Geschichtsquellen. 3. Aufl. II. 1887. p. 57. not. 4.

Chronikes = Chroniques.

Chronijk — Kronijk — Cronijek — Chronijeke — Chronijkje *etc.*

Chronijk, Brabandsche. 1288—1469.

Bei einer Feuersbrunst, welche i. J. 1822 die Archive de la Chambre des comptes en Brabant zerstörte, sind die Blätter mit den Begebenheiten der Jahre 1446-1455 aus der Chronik verschwunden. Heute ist die Handschrift im Kgl. Archiv zu Brüssel.

Ausg.: [1] ap. A.B.G. Schayes, Analectes archéologiques, historiques ... Anvers 1857. 8°. p.41. — [2] *wiederh. in* Annales de l'Acad. d'archéologie de Belgique. VII. p. 161. — [3] ed. Charles Piot *in* Chroniques de Brabant et de Flandre. (Collection des chroniques belges.) Bruxelles 1879. p. 49-62.

Kronijk, {De divisie, / De grote,} *vid.* Cronycke van Hollandt, Zeelandt ende Vrieslandt.

Cronyk der stad Brugge tydens het bestuer van Maximilian = Boeck, Het, van al.... *vid.* p. 161.

Cronycke, Die alder-excellentste, van Brabant, Hollant, Seelant, Vlaenderen int generael, —1486.

Ist nur Uebersetzung des Werkes Catalogus et cronica princ. et comit. Flandrie und auch von Andries de Smot gemacht sein.

Ausg.: [1] geprent i' Antwerpen by Rolandt van den Dorp 1497. fol. — [2] *wiederh. mit Zusätzen* Antwerpen 1518. fol. *Sehr selten, mit vielen interessanten Holzschnitten.* — [3] *unt.d.Tit.:* Dits die excellente croniko vā Vlaenderë. Beghinnende van Liederick Buc den eersten forestier tot den laetsten, achtervolghende die rechte afcomste der voorst grauen tot Keyser Carolo. Antverpen by J. van Doesborch 1530. fol. *Mit Fortsetzung bis 1507. (Mit den Holzschn. der früheren Ausg.; doch finden sich einige darunter, die an Dürer erinnern). Selten.*

Cronike, Die olde Freesche.
Geschrieben um 1474.

Fig. 19. POTTHAST, A., *Bibliotheca historica medii aevi.*

are extraordinarily detailed. On the modern period there is C. Bloch and P. Renouvin, *Guide de l'étudiant en histoire moderne et contemporaine* (Presses universitaires de France, Paris, 1949), and W. Kienart (editor), *Historische Zeitschrift* (Oldenbourg, Munich), a post-war periodical survey by countries with historiographical judgements (for definition of historiography, see below, p. 66).

There are very many guides to recent books only, or to current output, but as much of the material they index comes from periodicals, we may note first E. H. Boehm and L. Adolphus (editors), *Historical Periodicals* (Clio Press, Santa Barbara, 1961) which merely lists about 5000 serials from many countries. The *Jahresberichte der Geschichtswissenschaft* (Mittler, Berlin) covered historical output from 1878 to 1913 in a long series of annual volumes, and is now continued by the (selective) *International Bibliography of Historical Sciences* from 1926, this being published in Washington, and later Paris. The wartime gap (1940–6) in this publication is covered so far as material published in Great Britain is concerned by L. B. Frewer's *Bibliography of Historical Writings Published in Great Britain and the Empire, 1940–1945* (Blackwell, Oxford, 1947). This in its turn is continued by Joan C. Lancaster, *Bibliography of Historical Works Issued in the United Kingdom, 1946–56*, reissued 1964, and a similarly titled work covering 1957–60, 1962, compiled by William Kellaway. All these works are arranged by topics and published by the London University's Institute of Historical Research. Note also W. L. Langer and H. F. Armstrong's *Foreign Affairs Bibliography, 1919–1932* (Harper, New York), continued for 1932–42 by R. G. Woolbert, and for 1942–52 by H. L. Roberts. For current work English-speaking readers will probably find (Fig. 20) the Historical Association's *Annual Bulletin of Historical Literature* (1912–, In progress), of most general use. The 1964 number deals mainly with publications of 1962, and has very concise sections on general history, prehistory, ancient history, the earlier middle ages, the later middle ages, the sixteenth, seventeenth, eighteenth, nineteenth and twentieth centuries, Europe and the wider world, and American history. Each section is by a different authority and is in narrative form. Titles are clearly listed and there is some

Tunisia (Amer. Univ., Beirut), and J. Poncet describes *La Colonisation et l'Agriculture Européennes en Tunisie depuis 1881* (Paris: Mouton). R. Letourneau surveys *Évolution Politique de l'Afrique du Nord Musulmane, 1920–1961* (Paris: Colin, *NF.* 26), and D. C. Gordon reviews *North Africa's French Legacy, 1954–1962* (Harvard U.P., $2.50, Middle Eastern monogr., 9). J. Morizot writes on *L'Algérie Kabylisée* (Paris: Peyronnet, *NF.* 15), and A. C. M. Ross translates P. Bourdieu's *The Algerians* (Beacon Press, Boston, $3.95), publ. in French in 1958.

R. K. Kent considers the French period in *From Madagascar to the Malagasy Republic* (Thames & Hudson, 30s.), and J. Valette prints four reports on Madagascar in *Sainte Marie et la Côte Est de Madagascar en 1818* (Tananarive Impr. Nat.). R. F. Betts considers *Assimilation and Association in French Colonial Theory, 1890–1914* (Columbia U.P., 1961, $5).

F. E. LEESE.

XI.—AMERICAN HISTORY

(i) THE UNITED STATES OF AMERICA

The volume of publication in American history continues unabated, stimulated but also contained to some degree by fresh bibliographical guides to material. Two of these are outstanding. Harry J. Carman and Arthur W. Thompson, *A Guide to the Principal Sources for American Civilization, 1800–1900, in the City of New York; printed materials* (Columbia University Press, $15), is the second and concluding guide to source material in New York. The first volume, published in 1960, listed manuscript sources; the second inventories the printed material. Some sixty-six depositories have been surveyed and attention directed to valuable holdings in the lesser known collections. Kenneth W. Munden and Henry P. Beers, *Guide to Federal Archives relating to the Civil War*, (Washington D.C.: National Archives, $3) interprets its terms of reference broadly and is of great value for students of the Reconstruction period as well as of the Civil War. The volume is equipped with a full and accurate index and may well prove to be one of the most important books to emerge from the publishing frenzy of the Civil War centennial observances. In addition, it is a timely reminder of the wealth of material in the National Archives which is much less used than that in the Library of Congress. A major aid to research scholars in Southern history is Thomas D. Clark ed., *Travels in the New South: A Bibliography*. Vol. 1, *The Post-War South, 1865–1900: An Era of Reconstruction and Re-adjustment;* Vol. II, *The Twentieth Century South, 1900–1955: An Era of Change, Depression and Emergence* (University of Oklahoma Press, $20 the set). Travellers' accounts, promotional literature, guidebooks and directories are examined for their contributions to the cultural, social, economic and political history of the South as it changed from a predominantly rural to an urban industrial region. The more valuable books are commented on at length. Those of little value are dismissed in as little as a single sentence often

63

Fig. 20. *Annual Bulletin of Historical Literature.* (Copyright: Historical Association.)

EUROPEAN ECONOMIC COMMUNITY (Common Market) (cont.)

Economic Policy.

Businesses and supply of services, abolition of restrictions, programme (Oct. 1961), 18975 A

Capital, freedom of movement, directive, approval (May 1960) 18975 A

Cartels and Anti-Trust policy, regulations approved (Feb. 1962), 18975 A

Industrial import quotas (internal), abolition (Dec. 1961), 18975 A

Pay, equal pay for men and women, total discrimination to be eliminated by end 1964, 18975 A

Transport, common policy, proposed programme (Jun. 1962), 18975 A

Workers, movement of, directive approved (May 1960), 18975 A

European Development Fund.

(Previously referred to as " Overseas Development Fund.")

Activities (Jan. 1958-Dec. 1961) 18975 A

European Investment Bank.

Activities (to 30 Nov. 1961), 18975 A

Hallstein, Professor Walter.

Commission, president, re-apptmt., 18975 A

Membership.

Associate-Membership, see separate subhdg.

Denmark, membership application (Aug. 1961), 18975 A

Ireland, Republic of, membership application (Aug. 1961), 18975 A

Norway, membership application (May 1962), 18975 A

Portugal, membership application (Jun. 1962), 18975 A

United Kingdom, membership application (Aug. 1961), 18975 A

Tariffs (External).

(For bi-lateral agrmts. with non-member States, see subhdgs. individual countries, " Relations with.")

Common external tariffs, programme accelerated (1960-63), 18975 A

Tariffs (Internal).

Reductions, details (Jan. 1959, Jul. 1960, Jan. 1961, Jan.,

EUROPEAN POLITICAL UNION (cont.)

European Political Union.

to France (Jul.) and of President de Gaulle to W. Germany (Sep.) speeches and communiqués reaffirming decision to organize political unity of Europe, 18963 A

F

FRANCE

Algeria.

See separate main heading.

Atomic Energy and Research.

Euratom, participation in French projects, 18974 A

Cabinet.

Pompidou Cabinet, changes, corrigenda to previous references, 18983 A

Gaulle, President Charles de.

Adenauer, Dr. K., State visit to France (Jul. 1962), speech on Franco-German reconciliation and European political unity, 18963 A

European political union, speeches during Dr. Adenauer's visit to France (Jul.) and his visit to W. Germany (Sep.), 18963 A

Visits (W. Germany, Feb., Sep. 1962), 18963 A

W. Germany, State visit (Sep. 1962), speeches on Franco-German reconciliation and European political unity, 18963 A

German Federal Republic, Relations with.

Adenauer-de Gaulle talks (Baden-Baden, Feb. 1962), 18963 A

Adenauer, Dr. K., State visit to France (Jul. 1962), speeches and communiqué proclaiming final Franco-German reconciliation and intention to organize political unity of Europe, 18963 A

de Gaulle, President, State visit to W. Germany (Sep. 1962), speeches and communiqués proclaiming final Franco-German reconciliation and intention to organize political unity of Europe, 18963 A

United Arab Republic, Relations with.

French diplomats, arrest (Nov. 1961), trial on espionage charges, proceedings dropped, defendants released (Apr.

GERMAN FEDERAL REPUBLIC (cont.)

(WESTERN GERMANY)

France, Relations with.

Adenauer, Dr. K., State visit to France (Jul. 1962), speeches and communiqué proclaiming final Franco-German reconciliation and intention to organize political unity of Europe, 18963 A

de Gaulle, President, State visit to W. Germany (Sep. 1962), speeches and communiqués proclaiming final Franco-German reconciliation and intention to organize political unity of Europe, 18963 A

GHANA

Defence.

British personnel, jt. Services training mission, U.K. supply agrmt., 18981 C

United Kingdom, Relations with.

Defence, jt. Services training mission, U.K. provision, agreement, 18981 C

GREECE

European Economic Community,

Associate membership, ratification (Aug. 1962), 18975 A

GUAM

Polaris submarine base to be established at Apra in 1963, 18974 B

GUIANA (Dutch)

See main hdg. Netherlands West. Indies, subhdg. " Surinam."

H

HOLLAND

See main hdg. Netherlands.

I

INDIA

Constitution.

Amendments (14th), 18973 A

Goa, Daman and Diu.

(For events before the incorporation of Goa, Daman and Diu in the Indian Union on 14 March 1962 and for Indian relations with Portugal arising therefrom, see subheading Portugal, Relations with.)

Constitution, local legislature, approval, 18973 A

Himachal Pradesh.

Constitution, local legislature, approval, 18973 A

Manipur.

Constitution, local legislature,

Fig. 21. *Keesing's Contemporary Archives.* (Copyright: Keesing's Publications.)

evaluation of contents. There is a general index to the first 12 vols. Some, but not all, contributors mention material in periodicals; others record items in foreign languages. Current material appearing in periodicals is dealt with in *Historical Abstracts, 1775–1945* (Historisches Seminar, Vienna, 1955–, In progress) (note the limitation of period) more fully than in the *International Bibliography* (above, p. 55) though only 400–500 periodicals are abstracted—items briefly summarized so as to make their sense clear—compared with 3000 merely indexed in the latter. To bring our knowledge of current international affairs up to date we must have recourse to indexes of newspapers or services such as (Fig. 21) *Keesing's Contemporary Archives* (Keesing's, 1935–, In progress). This is arranged first by countries, then by topics. The main portion (white pages) is supplied weekly for insertion in a loose-leaf binder. When several topics are dealt with on a page, large capital letters are used to separate different subjects. Every second week a green-coloured subject index is supplied; this is always re-compiled and replaces its predecessor. Every thirteenth week the last of these fortnightly indexes is discarded, and its contents embodied in a quarterly yellow index. Keesing's folders last for two years; during the second year the quarterly index is salmon coloured. There is also a (pink) index of names. It is therefore quite easy to follow any topic through from its initiation up to about a fortnight ago, as there are numbered references to earlier entries. Keesing's reports are quite full, and do not require reference to a newspaper; they do not, of course, cover any news except that of national or international importance, nor plans of events ahead (details of forthcoming Royal tours, etc.). Keesing's is issued in languages other than English in Amsterdam, Brussels and Vienna, but these publications are quite independent of one another. Similar services are (Fig. 22), *Facts on File: the Index of World Events* (Facts on File, New York, 1940–, In progress), which has headings on topics such as Latin America, arts and science, sport, obituaries, rather than national heads, and a five-yearly index, and *Current Digest of the Soviet Press* (Joint Committee on Slavic Studies, New York, 1949–, In progress), issued weekly. The latter gives a complete weekly index to *Pravda* and *Izvestia*,

baby foods showed them to contain no more than 4% of the amount of strontium-90 considered a potential threat to infants' health. It said that no "change in normal dietary patterns" was warranted.

A sharp increase in the amounts of fallout-caused iodine-131 in fresh milk was reported by the PHS in figures issued May 23 and 30. The May 30 figures, based on readings taken May 14-18, showed the following levels (in terms of micro-microcuries of iodine-131 per liter of milk): Wichita, Kan. 660 mmc.; Kansas City, Mo. 600 mmc.; Des Moines, -Ia. 300 mmc.; Minneapolis 290 mmc.; Chicago 90 mmc.; St. Louis 80 mmc.; Cincinnati 50 mmc.; Denver 45 mmc.

Surgeon Gen. Terry said May 30 that the milk surveillance program had been increased but that "the readings do not call for protective measures of any sort."

Declines in the high midwestern readings were reported by the PHS in figures made public June 21. The midwestern readings, attributed to the U.S. atmospheric nuclear tests in the Pacific, had remained constant through June 14 but then showed the following reductions reported June 21: Wichita 80 mmc.; Kansas City, Mo. 155 mmc.; Des Moines 70 mmc.; Minneapolis 30 mmc.; Chicago 10 mmc.; St. Louis 35 mmc.; Cincinnati 10 mmc.

2 groups of children—10 each from Kansas City, Mo. and from St. Louis—were examined by the NYU Medical Center and were found to have absorbed only slight quantities of iodine-131 in their thyroid glands despite the relatively high levels reported in the milk they drank. The Kansas City group was tested June 22, the St. Louis group June 27. Dr. Merril Eisenbud of NYU reported to the PHS July 7 that the amounts of iodine-131 detected had not approached the recommended level for countermeasures.

Dr. G. D. Carlyle Thompson, Utah health director, reported Aug. 1 that milk from certain parts of northeastern Utah was being diverted from Salt Lake City because of increases in iodine-131 as a result of an atmospheric test carried out July 7 at the AEC's Nevada proving grounds. The level of radioactive iodine in milk supplied by the affected areas was not detectable July 6 but had risen to 1,660 mmc. a liter by July 20. It fell to 450 mmc. during the next few days, but rose again to 2,050 mmc. July 25.

The PHS reported Aug. 17 that the July 7 Nevada test had been responsible for an increase in the quantity of iodine-131 to 580 mmc. per liter of milk in the Salt Lake City area and 370 mmc. in Laramie, Wyo. milk supplies. Both figures were averages for the entire month of July. The July average for the entire PHS sampling network (61 stations throughout the U.S.) was 40 mmc. of iodine-131 per liter, compared with 30 mmc. in June.

Middle East

Saudi-Jordan Merger. A plan to merge the military forces of Jordan and Saudi Arabia and to coordinate the economic policies of both countries was announced in a joint communiqué Aug. 29. The agreement was reached at a 3-day meeting of Jordanian King Hussein and King Saud of Saudi Arabia in Taif, Saudi Arabia.

member states" and "can do nothing for the aspirations of the Arab struggle."

Khalil Kallas, deputy chairman of the Syrian delegation, reportedly asked the council to adopt a resolution condemning the UAR.

The league council Aug. 31 by a 10-1 vote (Syria opposed) approved a resolution saying that "it could not continue discussion of the Syrian complaint against UAR interference because the UAR had withdrawn." The council resolved to discuss Syria's complaints at its next meeting.

League Secy. Gen. Abdel Khalek Hassouna, an Egyptian, had gone to Beirut, Lebanon Aug. 28, on league instruction, in an unsuccessful effort to persuade Deiri and the UAR delegation to return to the Shtura conference. Deiri returned to Cairo Aug. 30. [See p. 218E3]

Cuba

JFK Pledge Vs. Cuban Force. Pres. Kennedy, citing concern "over the recent moves of the Soviet Union to bolster the military power" of Cuba, declared Sept. 4 that the U.S. was determined to prevent the Castro régime from "export[ing] its aggressive purposes by force or the threat of force." The President said it was "U.S. policy" to use "whatever means may be necessary" to bar Cuba "from taking action against any part of the Western Hemisphere."

The President issued his statement after he had consulted with Congressional leaders on alleged Soviet military aid to Cuba. Mr. Kennedy said: "Information has reached" the U.S. "in the last 4 days . . . which establishes without doubt that the Soviets have provided the Cuban government with a number of defensive missiles" and "radar and other electronic equipment . . . required for their operation." "We can also confirm the presence of several Soviet-made motor torpedo boats carrying ship-to-ship guided missiles" with a 15-mile range. "There is no evidence of any organized combat force in Cuba from any Soviet bloc country; of military bases provided for Russia; of a violation of the 1934 [Guantánamo] treaty; of the presence of ground missiles; or of other significant offensive capability either in

Fig. 22. *Facts on File.* (Copyright: Facts on File Inc.)

and a digest of news of all types from other sources, but the delay (minimum one month) is greater than that in the other services. Indexes to comprehensive national newspapers are more detailed still, but slower in publication; the (Fig. 23) *Index to "The Times"* (*The Times*, 1906–, In progress), now issued every two months, is some six months behind. Entries refer to columns on each page, and also, by a series of stars, to different editions. *The Times* has been indexed, though not on today's lines, back to 1790. *The Glasgow Herald* (from 1906) and *New York Times* (from 1913) also publish detailed indexes.

Such, then, are the tools by which we may dissect and discover history on a world-wide basis, throughout time. We will now say something about histories, comprehensive in themselves, made for reading directly.

HISTORY: COMPREHENSIVE WORKS

Once again (cf. pp. 34–6) we must refer initially to the great encyclopaedias; as they deal with the past they contain more history than anything else, especially the nineteenth-century editions; for example lengthy *Britannica* articles such as Macaulay's on Dr. Johnson and Ernest Barker's on the crusades have become standard works on their subjects. There are, however, works encyclopaedic in length, which deal with universal history exclusively, either the whole of it or a large span of it. A few of these were written by one person; more by syndicates. Works dealing with one or a group of countries only will be discussed in Chapters 3 and 4. The great value of these works lies not only in what they tell us, correct though it may well be, but in the references (bibliographical apparatus as they are called), sometimes to the sources the writer has used, sometimes to other works suggested for further reading. Such references are never as full as those given in the pure bibliographies in the previous section, but dropped in among readable narrative, they are perhaps more intelligible.

Perhaps the best-known comprehensive general works in English are the three Cambridge histories—ancient, mediaeval and modern.

THE TIMES INDEX

JANUARY—FEBRUARY

1962

A

A.A.M.C. Co., JAN. 22, 15c
A.B.C. Television Ltd.—gift to Coventry Cathedral Festival, FEB. 2, 13a
A.E.: see ASSOCIATED Engineering Ltd.
A.E. and G. Unit Trust Co., JAN. 16, 15b (5*)
A.E.I. Lamp and Lighting Co., Ltd.—fluorescent fillings: price reductions, JAN. 1, 17g;—Strike, FEB. 8, 7a; girls used to help spread, 12, 5c; girl pickets fail, 14, 5c; non-striker is union member, 15, 4f (5*); return to work, 19, 5d; non-union man continues work: sent to coventry, 28, 8f (5*)
A.G.J.—on Brig. R. C. H. Miers (tribute), FEB. 27. 15b
AMF Ltd., FEB. 10, 10b
AMF/Maxim Co., JAN. 15, 16c
A.N.R.—on Prof. M. A. Thomson (tribute), JAN. 29, 16d
A1 Nast Co., JAN. 11, 19a
A.P.V. Industries—casino plans, FEB. 21, 16e
A.V.P. Industries, JAN. 29, 15f
A.W. (Securities) Ltd., FEB. 19, 17a
AARS. Mr. K.: see IRAN: Norwegian Ambassador designate
ABARZUZA, Rear-Adm. D. F. de (Spain)—death, JAN. 10, 12e
ABBEY National Building Soc., JAN. 9, 15e; FEB. 1, 17e;—Torquay branch opened, FEB. 1, 17e
ABBEYDALE New Bone China Co. Ltd., JAN. 8, 15d; 16, 15e
ABBEYTOWN Mining Co., JAN. 15, 16c
ABBOTT, Very Rev. E. S. (Dean of Westminster)—on Dr. O. Peasgood (tribute), JAN. 29, 16e
ABBOUD, Ahmed (U.A.R.)—charge against dropped, JAN. 5, 8b (5*)
ABDI, Mr. A. O.—conviction quashed, FEB. 20, 13c
ABDULLAH, Prince: see JORDAN: Crown prince
ABDULLAH, Shaikh Mohammed: see INDIA: Kashmir: Chief Minister, former
ABDULMALIKI, Alhaji: see NIGERIA: Great Britain: High Commissioner
ABEL, Col. R. (Russia)—serving U.S. espionage sentence since 1957: exchange with Russian held prisoner: see POWERS, Capt. F. G.
ABERCONWAY, Lord—received by Queen Mother, FEB. 8, 14b
ABERDARE, Lady—son born, FEB. 6, 14b
ABERDEEN Edinburgh and London Trust, JAN. 2, 14b; FEB. 5, 18b
ABINGER, Lord—on medical auxiliaries (s.P.), JAN. 25, 14b
ABINGTON by-pass—road accident near, JAN. 3, 4g
ABORTION—sentence: appeal allowed, FEB. 27, 3e

ABOUD, Dr. El-Mehdi ben: see MOROCCO: United States: Ambassador
ABOUKHOFF, Mr. A.—death, FEB. 28, 14e
ABRAHAM, Mr. A.—marriage, JAN. 30, 6f (5*)
ABRAMOV, Mr.: see LAOS: Russia: Ambassador
ABSE, Mr. L.—on Criminal Justice Administration Bill (s.P.), JAN. 24, 14g
ABYSSINIA: see ETHIOPIA
ACCOUNTANTS, Assn. of Certified and Corporate—luncheon, JAN. 31, 12c
ACCOUNTANTS, Inst. of Chartered—examination results, FEB. 12, 18b; luncheon, 16, 14b
ACCOUNTANTS, Inst. of Cost and Works — dinner, JAN. 11, 12b; luncheon, FEB. 15, 14c
ACEVEDO, Sn. A.: see ARGENTINA: Public Works Minister
Achievement—company formed to expand sales, JAN. 16, 15e
ACHIEVEMENTS, first—light leading article, FEB. 2, 11d
ACKROYD, Sir C.—on Col. R. W. Hills (tribute), FEB. 13, 15a
ACME Missile Construction Co., FEB. 27, 19c
ACROW (Engineers) Ltd., JAN. 17, 16b (5*);—Steel moulds (photo.), FEB. 15, 20d
ACTON, Mr. H.—article on reading, JAN. 18, 13b
ACTUARIES, Inst. of—paper on computers, JAN. 23, 19a; president, FEB. 14, 20d
ACUTT, Sir K. C.—K.B.E., JAN. 1, 4b
ADAM, Gen. Sir R. F.—on U.N. bonds issue (l. with others), JAN. 25, 11e; on racial prejudice (l. with others), 27, 9e
ADAM, Robert—biog., FEB. 1, 13d
ADAM, Villiers de L.—*Axel*, FEB. 19, 14a
ADAMS, Mr. C. — *Hypocrites Anonymous*, FEB. 15, 8b
ADAMS, Sir G.: see WEST Indies: Prime Minister
ADAMS, Mr. J.—retirement, FEB. 13, 14g (5*)
ADAMS, Mr. J. C.—" The Globe Playhouse": illus., JAN. 18, 13d
ADAMS, Mr. R. S.—on engineering wage claim (l.), FEB. 16, 13d
ADAMS, Mr. S. (U.S.A.)—" First Hand Report," JAN. 18, 13d
ADAMS (Cyril) and Co., JAN. 18, 18f
ADAMSON (Daniel) and Co., FEB. 12, 17a
ADDIS, Mr. J.: see LAOS: Great Britain: Ambassador
ADDISON, Lord—on hospitals plan (s.P.), FEB. 15, 16c
ADDISON, Geoffrey R., JAN. 3, 4f; 9, 7d; 12, 7b; 25, 6e
ADDISON, Rev. W. R. F.—death, JAN. 9, 13b
ADDRESSOGRAPH-MULTIGRAPH CO., JAN. 11, 19b

Fig. 23. *Index to "The Times"*. (Copyright: *The Times* Publishing Co.)

CONTENTS

CHAPTER XVIII

ECONOMIC INTERDEPENDENCE AND PLANNED ECONOMIES

By ASA BRIGGS, *Professor of Modern History in the University of Leeds*

xix

Fig. 24. *The New Cambridge Modern History*. (Copyright: Cambridge Univ. Press.)

The other Cambridge histories—of India, of Poland, of the British Empire, etc.—are not relevant here. First to be published was *The Cambridge Modern History* (13 vols., Cambridge Univ. Press, 1902–26); the main work was completed in 1926, but a reprint without the bibliographies came out in 1934. This was largely planned by the historian Acton, and aimed at being "a narrative which is not a mere string of episodes, but displays a continuous development. It moves in a succession to which the nations are subsidiary". It aimed particularly at taking account of the scholarship of the nineteenth century, and of published sources such as the *Monumenta Germaniae historica*, the *Rolls Series*, and the *Dictionary of National Biography*. The bibliographies are a particularly valuable feature; in Vol. 1 they occupy 100 of the 807 pp. So are the tables in the index volume. By contrast (Fig. 24) *The New Cambridge Modern History* (14 vols., Cambridge Univ. Press, 1957–, In progress) of similar format excludes all bibliographies because so many are now available in contrast with the position sixty years ago. In general the new history follows out the lines laid down for its predecessor, but Sir George Clark's contributors, unlike those of Lord Acton, are not expected to conceal their own convictions. It was perhaps a mistake to take the work up to 1945, for Vol. XII, dealing with the period 1898–1945, is very scrappy on the later years. (Fig. 25) *The Cambridge Mediaeval History* (8 vols., Cambridge Univ. Press, 1911–36, now under revision) emulated Lord Acton's plan and claimed "Germany, indeed, has Heeren and Oncken, but in France even the great work of Lavisse and Rambaud deals with the Middle Ages on a much smaller scale than is here contemplated" (preface). This work, like its forerunners, has long bibliographies intended as aids to further reading, rather than as an indication of what the writer of the particular chapter had used, and was designed for the "general reader". *The Cambridge Ancient History* (12 text vols., and 5 of plates, Cambridge Univ. Press, 1923–39, now under revision) was the last of the trilogy to be published, though with the earliest time coverage. Naturally the Cambridge histories suffer from the defects of any composite work—unevenness—but they are a splendid starting

(vi) *Letters and Papers.*

Aeneas Sylvius Piccolomini (Pope Pius II). Commentarii. Ed. Gobellinus, J. Rome. 1584.
—— Der Briefwechsel des Eneas Silvius Piccolomini. Ed. Wolkan, R. (Fontes rerum Austriacarum. Abt. II. Vols. LXI–II, LXVII–VIII. Vienna. 1909–18.)
Caro, J. B. Aus der Kanzlei Sigmunds. AOG. LIX. 1879.
Christ Church Letters relating to the affairs of the Priory of Christ Church, Canterbury. Ed. Sheppard, J. B. (Camden Soc. n.s. Vol. XIX.) London. 1877.
Correspondence of Humphrey, Duke of Gloucester, and Pier Candido Decembrio, Ed. Borsa, M. EHR. XIX (1904). 509–26. [*See also* Newman, W. L. Correspondence of Humphrey, Duke of Gloucester, and Pier Candido Decembrio. EHR. XX (1905). 484–98.]
Le Cotton MS. Galba B.I. Ed. Scott, E. and Gilliodts van Severen, L. (Acad. Roy....de Belgique.) Brussels. 1896.
Epistolae Academicae Oxon. (1421–1509.) Ed. Anstey, H. 2 vols. (Oxford Hist. Soc. XXXV, XXXVI.) Oxford. 1898.
Historical Papers and Letters from the Northern Registers. Ed. Raine, J. (Rolls.) 1873.
Letters of John Tiptoft, Earl of Worcester,...to the University of Oxford [1460.] Ed. Tait, J. EHR. XXXV (1920). 570–2.
Letters and Papers of John Shillingford, Mayor of Exeter, 1447–50. Ed. Moore, S. A. (Camden Soc. n.s. Vol. II.) London. 1871.
Letters of the fifteenth and sixteenth centuries. Ed. Anderson, R. C. (Southampton Record Soc.) Southampton. 1921.
Letters of the Kings of England. Ed. Halliwell-Phillipps, J. O. 2 vols. London. 1846. [Translations only.]
Letters of Queen Margaret of Anjou and Bishop Beckington and others, written in the reigns of Henry V and Henry VI. Ed. Munro, C. (Camden Soc. LXXXVI.) London. 1863.
Lettres de rois, reines, et autres personnages des cours de France et d'Angleterre. Ed. Champollion-Figeac, A. Vol. II. (Coll. doc.) Paris. 1847.
Literae Cantuarienses. Ed. Sheppard, J. B. Vol. III. (Rolls.) 1889.
Mediaeval Post-Bag. Ed. Lyell, L. London. 1934. [Contains a few letters not before published.]
Memorials of St Edmund's Abbey. Ed. Arnold, T. Vol. III. (Rolls.) 1896. [Letters from Register of Abbot Curteys, 1440–1444, pp. 241–79.]
Memorials of the reign of Henry VI. Official Correspondence of Thomas Bekynton, Secretary to Henry VI and Bishop of Bath and Wells. Ed. Williams, G. 2 vols. (Rolls.) 1872. [*See also* Journal by one of the Suite of Thomas Beckington, 1442. Ed. (in transl.) Nicolas, N. H. London. 1828.]
Original Letters illustrative of English History. Ed. Ellis, H. Three series. 11 vols. London. 1824–46.
Paston Letters, 1422–1509. Ed. Gairdner, J. (Library edn.) 6 vols. London. 1904.
Plumpton Correspondence. A series of letters, chiefly domestick, written in the reigns of Edward IV, Richard III, Henry VII, and Henry VIII. Ed. Stapleton, T. (Camden Soc. IV.) London. 1839.
Poggio Bracciolini, F. Epistolae. Ed. Tonelli, T. 3 vols. Florence. 1832–61.
Royal and historical letters during the reign of Henry IV. Ed. Hingeston, F. C. (Rolls.) 1860. [This covers the years 1399–1404. A second volume was suppressed but can be obtained in the larger libraries.]
Some Literary Correspondence of Humphrey, Duke of Gloucester. Ed. Creighton, M. EHR. X (1895). 99–104.
Stonor Letters and Papers, 1290–1483. Ed. Kingsford, C. L. 2 vols. (Camden Soc. 3rd ser. Vol. XXIX, XXX.) London. 1919. The editor afterwards published a supplement in Camden Miscellany, XIII. (Camden Soc. 3rd ser. Vol. XXXIV.) 1924.
Trevelyan Papers. Ed. Collier, J. P. 3 vols. (Camden Soc. LXVII, LXXXIV, CV.) London. 1857–72.

Fig. 25. *The Cambridge Mediaeval History.* (Copyright: Cambridge Univ. Press.)

point for any aspect of history, particularly the original editions
with long bibliographies. As with the *Britannica*, there are chapters
such as that in the *Cambridge Modern* (Vol. 2) by F. W. Maitland, on
the "Anglican settlement and the Scottish reformation", which set
a standard that it would be impossible to follow throughout. A
similar French work is E. Lavisse and A. Rambaud (editors),
Histoire générale du IVe s. à nos jours (12 vols., Colin, Paris, 1893–
1905), and the corresponding German work is W. Oncken,
Allgemeine Geschichte in Einzeldarstellungen (48 vols., Grote, Berlin,
1879–92). Seventy scholars had a hand in Lavisse–Rambaud and
twenty-one were associated with Oncken. The French have taken
the lead recently in large composite works:

> BERR, H. (editor), *Evolution de l'humanité*, Michel, Paris,
> 1920–, In progress. Over 100 vols. have appeared.
> CAVAIGNAC, E. (editor), *Histoire du monde*, de Boccard, Paris,
> 1924–, In progress.
> GLOTZ, G. and COHEN, R. (editors), *Histoire générale*, Presses
> universitaires de France, Paris, 1926–, In progress. Ancient
> and mediaeval only.
> HALPHEN, L. and SAGNAC, P. (editors), *Peuples et civilisations*,
> Presses universitaires de France, Paris, 1926–, In progress.
> Over 20 vols. have appeared.
> *Clio; Introduction aux études historiques*, 14 vols, Presses uni-
> versitaires de France, Paris, 1934–52.

A peculiar, perhaps typically American, work universal in
scope, is J. N. Larned's *New Larned History for Ready Reference* (12
vols., Nichols, Springfield, 1922–4). This is arranged by subject,
but thereunder gives not an original article but an extract from a
recognized authority. The work may, therefore, be used as an
index. Resurrecting the standard historians in encyclopaedic form
does not, perhaps, serve many interests if the number of surplus
copies of the *Historians' History of the World* (15 vols., Encyclopaedia
Britannica, 1926) is any criterion. A useful epitome of world
history is W. L. Langer, *An Encyclopaedia of World History*[1] (3rd

[1] See also p. 198.

edition, Harrap, 1956), this being chronological in arrangement. This is now easily available in paperback from 1964 (Penguin). There is also a *Dictionary of Modern History, 1789–1945* (Cresset Press, 1962) by A. W. Palmer, *Larousse Encyclopaedia of Modern History from 1500* (Hamlyn, 1964), and a *Concise Dictionary of Mediaeval History*, by H. E. Wedeck (Philosophical Library, New York, 1964). The *Handbook for History Teachers* (Methuen, 1962) is a cross between a bibliography and a comprehensive work, published by the Institute of Education of London University. G. A. Williams, *Guide to Sources of Illustrative Material for use in Teaching History* (Historical Association, 1962) gives information on how to obtain postcards, filmstrips, models, etc. The periodical *Foreign Affairs* (U.S.A.) is universal and international in scope.

Before turning to different aspects or more restricted concepts of world history, we must give some attention to the great universal histories by single authors, despite their limitations. It is true that we did not carry out this service for comprehensive universal biography, for lack of examples, though we shall when we come on to specialized biographies (pp. 186–90). There have been many great universal histories by individuals, all seminal, too, in leading on to other works, but of more value, generally speaking, for the stimulation of ideas than for the discovery of facts. Sir Walter Raleigh's *History of the World* (1614) is perhaps the best known though not the earliest attempt at a universal history. Voltaire (*Essai sur les moeurs*, 1756) and Ranke (*Weltgeschichte*, 1881–8) should be known for their influence on others though they are not read nowadays. If Spengler's *Decline of the West* (Routledge, 1934) be inadmissible as insufficiently broad in treatment, then (Fig. 26) A. J. Toynbee's *A Study of History* (10 vols., Oxford Univ. Press, 1934–52), abridgement in 2 vols., remains the one great contemporary example of a true universal history.

We had something to say of historiography (the science of writing history), though not calling it by that name, when discussing the atmosphere of history above. Although intended for the general reader, such works as H. Butterfield's *History and Human Relations* (Collins, 1951) and G. Barraclough's *History in a Changing World*

THE GENESES OF CIVILIZATIONS

A. THE PROBLEM OF THE GENESES OF CIVILIZATIONS

HAVING satisfied ourselves that societies of the species called civilizations are intrinsically comparable with one another, and having decided to attempt a comparative study of the twenty-one representatives of the species which we find at our command, we may now start our inquiry, at the natural starting-point, by considering how civilizations come into existence, or, in subjective terms, how they emerge above the lower limit of our mental field of vision. In this inquiry, we must take account of the different modes in which they emerge; and if we attempt to give some general description and explanation of the phenomenon, it must be such as to cover all the modes of emergence which we have observed.

When we were identifying representatives of the species,[1] our explorations revealed certain features in the backgrounds of civilizations which first served us as landmarks for a survey of the historical landscape and afterwards enabled us to make a provisional classification of the specimens which we had identified. This classification was determined by two criteria.

Our primary criterion was the origin of a society's religion; our secondary criterion was the original range of its geographical habitat. On the religious criterion, we classified our twenty-one civilizations into five groups: first, civilizations which carried on the traditions of earlier civilizations by taking over the religions of these earlier civilizations' dominant minorities; second, civilizations which 'affiliated' themselves to earlier civilizations by growing up within chrysalides constituted by churches which had been created by these earlier civilizations' internal proletariats. Such 'affiliated' civilizations fell into two sub-groups: one in which the germs out of which the chrysalis-churches had been created by the internal proletariats of the 'apparented' societies had been indigenous to these 'apparented' societies, and another in which those germs had been alien from them. The fourth group consisted of civilizations which were related to earlier civilizations by the looser tie of having derived their religions from these earlier civilizations' external proletariats. In the fifth place, we found civilizations

[1] In I. C (i), above.

Fig. 26. TOYNBEE, A. J., *A Study of History*. (Copyright: Oxford Univ. Press.)

(Blackwell, Oxford, 1956) are indeed universal in concept. An excellent guide to nineteenth-century historiography is G. P. Gooch's *History and Historians in the Nineteenth Century* (2nd edition, Longmans, 1952). There is a *History of Muslim Historiography* by F. Rosenthal (2nd edition, Heinman, New York, 1966).

We list now a few works which, though universal in space, are not in time:

Archaeology

DÉCHELETTE, J., *Manuel d'archéologie pre-historique celtique et gallo-romaine*, 2nd edition, 6 vols., Picard, Paris, 1924–7. Continued by A. Grenier (4 vols., 1931–60).

EBERT, M., *Reallexikon der Vorgeschichte, unter Mitwirkung zahlreicher Fachgelehrter hrsg. von Max Ebert*, 15 vols., de Gruyter, Berlin, 1924–32.

COTTRELL, L. (editor), *The Concise Encyclopaedia of Archaeology*, Hutchinson, 1960.

Note the following periodicals:

Revue archéologique (France).
Journal of the Pre-Historic Society (Great Britain).

Antiquity

CARY, M. (editor), *Oxford Classical Dictionary*, Clarendon Press, Oxford, 1949.

SMITH, Sir W., *Dictionary of Greek and Roman Biography and Mythology*, 3 vols., Murray, 1880.

MULLER, I. VON, and others (editors), *Handbuch der Altertumswissenschaft*, Beck, Munich, 1886–, In progress. Over 60 vols. have appeared.

PIGHI, G. B., and others (editors), *Enciclopedia classica*, Soc. ediz. intern., Turin, 1959–, In progress.

PAULY, A. F. VON., *Pauly's Real-Encyclopadie der classischen Altertumswissenschaft*, Druckenmüller, Stuttgart, 1894–, In progress. The fullest work with a complicated method of issuing supplements. Over 70 vols. or separate portions of volumes have appeared.

SANDYS, *Sir* J. E. (editor), *Companion to Latin Studies*, 3rd edition, Cambridge Univ. Press, 1925.

WHIBLEY, L. (editor), *Companion to Greek Studies*, 4th edition, Cambridge Univ. Press, 1931.

DAREMBERG, C., and SAGLIO, E., *Dictionnaire des antiquités grecques et romaines*, 6 vols., Hachette, Paris, 1877–1919. Has line block illustrations, but is still useful.

History of the Greek and Roman World (general editor, M. Cary), Methuen, 1947–, In progress. The best-known multi-volumed work in Great Britain; six of seven volumes available.

The following classical periodicals should be noted:

Journal of Hellenic Studies and *Journal of Roman Studies* (Great Britain); *Revue des études grecques* and *Revue des études latines* (France); *Rivista di studi classici* (Italy).

Mediaeval Times

Progress of Mediaeval and Renaissance Studies in the United States and Canada, University of Colorado, Colorado, 1923–, annual. This is a continuous narrative survey of papers read to learned societies, books in the press, etc. Note also *The Larousse Encyclopedia of Ancient and Medieval History*, Hamlyn, 1963.

Modern History

NEVINS, A., and EHRMANN, H. M., *The University of Michigan History of the Modern World*, 15 vols., University of Michigan, Ann Arbor, 1958–, In progress.

FUETER, E., *World History, 1815–1920*, Methuen, 1923.
Periodicals on later history are so numerous that a selection will be given under different countries.

The difference between the comprehensive general works on modern times that we propose to mention now and such services as *Keesing's* (above, pp. 57–8) is that they are designed for continuous reading; obviously they will include good general newspapers such as *The Times*, *The Guardian* (London), *New York Times*, *Le Soir* (Paris), *Berliner Tageblatt* (Berlin), etc. An unindexed newspaper is always less useful than one of the indexed ones, described above (p. 60), but in default of an index one can sometimes usefully use a daily contents summary, or a chronology of the year which many papers publish round about Christmas. Many of the encyclopaedias listed above (pp. 34–6) issue "books of the year" (*Britannica*, *Chambers's*, *Collier's*, *Americana*, etc.). The *New International Year Book* (Dodd, New York, 1908–, In progress) is a work of this type that is quite independent of its parent encyclopaedia. (Fig. 27), *The Annual Register* (Longmans, London, 1761–, In progress), is the oldest established annual survey, and has varied greatly in scope and coverage during its long history. It still has a strong United Kingdom bias, but has long sections on Commonwealth and foreign history, science, literature, documents, obituary. It is probably the most useful source for the developments of the last ten or more years that are too recent to have got into the encyclopaedias or monographs. Although the contributors are authorities in their own fields, the work is not as unbiased as a more considered work of history might be expected to be, but a recent number includes such useful subjects as weather and world population trends.

Finally we may mention two quarterly periodicals of world coverage, *Journal of World History* (Paris, 1953–, In progress), in three languages and *Journal of Contemporary History* (1966–, In progress).

Chapter 3

INTERNATIONAL DEFENCE ORGANIZATIONS

DURING 1962 the dominant fact of international politics remained the division of the States of the world into three groups: those who, principally through NATO, SEATO, and CENTO, were allied with the United States; those who, through the Warsaw Treaty and the world Communist movement, were allied to the Soviet Union; and those who, in relation to the conflict between the first group and the second, were neutral. But alignments and antagonisms other than these were increasingly making themselves felt. Within the Western block the United States found itself in conflict with its European allies over nuclear policy, and with France and Germany also on relations with the Soviet Union. Within the Communist block, the Soviet Union openly disagreed with China and Albania over ideological questions and the Sino-Indian border dispute. The United States and the Soviet Union, though experiencing a major crisis in their relations over Cuba, took some tentative steps towards a *détente*: and the more these two great Powers drew together, the more each of them imposed a strain on relations with its allies, who feared that a bargain struck between the United States and the Soviet Union would be at the expense of third parties.

THE NORTH ATLANTIC TREATY ORGANIZATION

The shift in the balance of economic strength within NATO away from North America and towards Europe caused the alliance to concentrate its attention on debating the military implications of this new situation. At one extreme the United States opposed the possession, by its European allies, of independently-controlled strategic nuclear forces, contending that they had no need of them and that such forces could not constitute a credible deterrent. At the other extreme France and Britain showed themselves determined to maintain their own strategic nuclear forces, arguing that situations could arise in which the United States deterrent would not protect them, and that they were in fact capable of deterring the Soviet Union with these forces. Western Germany put forward no demands for nuclear weapons of its own, but expressed interest in sharing in the multilateral control of a NATO strategic nuclear force. This disagreement was connected with another, about the importance of increasing the conventional forces of the alliance: the United States pressing its European

Fig. 27. *The Annual Register.* (Copyright: Longmans.)

Europe in General. The United Kingdom. The British Commonwealth

INTRODUCTION

In a book addressed to the English speaking world, we make no excuse for devoting most of this chapter to different aspects of the biography and history of the United Kingdom. For every one who wishes to study some aspect of universal history, there will be ten concerned with their own homeland, and despite the present-day stigma attached to colonialism, the study of British history remains of great concern to a large slice of the world. Why can we not study national history from the works surveyed already? We can and will, of course, if we have no fuller ones, and maybe for purposes of comparison or convenience if we possess them. But it is generally best to study national bibliography from national works, which are generally fuller, more detailed, and nearer to the heart of their compilers than those of wider scope. This is only natural; early in life students are taught the history of their own country; later, perhaps, that of their own village or local industry. Advanced studies for higher degrees also centre on national and local history because scholars can write more realistically and accurately about an area they can comb in detail while doing their research. True there are great exceptions such as the German Halévy's *History of the English People*, and Gibbon's *The Decline and Fall of the Roman Empire*, but both these historians spent much time among the scenes about which they wrote. Even so, the writer on his own country is able to master his sources and reflect his own national spirit of progress much more easily than he can portray international influences. Despite the great work of UNESCO in publishing innumerable international bibliographies, the sympathies of individuals remain essentially national or local. Whenever we go abroad we reveal our ignorance in the fervour with which we purchase local guide books and histories, regardless of their quality. William the Conqueror, 1066; Declaration of Independence, 1776; Sedan, 1876; Versailles, 1918; can we give such significant dates for even *one* foreign country?

EUROPE

Before starting national bibliography we must note one or two works, historical rather than biographical, that deal with the whole of Europe. W. L. Langer's series, *The Rise of Modern Europe* (12 vols., Houghton Mifflin Co., Boston, 1934–53), Methuen's *History of Mediaeval and Modern Europe* (8 vols., Methuen, 1931–56), and the *Oxford History of Modern Europe* (Clarendon Press, 1954– In progress), are very useful. With an emphasis on earlier periods is E. Eyre (editor), *European Civilisation, its Origin and Development* (7 vols., Oxford Univ. Press, 1935–7). H. A. L. Fisher's *History of Europe* (Arnold, 1936) is probably the best-known one-volume history, but Pirenne and others have contributed in this way. A modern compendium is John Calmann (editor), *Western Europe* (*Handbooks to the Modern World*), Blond, 1966. L. J. Ragatz, *Bibliography for the Study of European History, 1815–1939* (Edwards, Ann Arbor), and A. Bullock and A. J. P. Taylor (editors), *A Select List of Books on European History, 1815–1914* (2nd edition, Oxford Univ. Press, 1957) are useful bibliographies. The briefer Historical Association bibliographies (*Helps for Students of History*), covering A.D. 395–1500, 1494–1788 and 1789–1945, are useful introductions. A similar work from the same publishers for 1715–1815 has been compiled by J. S. Bromley and A. Goodwin (1956). *Who's Who in Central and East Europe* (2nd edition, 1935–6, 1937) (no more published) is still worth consulting for those states that do not have their own Who's Whos.

UNITED KINGDOM: BIOGRAPHY. NATIONAL

Pride of place in this section among the comprehensive works (there are few bibliographies as such) must be given to the great (Fig. 28) *Dictionary of National Biography* (22 vols., Oxford Univ. Press, 1908–9).

There are various editions and supplements to this work, and its complicated bibliography calls for some attention. Like Sonnenschein's *Best Books*, it was the product of a dedicated man of wealth, who was prepared to devote all his leisure to it for many years. George Smith, partner in the publishers Smith, Elder & Co., decided about 1882 to produce a British national dictionary of biography, by which time many nations had embarked on similar works. There was, it is true, the folio *Biographia Britannica* (6 vols., 1747–66), and this had gone into an incomplete second edition, but, considerable undertaking as it was a century ago, it was by now entirely inadequate. At first Smith hoped to emulate Michaud by bringing out a universal biography. But his literary associate Leslie Stephen, editor of the *Cornhill Magazine* which Smith published, dissuaded him from the task. As it turned out, the national work was big enough; the original edition ran to 63 vols., appearing punctually each quarter for fifteen years. It contained close on 30,000 entries, more than in any other national dictionary; one Englishman or woman in every 5000 who reached adult life through the ages claims a place. The 22-volume thin-paper edition includes a supplement of persons who died while the main work was being written. There have been further supplements covering 1901–11 (3 vols., or 3 vols. in 1), 1912–21, 1922–30, 1931–40, and 1941–50, each containing cumulative entries for the twentieth century. A review of the last but one of these volumes in the *Times Literary Supplement* for 16 December 1949 states "the D.N.B. is an achievement the greatness of which it is easy to underestimate today. When the first volume appeared, the study of even political history was on a modest scale in the universities and colleges; when the last volume appeared, literary, social and economic history were still in their infancy in our seats of learning; music and the

of Sir Chichester with Lady Anne they became possessors of Tawstock, thenceforth the family seat.

Sir Bourchier Wrey commanded a regiment of horse after the Restoration, and served under the Duke of Monmouth. He was M.P. for Liskeard from 1678 to 1679, was returned for the county of Devon 1685, and sat for Liskeard 1689 to 1696. He fought a duel with Thomas Bulkeley, M.P. for Beaumaris, in Hyde Park on 4 Feb. 1691–2, in which Luttrell notes that of the six men engaged as principals and seconds five were M.P.s. Two of the seconds were slightly wounded. In May 1694 he fought another duel with James Praed of Trevethowe, M.P. for St. Ives, at Falmouth, and 'was run through the body, Mr. Praed being only hurt slightly in the face.' On 1 June he was reported dead of his wound, but lived until 21 July 1696, when Luttrell notes that Sir Bourchier Wrey and Captain Pitts, both M.P.s, are dead. He was buried in Tawstock church. He married Florence, daughter of Sir John Rolle.

His grandson, SIR BOURCHIER WREY (1714–1784), dilettante, born in 1714, became fifth baronet on the death of his father, Sir Bourchier Wrey, in 1726. His mother, Diana, was daughter of John Rolle of Stevenstone. After attending Winchester College, he matriculated from New College, Oxford, on 21 Oct. 1732. He was elected M.P. for Barnstaple, 20 Jan. 1747–8, and became a member of the Society of Dilettanti in 1742. He went to Bremen, Hamburg, and Lübeck in 1752 as a delegate of the 'Society for carrying on the Herring Fishery,' and succeeded in these ports and at Copenhagen in arranging better terms for the English fishermen. He rebuilt the pier at Ilfracombe in 1761. There are several of his letters among the Newcastle correspondence in the British Museum manuscripts. In them he speaks of his zeal for his majesty and his ministers; asks for a living in Devon for his brother as 'a proof that those that exert themselves towards the support of Liberty in Times of Confusion and Rebellion are entitled to its benefits in the days of Tranquillity,' dated November 1748, alluding apparently to 'the '45' when there were some disturbances in Exeter. He died on 13 April 1784, and was buried in Tawstock church, where is a pyramidal monument to him and his two wives, for the first of whom there is a long Latin epitaph in the 'Gentleman's Magazine' of 1751. He married, first, in 1749, Mary, daughter of John Edwards of Highgate (she died without issue in 1751); and secondly, in 1755, Ellen, daughter of John

Thresher of Bradford in Wiltshire. He was succeeded as sixth baronet by his eldest son Bourchier. His portrait was painted by George Knapton in 1744; he is represented with a punch-bowl, on which is inscribed 'Dulce est desipere in loco.'

[Luttrell's Brief Relation; Cal. State Papers, Dom.; Lysons's Devon; Cust and Colvin's History of the Society of Dilettanti; Notes and Queries, 5th ser. viii. 473.] E. L. R.

WRIGHT, ABRAHAM (1611–1690), divine and author, son of Richard Wright, silk-dyer, of London, was born in Black Swan Alley, Thames Street, 23 Dec. 1611; apparently his father was the Richard Wright who was warden of the Merchant Taylors' Company, 1600–1, 1606–7, and master 1611–1612. He was sent to the Mercers' chapel school in Cheapside, and was afterwards from 1626 at Merchant Taylors' school. He was elected scholar of St. John's College, Oxford, on 11 June 1629, and matriculated on 13 Nov. (certificate of his signing the articles in *Hist. MSS. Comm.* 2nd Rep. App. i. 78). He was especially favoured by Juxon for his good elocution. He was elected fellow of his college in 1632, graduated B.A. on 16 May 1633, and M.A. on 22 April 1637.

When Laud received Charles I in St. John's on 30 Aug. 1636, Wright delivered the speech welcoming the king to the new library (the verses are printed in his *Parnassus Biceps*, 1656), and after dinner he acted in the play 'Love's Hospital,' by George Wild [q.v.], before the king and queen. St. John's had long been famous for its plays (see *The Christmas Prince*, London, 1816; and *Narcissus*, London, 1893), and 'was at that time so well furnished as that they did not borrow any one actor from any college in town' (LAUD, *Hist. of his Chancellorship of Oxford*). Wright is said himself to have written a comic interlude called 'The Reformation,' acted at St. John's about 1631 (WARTON's edition of Milton's *Poems*, 1785, pp. 602–3).

On 27 Sept. 1637 Wright was ordained deacon by Francis White (1564?–1638) [q.v.], bishop of Ely, in the chapel of Ely House. In the same year he published at Oxford a collection of sixteenth and seventeenth century epigrams, which he called 'Delitiæ Delitiarum.' On 22 Dec. 1639 he was ordained priest by Bancroft, bishop of Oxford, in Christ Church Cathedral. He soon became a popular preacher, and preached before the king, before the university, and at St. Paul's (WOOD, *Athenæ Oxon.* iv. 275; cf. *Hist. MSS. Comm.* 2nd Rep. App. i. 79).

In August 1645 he was presented to the

H 2

educated at Harrow and Christ Church, Oxford; conservative M.P., North Wiltshire, 1880–85; East Wiltshire, 1885–92; West Derby division of Liverpool, 1893–1900; South Bristol, 1900–6; South County Dublin, 1906–10; Strand division of Middlesex, 1910–18; St. George's, Westminster, 1918–21; belonged to 'country party' on entry into parliament, 1880; parliamentary secretary to Local Government Board, 1886–92; took large part in framing and getting through House of Commons Local Government Act, which created county councils throughout Great Britain, 1888; president of Board of Agriculture, with seat in cabinet, 1895–1900; popularity of his appointment soon impaired by his vigorous and successful measures to stamp out rabies, which met with violent opposition; president of Local Government Board, 1900–5; secured passing of Metropolitan Water Act, in teeth of bitter opposition, 1902; successful chief secretary for Ireland, 1905; created Union Defence League, 1907; president of Local Government Board, 1915–16; secretary of state for colonies, 1916–18; first lord of Admiralty, 1919–21; F.R.S., 1902; created viscount, 1921.

LONGHURST, WILLIAM HENRY (1819–1904), organist and composer; chorister (1828), assistant organist (1836), and organist (1873–98) of Canterbury Cathedral; Mus.Doc., 1875; published church music.

LONSDALE, fifth EARL OF (1857–1944), sportsman. [See LOWTHER, HUGH CECIL.]

LOPES, SIR LOPES MASSEY, third baronet (1818–1908), politician and agriculturist; educated at Winchester and Oriel College, Oxford; B.A., 1842; M.A., 1845; conservative M.P. for Westbury, 1857–68, for South Devon, 1868–85; urged grievance of burden of local taxation; helped to carry Agricultural Ratings Act, 1879; civil lord of the Admiralty, 1874–80; P.C., 1885; alderman of Devonshire county council, 1888–1904; a scientific farmer, he spent much money on improving his estates.

LORD, THOMAS (1808–1908), Congregational minister; held Midland pastorates (1834–79) till he settled at Horncastle, when he preached in his 101st year; original member of Peace Society; published devotional works.

LOREBURN, EARL (1846–1923), lord chancellor. [See REID, ROBERT THRESHIE.]

LORIMER, SIR ROBERT STODART (1864–1929), architect; son of Professor James Lorimer [q.v.]; apprenticed to Sir Rowand Anderson, architect, 1885; entered office of G. F. Bodley [q.v.], 1889; returning to Edinburgh, began long series of restorations, which were among his most pleasing works, 1892; designed many large Scottish

country houses; his churches include St. Peter's (Roman Catholic), Morningside, Edinburgh (1906); designed chapel of Order of the Thistle, St. Giles' Cathedral, Edinburgh, 1909–11; recognized as leading architect of Scotland, 1914–18; after European war chiefly occupied on memorials, most important being Scottish National War Memorial, Edinburgh (1918–27); knighted, 1911; saviour of crafts in Scotland; restored to Scotland vital and characteristic architecture.

LOTBINIÈRE, SIR HENRY GUSTAVE JOLY DE (1829–1908), Canadian politician. [See JOLY DE LOTBINIÈRE.]

LOTHIAN, eleventh MARQUESS OF (1882–1940), journalist and statesman. [See KERR, PHILIP HENRY.]

LOUISE CAROLINE ALBERTA (1848–1939), princess of Great Britain and Ireland, Duchess of Argyll; sixth child of Queen Victoria; married (1871) the Marquess of Lorne (later ninth Duke of Argyll, q.v.); a gifted sculptress; made home an artists' rendezvous; wrote · magazine articles as 'Myra Fontenoy'; first president of National Union for the Higher Education of Women.

LOUISE VICTORIA ALEXANDRA DAGMAR (1867–1931), princess royal of Great Britain and Ireland, Duchess of Fife; third child of Prince and Princess of Wales; married (1889) the sixth Earl of Fife, created duke on his marriage; declared princess royal, 1905; rescued from shipwreck off Cape Spartel, 1911.

LOVAT, fourteenth (sometimes reckoned sixteenth) BARON (1871–1933). [See FRASER, SIMON JOSEPH.]

LOVE, AUGUSTUS EDWARD HOUGH (1863–1940), mathematician and geophysicist; second wrangler (1885), fellow (1886–99), St. John's College, Cambridge; F.R.S., 1894; Sedleian professor of natural philosophy, Oxford, 1898–1940; investigated theory of elasticity of solids in its mathematical setting and its application to problems of the earth's crust; discovered 'Love waves', 1911; formulated a theory of biharmonic analysis, 1929; his *Treatise on the Mathematical Theory of Elasticity* (1892–3) a standard work.

LOVELACE, second EARL OF (1839–1906), author of *Astarte*. [See MILBANKE, RALPH GORDON NOEL KING.]

LOVETT, RICHARD (1851–1904), author; spent boyhood (1858–67) in United States; B.A. London, 1873; M.A., 1874; book editor of Religious Tract Society, 1882; secretary, 1899; wrote centenary history of London Missionary Society, 1899; wrote lives of James Gilmour (1892)

269

Fig. 29. *The Concise Dictionary of National Biography.* (Copyright: Oxford Univ. Press.)

arts were barely recognized. Leslie Stephen and Sidney Lee (the successive editors) had to rely mainly on amateurs who had to get along without the help of many works of reference now taken as a matter of course". This reviewer goes on to speak of the need for a new edition and mentions the article on Horace Walpole as one which the progress of scholarship and subsequent publication have greatly affected. Not everyone in the *D.N.B.*, however, has received as extensive subsequent attention as W. S. Lewis has given to Walpole. At their worst, the articles and their bibliographies are a starting point; at their best they are very much more.

(Fig. 29), *The Concise Dictionary of National Biography* (2 vols., Oxford Univ. Press, 1903–61), though based on the main work, deserves separate treatment. In the latest reissue (these take place every decade), Vol. 1 covers the period to 1900; Vol. 2, 1901–50. This is both an index to the main work and an independent reference work; the entries are about a fourteenth as long as the originals. When referring to the main work, the *date of death* is the indexing factor. It cannot be established whether an entry in Vol. 1 of the *Concise D.N.B.* is in the main or supplementary sequence in Vols. 1–22 of the main work without searching. In which of the five twentieth-century volumes a person recorded in Vol. 2 occurs depends on whether he died before 1911, 1921, 1930, 1940 or 1950. A new feature in thi volume is a subject index which even includes a heading for *Dictionary of National Biography*, referring to Sidney Lee, George Smith and Leslie Stephen.

Before leaving the *D.N.B.* we must refer to the method of issuing corrections; these are printed every few years in the *Bulletin of the Institute of Historical Research* and a cumulated volume is *Dictionary of National Biography corrections and additions, cumulated from the Bulletin of the Institute of Historical Research, 1923–63*, Hall, Boston, 1965.

The *D.N.B.* does not include many people of lesser eminence, and for these (Fig. 30) *Men and Women of the Time* (15th edition, Routledge, 1899) is useful. This appeared first in 1852, and the third edition of 1856 included women for the first time. Strictly this should be regarded as contemporary biography, as all the persons recorded in it were alive at the time, but it is more convenient

MEN AND WOMEN OF THE TIME

ABBAS PACHA, Khedive of Egypt, K.G.C.B., is the eldest son of the late Tewfik Pacha. He was born on July 14, 1874, and succeeded his father in January 1892, when he was eighteen years of age. He had previously studied with his brother, Mehemet Ali, at the Theresianum Academy, in Vienna, and was still there at the time of his father's death. He studied law and politics, for which he displayed great aptitude. Prince Abbas Pacha was made Hon. K.G.C.B. by the Queen in 1892. His attitude towards Great Britain is not considered a friendly one, he having early in 1893 substituted statesmen of anti-English sympathies for those appointed by England. Lord Cromer remonstrated with him, and the Khedive was persuaded to compromise; but he is still not really friendly towards England. In July 1893 he paid a visit of homage to the Sultan of Turkey. In 1895 a daughter was born to him in his harem, and he afterwards married the mother.

ABBE, Cleveland, born in New York City, Dec. 3, 1838, is the son of George Waldo Abbe and Charlotte Colgate, both natives of the United States of America, and of purely English ancestry. The earliest American ancestry of this family was John Abbey, of Salem, Massachusetts, in 1637. Mr. Cleveland Abbe graduated in 1857 at the College of the City of New York, studied astronomy under Brünnow at the University of Michigan, 1859-60, also under Gould at Cambridge, Massachusetts, 1860-64, and under Struve at Poulkova, 1865 and 1866. He took the degree of A.B. 1857, A.M. 1860, LL.D. (Michigan University) 1889, Ph.D. 1892; was Director of the Cincinnati Observatory, 1868-74, Professor of Meteorology in the Signal Service, and Assistant to the Chief Signal Officer, 1871 to 1891, and is now (1893) Senior Professor of Meteorology in the "Weather Bureau of the Department of Agriculture." He is a Member of the National Academy of Sciences, and of numerous other scientific societies in America and Europe; author of "The Weather Bulletin of the Cincinnati Observatory," 1869; "Annual Summary and Review of Progress in Meteorology," 1878 annually to 1889; "Report on the Signal Service Observations of the Total Eclipse of 1878"; "Treatise on Meteorological Apparatus and Methods," 1887; "Preparatory Studies for Deductive Methods in Storm and Weather Predictions," 1890; "The Mechanics of the Atmosphere," 1891; and numerous smaller memoirs. He was Delegate to the International Convention of 1893 in Washington on Prime Meridian and Standard Time; and to the International Conference of Meteorologists in Munich, 1891. As Meteorologist to the United States Scientific Expedition to the West Coast of Africa, 1889-90, he made the first extensive set of accurate observations at sea of the movements of upper and lower clouds—using a marine nephroscope devised by him for this purpose.

ABBEY, Edwin Austin, R.A., R.I., was born April 1, 1852, at Philadelphia, U.S.A., and was a pupil of the Pennsylvania Academy of Fine Arts. In 1871 he began drawing for the publications of Harper Brothers. In 1878 he became a Member of the American Water-Colour Society. In 1878 he removed to England. He has illustrated the following works: "Selections from the Hesperides and Noble Numbers of Robert Herrick," 1882; "She Stoops to Conquer," 1887; "Old Songs," 1889; "Sketching Rambles in Holland," 1885 (in conjunction with G. H. Broughton, A.R.A.); "The Quiet Life," 1890 (in conjunction with Alfred Parsons). The following are his principal water-colour pictures; "The Stage Office," 1876; "The Evil Eye," 1877; "The Sisters." 1881; "The Widower," 1883; "The Bible Reading," 1884; "An Old Song," 1886; "The March Past," 1887; "Visitors," 1890. His oil-paintings are as follows: "May-

Fig. 30. *Men and Women of the Time.* (Copyright: Routledge.)

to treat old contemporary works along with retrospective biographies. There are 4 pp. on Florence Nightingale, but the extent to which these are padded is shown by the concluding sentence: "towards the close of last year, her Majesty presented to Miss Nightingale a diamond ornament, adapted to be worn as a decoration, of the most costly and elegant description". Great changes were made in the 1899 edition, though this still contained entries for a number of foreigners, mostly rulers and statesmen. The entry for Abbas Pacha on the page illustrated, though cynically amusing, does not inspire confidence, and one can only surmise what diplomatic démarches would result from a similar treatment today of President Nasser. The first edition contained 300 biographies; the last over 3400; it also had an interesting supplement of the "Who Was Who" type; this listed some 3300 entries removed by death, and gave the last edition in which the life appeared. In 1901 *Men and Women of the Time* was incorporated with (Fig. 31) *Who's Who* (Black, 1849–, In progress), an extremely comprehensive annual, recording prominent British persons. A few other lives are included (e.g. Marshal Timoshenko). The basis of inclusion in *Who's Who* is kept a close secret. Information about individuals is entirely factual and based on a form sent to them; absolute consistency is not insisted upon so that the heading "recreations" is sometimes used facetiously or excluded, and educational details (honours attained in degrees, etc.) are sometimes glossed over. After a list of abbreviations used follows an obituary (while work was in press), the Royal Family, supplement (newly honoured individuals as well as extra details of persons already included), and the main sequence. Well over 20,000 names are included, and it may be said that in the United Kingdom one's chances of getting into *Who's Who* are less than 1 in 2000. It is much less than half as difficult to get into it as into the *D.N.B.*, where one will have to await death but can get an appraisement and not a mere string of facts; these, however, often include a complete list of an author's publications. Linked to *Who's Who* and of similar format is *Who Was Who*, by the same publisher. Of this, 5 vols. have now appeared covering entries removed from *Who's Who*, 1897–1915,

Newcastle upon Tyne 2. *T.:* Newcastle 81-4441.

EVERSHED, family name of **Baron Evershed.**

EVERSHED, 1st Baron, *cr.* 1956, of Stapenhill; **Francis Raymond Evershed,** P.C. 1947; Kt., *cr.* 1944; F.S.A. 1950; A Lord of Appeal in Ordinary since 1962; a United Kingdom Member of the Permanent Court of Arbitration at The Hague since 1950; Chairman of The Pilgrim Trust since 1960; *b.* Burton-on-Trent, 8 Aug. 1899; *s.* of late Frank Evershed and Helen Lowe; *m.* 1928, Joan, *o. d.* of late Hon. Mr. Justice Bennett. *Educ.:* Clifton; Balliol Coll., Oxford. Served European War, 1918-19, R.E., 2nd Lt. (France); B.A. degree, 2nd class Litt. Hum., 1921; Hon. Fellow Balliol Coll., 1947; Hon. LL.D.: Leeds, 1950; Nottingham, Melbourne, Adelaide and New York, 1951; Birmingham, 1953; Southampton, 1955; London, 1956; Columbia, N.Y., 1960; Hon. D.C.L. Oxford, 1955; Hon. D.Litt. Bristol, 1959; Hon. Fell. Nuffield College, Oxford, 1962; Hon. Freeman of Borough of Burton-on-Trent, 1952; Called to Bar, Lincoln's Inn, 1923, K.C. 1933, Bencher, 1938; Treasurer, 1958. Chm. Central Price Regulation Cttee., 6 Grosvenor Gardens, S.W.1, 1939 - 42; Regional Controller, Nottinghamshire, Derbyshire and Leicestershire coal-producing region, 1942-1944; Judge of Chancery Division, High Court of Justice, 1944-47; a Lord Justice of Appeal, 1947-49; Master of the Rolls, 1949-62. Member of Committee appointed by Minister of Works and Buildings on Compensation and Betterment, 1941; member of Industrial and Export Council appointed by Pres. of Board of Trade, 1941; Chairman Commission on Wages and Conditions of Labour in Cotton Spinning Industry, 1945-46; Chairman of Committees of Enquiry into Dock Wages, 1945, and into prices and production on Textile Machinery, 1946; Chm. Cttee. on Practice and Procedure in Supreme Court, 1947; President of Clifton College, 1951; Chairman Royal Commission on Historical Manuscripts, 1949-62; Trustee of Pilgrim Trust, 1952; Member Council of Legal Education, 1953; Chairman Law Advisory Committee, British Council, 1956. Freeman of City of London, 1953; Hon. Member American Academy of Arts and Sciences, 1956. Vice-Pres. Richmond Football Club; Patron, Derbyshire County Cricket Club; Hon. Member All-England Lawn Tennis Club. *Recreations:* usual. *Heir:* none. *Address:* Wornegay Grange, Setch, King's Lynn. *T.:* Watlington 250; 22 Old Buildings, Lincoln's Inn, W.C.2. *T.:* Chancery 5262. *Club:* Garrick.

EVERSHED, Rear-Adm. (retd.) Walter, C.B. 1959; D.S.O. 1940; J.P.; *b.* 19 April 1907; 2nd *s.* of late Edward Evershed and Lilian Johnstone, of 48 Handsworth Wood Road, Birmingham; *m.* 1944, Susan Mary, *d.* of Rev. A. R. Browne-Wilkinson; two *s.* three *d. Educ.:* R.N.C., Osborne and Dartmouth. Admiral Superintendent; H.M. Dockyard, Rosyth, 1957-60. In command H.M.S. Gambia, 1954-56; Director of Operations Division, Admiralty, 1956-57; Admiral Superintendent, Rosyth Dockyard, 1957-60. Controller, S.E. Sub-Region, London Civil Defence Region, 1961-. J.P. 1961. Hon. Burgess of Dunfermline, 1960. *Address:* Tillington Old Rectory, Nr. Petworth, Sussex. *Club:* United Service.

EVERSON, Frederick Charles, C.M.G. 1956; Commercial Counsellor, British Embassy, Stockholm, since 1960; *b.* 6 September 1910; *s.* of Frederick Percival Everson; *m.* 1937, Linda Mary Clark; three *s.* one *d. Educ.:* Tottenham County School, Middlesex. B.Sc. (Econ.) London. Entered
978

Civil Service, July 1928; Consular Service, Dec. 1934. Chief Administrative Officer, British Embassy, Bonn, Germany, 1953-56; Ambassador to El Salvador, 1956-60. *Address:* c/o Foreign Office, S.W.1.

EVERY, Sir John (Simon), 12th Bt., *cr.* 1641; Director of a number of private companies; *b.* 24 April 1914; *er. s.* of Sir Edward Oswald Every, 11th Bt. and Lady Ivy Linton Every; *S.* father, 1959; *m.* 1st, 1938, Annette Constance (marr. diss., 1942), *o. c.* of late Maj. F. W. M. Drew, Drewscourt, Co. Cork; 2nd, 1943, Janet Marion, *d.* of John Page, Blakeney, Norfolk; one *s.* two *d. Educ.:* Harrow. Served War of 1939-45, Capt., Sherwood Foresters. Business Co. Director, 1945-60. *Recreations:* cricket, tennis, shooting. *Heir: s.* Henry John Michael Every; *b.* 6 April 1947. *Address:* Egginton, nr. Derby. *T.:* Etwall 245. *Club:* M.C.C.

EVETTS, Lieut.-Gen. Sir John (Fullerton); Kt. 1951; C.B. 1939; C.B.E. 1937; M.C.; Pres., Chm. Council, Three Counties Industrial Education Assoc.; *b.* 30 June 1891; *s.* of late Lieut.-Colonel J. M. Evetts, Tackley Park, Oxon; *m.* 1916, Helen Phyllis, *d.* of late Capt. C. A. G. Becher, Burghfields, Bourton on the Water, Glos.; one *s. Educ.:* Temple Grove; Lancing; Royal Military Coll., Sandhurst; Staff Coll., Camberley. Entered Army, 1911; joined The Cameronians (Scottish Rifles); served European War, 1914-18 (M.C., despatches); Lieut. 1913; Capt. 1915; temp. Major Machine Gun Corps, 1916; Bt.-Maj. 1929; Substantive, 1929; Bt. Lt.-Col. 1931; Substantive, Lt.-Col. Royal Ulster Rifles, 1934; Col. 1935; Maj.-Gen. 1941; employed with Iraq Army, 1925; D.A.A.G. War Office, 1932; Commander British Troops in Palestine, 1935; G.S.O. 1. Palestine, 1936; Brig. Comd. 16th Inf. Bde., Palestine and Trans-Jordan, 1936-1939 (despatches); B.G.S., H.Q., Northern Command, India, 1939-40; Comdr. Western (Indept.) Dist., India, 1940-41; Divl. Comdr., 1941 (despatches); Asst. C.I.G.S., 1942; Senior Military Adviser to Minister of Supply, 1944-46; retired pay, 1946; Head of British Ministry of Supply Staff in Australia, 1946-51, and Chief Executive Officer Joint U.K. - Australian Long Range Weapons, Board of Administration, 1946-49. Managing Director, 1951-58, Chm., 1958-60, Rotol Ltd. and Brit. Messier. O.St.J. Legion of Merit (U.S.), 1943. *Address:* Pepper Cottage, Kemerton, Nr. Tewkesbury, Glos. *Club:* Naval and Military.

EVILL, Air Chief Marshal Sir Douglas Claude Strathern, G.B.E., *cr.* 1946; K.C.B., *cr.* 1943 (C.B. 1940); D.S.C. 1916; A.F.C. 1919; *b.* 1892; *m.* 1920, Henrietta Hortense, *d.* of Sir Alexander Drake Kleinwort, 1st Bt.; one *s.* two *d. Educ.:* Royal Naval Colleges, Osborne and Dartmouth. Served European War, 1914-19 (D.S.C., A.F.C.); War of 1939-45 (despatches twice, C.B., K.C.B.). Head of Royal Air Force Delegation in Washington, 1942; Vice-Chief of the Air Staff, and addtl. Member of the Air Council, 1943-46; Air Chief Marshal, 1946; retired 1947. *Address:* South Lawn, Cheriton Close, Winchester, Hants. *Clubs:* United Service, Lansdowne.

EVOE; *see* Knox, Edmund G. V.

EWALD, Paul P., F.R.S. 1958; Dr.phil.; Professor emeritus of Physics, Polytechnic Institute of Brooklyn, since 1957; Professor of Physics and Head of Department, Polytechnic Institute of Brooklyn, 1949-57; *b.* Berlin, Germany, 23 January 1888; *s.* of Paul Ewald, Historian (Univ. Berlin), and Clara Ewald, Portrait-Painter; *m.* 1913, Ella (Elise Berta) (*née* Philippson); two *s.* two *d. Educ.:* Victoria Gymnasium, Potsdam; Univs. of Cambridge, Göttingen and Munich

Fig. 31. *Who's Who.* (Copyright: A. & C. Black.)

1916–28, 1929–40, 1941–50 and 1951–60. It is intended to continue publishing each decade. Some entries are removed from *Who's Who* for reasons other than death, and these never get into *Who Was Who*.

There are many—were not people so important one might say too many—British biographical dictionaries of one sort or another. *Men of the Reign* (Routledge, 1885) stands in a similar relationship to *Men and Women of the Time*, as does *Who Was Who* to *Who's Who*. "A large number of the names have occurred in one or other of the eleven (1885) editions of 'Men of the Time'. But it must not be supposed that in these cases we have always been content with a mere reprint. Many of the lives occurring in that book have been omitted altogether; all have been carefully revised; and the majority have been rewritten" (preface). The 3000 names in the work have also been drawn from other sources such as *The Times* obituaries, and these have been published separately. Peerages and companionages will be considered separately in Chapter 5. Many nineteenth-century works were built around the growing prestige of the illustrator; E. Lodge's *Portraits of Illustrious Personages* (12 vols., Harding & Lepard, 1823 and other editions) is perhaps the best known; others were *Portraits of Men of Eminence* (6 vols., 1863–7), *Men of Mark* (7 vols., 1876–83), and *Men and Women of the Day* (7 vols., 1888–94). The most individual of these productions is T. G. Bowles (Jehu junior, *pseud.*), *Vanity Fair Album: a Show of Sovereigns, Statesmen, Judges and Men of the Day* (35 vols., 1869–1903) with coloured cartoons by Spy and others; the text is insubstantial. Two modern works by William Matthews of the University of California are of great interest: *British Diaries* (Berkeley, California Univ. Press, 1950) (chronological; each item annotated; author index), and (Fig. 32) *British Autobiographies* (same publisher, 1955). Almost as valuable as the main sequence is the subject index which refers to the individually numbered main entries; subjects such as corn laws, detectives and policemen, entertainers, and locations (English counties, etc.) all have numerous entries. Matthews' *Diaries* lists unpublished manuscripts and their whereabouts, not so his later book.

country sports from 70's.   279   British Agent; escape.   288

GRIMSHAW, Beatrice Ethel. Isles of Adventure (1930). Her thirty years in New Guinea and South Seas;travels and native life; journalism.   280

GRIMWOOD, Ethel St. Clair. My Three Years in Manipur (1892). Experiences of wife of political agent in Manipur court, domestic and social life; the Mutiny; adventures and escape.   281

GRINNELL-MILNE, Duncan William. An Escaper's Log(1926);Wind in the Wires (1933). Prison experiences in Germany in WW1 and escape to Holland;training as airman and service with RFC in WW1 capture and escape.   282

GRONOW,Capt. Rees Howell. Reminiscences (L. 1862); Recollections (1863) Celebrities of London and Paris(1865) Last Recollections (1866). Collected form: Recollections and Reminiscences (1889).Social life in Grenadiers; his clubs and life as a buck;society life sport, gallantry, gossip about society, literary, political personages in first half of the century.   283

GROSSEK,Mark. First Movement (1937) Polish-Jewish boy in London elementary schools; family background; his early literary interests.   284

GROSER, Fr. St.John B. Politics and Persons (1949).Catholic priest's life and work in Stepney from 1930's;social work;poverty, unemployment, Labour Party, Communist Party; a sympathetic record.   285

GROSSMITH, George. A Society Clown (Bristol, 1888); Piano and I (1910); "G.G." (1933). Long career as entertainer; tours in England and America; work in musical comedy and in Gilbert and Sullivan operas; social life and theatrical scene.   286

GROSSMITH, Weedon. From Studio to Stage (1913). Schools; study as painter;amateur theatricals and career in theatre from 1885; Savage Club; social life in London.   287

GROUNDSELL,Frank. Lunatic Spy(1935) His tours and travels as an entertainer; in Germany during WW1 and work as

GROVES,Anthony Norris. Diary, 1829-1852;work and travels of a missionary in India and Bagdad; educational work missionary rivalries; native life and poverty; medical affairs. Memoir, by Mrs. Groves (1856); Journal of a Residence at Bagdad (1832).   289

GRUBB, Wilfrid Barbrooke. Among the Indians of the Paraguayan Chaco(1904) Missionary work in Paraguay in 90's at the Chaco mission; ethnography;Indian ways.   290

GRUNDY, Anthony George. My Fifty Years in Transport (1944). His career as a pioneer in passenger transport on railways and trams.   291

GRUNDY, Francis H. Pictures of the Past (1879). Lancs boyhood; work as a civil engineer on railways in Lancs & Yorks;friend of Patrick Bronte; later experiences in Australian goldfields; Brisbane, Sydney.   292

GRUNDY, George Beardoe. Fifty-Five Years at Oxford (1945). School; student at Oxford; tutor in ancient history; Brasenose and Corpus; scholars & celebrities; books; good.   293

GUBSKY, Nikolai. Angry Dust (1937); My Double and I (1939). Youth in Russia; misfortunes in Revolution; exile in England and struggles;unemployment and odd jobs; writing in London.   294

GUERIN, Eddie. Crime (1928); I Was a Bandit (1929). Life of a criminal; slums and poverty; prison life in USA France and England; has some sociological value.   295

GUGGISBERG,Sir Frederick Gordon. We Two in West Africa(1909). Travel with his wife on Gold Coast and in Central West Africa.   296

GUILLEMARD, Francis H. H. The Years that the Locusts Have Eaten (MS, Bodleian Library, Eng. Misc. d. 189-192, 196, 236). Childhood at Eltham; youth at Cambridge; medical study at Barts; residence in S.Africa and Madeira and travels; discursive reminiscences.297

GUILLEMARD, Sir Laurence N. Trivial

Fig. 32. MATTHEWS, W., *British Autobiographies*. (Copyright: California Univ. Press.)

(Fig. 33), D. H. Simpson's *Biography Catalogue of the Library of the Royal Commonwealth Society* (the Society, 1961), though only an index, is an extremely valuable one. It lists biographies under their subjects, including references in periodicals; the British Empire is included as a subject, and General Gordon, for example, has two full columns of entries. There is a list of collective biographies, including some titles later than those Riches (above, pp. 32–3) has included, and a comprehensive subject index, listing lives relating to all parts of the Commonwealth. This is a good example of how the catalogue of a large specializing library can in many ways equal or exceed in value a subject bibliography which may well contain many "ghost" entries, extracted from doubtful authorities (book-sellers' catalogues, etc.). At least the user of Simpson knows that all he reads about can be produced in one library.

Three final works on a national scale which we propose to mention here are firstly Frederick Boase's *Modern English Biography* (6 vols., Netherton, Truro, 1892–1921, reissued 1965, by Frank Cass), which includes a good number of names not in other works and has a subject index, lists of pseudonyms, etc.

"The six volumes in over 4000 pages contain some 30,000 short biographical sketches of persons who died between 1851–1900 who achieved any public importance whatsoever. Each biography is accompanied by a note of the particular sources used in each entry so that further research can be greatly facilitated. Boase made a special study of the existence of portraits and photographs of his subjects and gives details where these can be found. He also placed a great emphasis on exact detail particularly of births and deaths, a list of published works or theatre performances, and other facts which are sometimes omitted in larger works of reference, but which are all available here.

"As Boase stated in his preface his object was to cover the careers of not only the well-known people such as judges, members of parliament, bishops, privy councillors, members of the armed services, knights of the realm, stipendiary magistrates and others but also to survey the lives of other interesting people such as architects, engineers, inventors, businessmen, shipbuilders, pub-

4

BOURINOT, *Sir* J. G.   Lord Elgin [Makers Can.]
[iv]276*pp. p. Tor.* 1903.

DOUGHTY, *Sir* A. G.   The Elgin-Grey papers, 1846–
1852; ed. with notes and appendices by Sir
A. G. D. [Can. Pub. Archiv.] 4*v. Ott.* 1937.

GRANT, W. L.   Lord Elgin [U.E., *v.*4, *pp.*309–11,
1913] *p.*

KENNEDY, W. P. M.   Lord Elgin [Makers Can.
Anniv. Ed., *v.*6.]   vi.272*pp.* [*bibliog.*]*p. & i.* 1926.

LEMOINE, *Sir* J. MacP.   Le Comte d'Elgin,
Gouverneur-Général du Can. [Can. R. Soc., *v.*12,
*sect.*1, *pp.*193–200, 1894]*

MORISON, J. L.   The eighth Earl of Elgin: a
chapter in nineteenth-century imperial history.
318*pp. p. & i.* 1928.

OLIPHANT, L.   Narrative of the Earl of Elgin's
mission to China and Jap. in the years 1857, '58,
'59.   2*v. i.* 1860.

SAIGAL, B.   Lord Elgin and Afghanistan [Jour. Ind.
Hist. *v.*32, *pt.*1, *pp.*61–81, 1954]

WALROND, T.   Letters and journals of James,
eighth Earl of Elgin, Governor of Jamaica,
Governor-General of Canada, Envoy to China,
Viceroy of India.   xii.467*pp.* 1872.

WRONG, G. M.   The Earl of Elgin.   xii.300*pp. m.,
p. & i.* 1907.

Elibank, Gideon Murray, *2nd Visc.* [1877–1951] *Col.
admin.*

ELIBANK, *2nd Visc.*   A man's life: reflections and
reminiscences of experiences in many lands.
304*pp. p. & i.* 1934.

Eliot, Edward Carlyon [1870–1940] *Comm., Gilbert
& Ellice Is.: Admin. of Dominica*

ELIOT, E. C.   Broken atoms.   254*pp.* 1938.*

Eliot, *Rev.* **John** [1604–c. 1687] *Miss. in Can.*

John Eliot [Scot. Miss. & Phil. Reg. *v.*4, *pp.*40–46,
1823]

Life of the Rev. John Eliot, the apostle of the North
American Indians [Miss. Reg. *v.*2, *pp.*305–14,
345–51, 385–400, 425–31, 1814; *v.*3, *pp.*109–17,
169–80, 640–49, 1815]

Elizabeth I [1533–1603] *Queen of England 1558–1603*

BEESLY, E. S.   Queen Elizabeth [Twelve English
Statesmen ser.] vii.245*pp.* 1892.

NEALE, J. E.   Elizabeth and her parliaments, 1559–
1581.   434*pp. p. & facs.* 1953.

,,   Queen Elizabeth.   402*pp. p. & facs.* [1934]
1950.

ROWSE, A. L.   The Elizabethan Age [The England
of Elizabeth *and* The Expansion of Elizabethan
England] 2*v. m., p., pl. & facs.* 1951–55.

STRACHEY, L.   Elizabeth and Essex; a tragic
history.   288*pp.* [*bibliog.* 2*pp.*] *p.* 1930.

Elizabeth II [1926–   ] *Queen of Great Britain
& N. Ireland*

Collection of programmes, invitations, photographs
and other items relating to the Royal Tour of the
Commonwealth 1953–1954 [*Further material on
the Royal Tour and on the tours of Prince Philip,
Duke of Edinburgh, appear in the Library's
catalogue under BRITISH EMPIRE—Crown*]

The Royal Tour, Canada, 1951 [Photographs]
[96]*pp. m. Tor.* 1952.

L.C.—I

The Royal Tour of Canada [R.C.M.P. Quart. *v.*17,
*pp.*204–68, 1952] *i.*

BOLITHO, H. H.   The Queen's American ancestors
[*from* Past and Future, *v.*1, *no.*4, *pp.*7–10, 1958]

DEVON, S.   The golden souvenir of the royal tour
of Canada; with Daily Graphic photographs.
22*pp. m., p. & i.* 1951.

,,   The royal Canadian tour—The complete pictorial
story.   89*pp. m. p., & i.* [1951]

FAULKNER, A.   Princess Elizabeth in North
America [Eng. Speak. World, *v.*33, *pp.*26–30, 1951]

KISSAUN, M.   Elizabeth II [in Maltese: includes
accounts of Her Majesty's visits to Malta as
Princess]   120*pp. i. Malta.* 1954.

MORRAH, D. M. MacG.   The work of the Queen.
191*pp. p.* 1958.

OUIMET, J. T. J.   My impressions of the Royal
visit [R.C.M.P. Quart. *v.*17, *pp.*206–34, 1952] *i.*

STANHOPE, J.   The royal tour of Kenya: [Account
by J. S.]—Pictorial souvenir.   22*pp. i.* [1952]

Elizabeth, [1900–   ] *Queen Consort of George VI*

ASQUITH, *Lady* C.   The queen: an entirely new and
complete biography written with the approval
of her Majesty.   239*pp. p. & i.* 1937.

Ellegood, Jacob [1824–1911] *Rector of St. James the
Apostle, Montr.*

HOWARD, O. W.   Illustrated interviews. XII.—
The Rev. Canon Ellegood [Westm., *v.*5, *pp.*1–7,
1904] *p. & i.*

Ellenborough, Edward Law, *1st Earl of* [1790–
1871] *Gov.-Gen. of Ind., 1841–44*

The administration of Lord Ellenborough [Calc.
Rev., *v.*1, *no.*2, *pp.*508–62, 1846]

India and Lord Ellenborough.   123*pp. c.* 1844.

CHATTERJI, N.   Lord Ellenborough and the Taluq-
dars of Oudh [Ind. Hist. Jour., *v.*16, *pp.*78–82,
1937]

GARRETT, K. I.   Lord Ellenborough's ideas on
Indian policy. [M.A. thesis Univ. of London, 1936]
330.5*pp.* [*bibliog.*] [1936] 1949.   *Typewritten copy.*

IMLAH, A. H.   Lord Ellenborough; a biography of
Edward Law, Earl of Ellenborough, Gov.-Gen.
of India [Harvard Hist. Stud., *v.*43] xii.295*pp.,*
[*bibliog.* 10*pp.*] *p. & i. Camb., Mass.* 1939.

LAW, *Sir* A.   India under Lord Ellenborough,
March 1842—June 1844: a selection from the
hitherto unpublished papers and secret despatches
of Edward Earl of Ellenborough; ed. with introd.
by Sir A. L.   [64]. 211*pp. p.* 1926.

Ellenborough, Jane [*née* Digby] *Countess of* [1807–
1881] *Trav.*

BLANCH, L.   Jane Digby el Mezrab.   Matrimonial
theme and variations [The wilder shores of love,
*pp.*131–96, 1954] *p. & pl.*

Ellery, William [1727–1820] *Signatory of Amer. Dec.
of Indep.*

FRANKLIN, S. B.   William Ellery, signer of the
declaration of Independence [Rhode Is. Hist.
Soc. *v.*12, *pp.*110–19, 1953; *v.*13, *pp.*11–17, 44–52,
1954] *p.*

Ellice, Edward [1783–1863] *Can. polit. & businessman*

GALBRAITH, J. S.   Edward ' Bear ' Ellice [Beaver,
*pp.*26–29, June, 1954] *p.*

Fig. 33.   *Biography Catalogue of the Royal Commonwealth Society.*
(Copyright: the Society.)

lishers, authors, actors, dramatists, physicians, surgeons, musicians, music-hall artists, electricians, railway managers, painters, sculptors, engravers, explorers, sporting celebrities, eccentric characters and notorious criminals . . . in fact anyone who has been well known. Additionally, many foreigners living in England and nationals of British colonies have also been included.

"Boase gathered his material from obituaries and reports published in *The Times*, *Illustrated London News* and other journals; he consulted local newspapers, the transactions of learned societies, parish and church registers, the records of the registrar-general at Somerset House, published memoirs, correspondence with private individuals and many other sources. The whole series, therefore, has a greater coverage of national and local celebrities who died in the latter part of the nineteenth century than the *Dictionary of National Biography*" (reissuing publisher's announcement). Sir William Musgrave's *Obituary Prior to 1800* (6 vols., Harleian Society, 1899–1901) reprints extracts from the life-work of its author from his manuscripts in the British Museum. Entries are very brief, consisting of the biographee's name, profession, date of death, and reference to a source where fuller information may be found. Unfortunately Musgrave died, leaving his work unfinished, and some of his sources are unidentifiable. However, the work, which covers British names only, includes references in such works as the *Annual Register*, *Biographia Britannica*, and the *Gentleman's Magazine* which are easily accessible in libraries. It is the most generally useful of surviving British works based on eighteenth-century scholarship. The *Gentleman's Magazine* has a biographical index of its own (*An Index to the Biographical and Obituary Notices in the Gentleman's Magazine, 1731–1780*, British Record Society, London, 1891). Both this index and Musgrave have useful supplementary keys, the former to the volumes of the *Gentleman's Magazine*, with its extraordinarily complicated numeration, down to 1868, "at which date this periodical ceased to have any practical value!" A "popular" modern biography confined to historical figures is *Who's Who in History* (Routh, C. R. N. (editor), Blackwell, Oxford, 1960–, In progress), planned to cover Great Britain in 4 vols.

There are excellent works for Scotland, Wales, Ireland and Jersey:

> CHAMBERS, R. (editor), *Biographical Dictionary of Eminent Scotsmen*, 5 vols., Blackie, Edinburgh, 1855. Includes persons living at the time and others back to the earliest times. Vol. 5 is a supplement.
>
> HONOURABLE SOCIETY OF CYMMRODORION, *Y bwygraffiadur Cymreig hyd 1940*, The Society, 1953 (3500 biographies A.D. 400–1940). There is an English translation of this Welsh work, containing much revision (1959). Ten-yearly supplements in both languages are planned.
>
> CRONE, J. S., *A Concise Dictionary of Irish Biography*, 2nd edition, Talbot Press, Dublin, 1937. Brief entries on all periods.
>
> EAGER, A. R., *A Guide to Irish Bibliographical Material*, Library Association, 1964. Pp. 223–337 relate to biography, history (including local history arranged by counties) and allied subjects.
>
> BALLEINE, G. R., *A Biographical Dictionary of Jersey*, Staples Press, 1948 (300 biographies). Excludes living persons.

UNITED KINGDOM: BIOGRAPHY. LOCAL

Before turning from British biography to British history, we must give some indication of guides to local biography, in view of the importance of local history studies. Unfortunately, these have not been published in a very systematic manner. There are various borough *Who's Whos* (Hull, Luton, Norwich, Sheffield), compiled on a basis of contributors' copy, which often signifies that the more eminent local worthies do not trouble to send in entries. Directories, official diaries of local councils, etc., contain useful lists of officials and men and women in public life; long files of those relating to the immediate neighbourhood are to be found in most British provincial central libraries. Individual biographical works of local or regional interest include *Public Men of Ipswich and East Suffolk* (1875); *Gloucestershire Biographical Notes* (1887);

Birmingham Faces and Places (1888–94) (there is still a *Birmingham Post Who's Who and Directory*); and *Manchester Faces and Places* (1889–1906).

The illustrated record of local worthies printed on special paper had a comparatively short life in Great Britain (1890–1914), owing to ever-increasing printing costs. There are two main groups, though these were printed by a wide range of firms, and volumes in the various series are not easily recognized as such. What may be called the Press–Gaskell series, after the names of the successive compilers, includes volumes covering most English counties styled usually *(Blank)shire Leaders; Social and Political.* Some of these went into more than one edition, and there are also volumes on Ulster, the Lothians, etc. The importance of these works is their inclusion of local businessmen as well as the peers and country gentry extracted from more comprehensive biographical dictionaries. These were obtained from local journalists or the subjects themselves. The other series, *Pike's New Century*, is represented by much more sumptuous works on art paper. They were with one or two exceptions styled *(Blank)shire at the Opening of* (later *in*) *the Twentieth Century; Contemporary Biographies.* Over 30 vols. were published between 1898 and 1912; sometimes neighbouring English counties were grouped. There are volumes covering Bristol, Manchester, Birmingham, Liverpool, Sheffield, Edinburgh and the Lothians, London, South Wales, British engineers, Dublin and other Irish localities. (Fig. 34), Hopper, E. C. (editor), *Norfolk and Suffolk in East Anglia* (Pike, Brighton, 1911), is typical of the series. It commences with full-page portraits of Edward VII, recently deceased, and George V. The frontispiece is of the royal Norfolk home at Sandringham, and there is full-page treatment, including biographical material and large portraits of the two lord lieutenants and two bishops at that time responsible for the area. A well-illustrated descriptive section (130 pp.) following has a large number of illustrations not found elsewhere; even the emphasis in this section is biographical, the owners of country seats being given as full treatment as their stately homes. The biographical section is made up as follows: nobility and gentry

Contemporary Biographies   309

Recreations : natural history, and meteorology. Married, in 1868, Sara A., eldest daughter of the late John Aldrich, J.P., of Diss, and has issue two sons and three daughters. ` Club : National Liberal.

Mr. B. E. Gough.

Gough.—BERNARD EDGAR GOUGH, 39, High Street, Ipswich ; son of the late George Gough, of Woodbridge, and grandson of the late Captain Fitzpatrick, R.A., of Ipswich ; born at Woodbridge, in 1873 ; educated at Woodbridge Grammar School ; holds various certificates for mathematics, etc. ; B.M.G. (Banjo, Mandoline, Guitar) diploma. Commercial traveller and accountant ; also banjoist ; Conductor of St. Pancras Catholic Church Choir, Ipswich, from 1900-1905 ; in 1904 started a banjo-mandoline band in Ipswich, being the first of its kind in the locality ; Conductor of " Bernard Gough's Sextette Party " (banjoists and mandolinists) ; a violin player, and has assisted in the Orchestra of the Ipswich Choral Society, the Ipswich Philharmonic Society, and other musical societies. Married, in 1905, Sarah Hamblin (née King), who at the time had a son aged four years, named Arthur James King Hamblin, whose father was the late Arthur Hamblin.

Mr. John W. Greene.

Greene.—JOHN WOLLASTON GREENE, The Panels, Bury St. Edmunds ; son of the late John Smythies Greéne, solicitor, of Bury St. Edmunds, and grandson of John Greene, solicitor, of Bury ; born at Bury St. Edmunds, September 1st, 1869 ; educated at King Edward VI. School, Bury St. Edmunds. Admitted a solicitor, October, 1890 ; senior partner in the firm of Greene and Greene, Bury St. Edmunds ; Clerk to the Borough Justices ; Registrar of the Archdeaconry of Sudbury ; Clerk to the Governors of the Grammar School ; Deputy Coroner for the borough ; Notary Public, Perpetual Commissioner, and Commissioner for Oaths ; member of the Law Society and the Justices Clerks' Society ; member of the Solicitors' Benevolent Association and of the Incorporated Society of Provincial Notaries Public of England and Wales ; a Director of the Bury St. Edmunds Gas Company ; a Local Director of the Alliance Assurance Company. Recreation : motoring, and is a member of the Suffolk Automobile Club. Club : West Suffolk County.

Mr K. W. Greene.

Greene.—KENNETH WOLLASTON GREENE, Grey Friars, Bury St. Edmunds ; son of the late John Smythies Greene, solicitor, of Bury ; born at Bury St. Edmunds, January 17th, 1880 ; educated at Lancing College, Sussex. Admitted a solicitor, February, 1903 ; partner in the firm of Greene and Greene, of Bury St. Edmunds ; member of the Bury St. Edmunds Corporation ; Captain in the 5th Battalion Suffolk Regiment ; Commissioner for Oaths ; member of the Law Society. Recreations : motoring, and yachting ; member of the Royal Norfolk and Suffolk Yacht Club, and the Suffolk Automobile Club. Married, September, 1909, Constance Agnes, younger daughter of the late Robert Jackson. Club : West Suffolk County.

Fig. 34. Pike's *New Century Series. Norfolk and Suffolk.*

(22 pp.), unspecified (61 pp.), clergy (suffragan bishops leading) (36 pp.), the professions (judges leading) (85 pp.), commercial (39 pp.), After a few pages of obituaries, the work concludes with indexes of places and persons. A typical page has three factual biographies, generally with portraits. The value of this and similar works is that they include persons about whom it would be extremely difficult to find information elsewhere such as the "banjoist" on the page illustrated.

Pike's series were imitated, but none of his rivals achieved comprehensive coverage. Owing to rising costs there was a movement towards non-illustrated county Who's Whos, arranged strictly alphabetically, without the class distinctions of the pre-1914 examples. The largest number of these was produced by Baylis of Worcester, but many odd volumes of local interest by other publishers are available in libraries in their respective localities.[1]

UNITED KINGDOM: HISTORY. NATIONAL

The great *Oxford Bibliography of British History* is the natural starting point for detailed work on Great Britain, though only the volumes for 1485 to 1789 have appeared. Before we consider them we should note W. Bonser (editor), *An Anglo-Saxon and Celtic Bibliography* (A.D. 450–1087) (Blackwell, Oxford, 1957), and *A Romano-British Bibliography* (55 B.C.–A.D. 449) (same publisher, 1964). The first of these lists close on 12,000 items drawn from periodicals and individual and collected works; the arrangement is by topic. (Fig. 35), C. Gross, *Sources and Literature of English History from the Earliest Times to About 1485* (2nd edition, Longmans, 1915), though not part of the Oxford bibliography, has never been replaced. It is a remarkable pioneer work based on the dictum of the historian Frederic Harrison that "just as a real history is not a series of annals, so a real bibliography is not a mere catalogue of

---

[1] This section is largely based on an extremely useful article by H. J. Hanham, "Some neglected sources of bibliographical information: county biographical dictionaries, 1890–1914", *Bulletin of the Institute of Historical Research*, **34** (1961), pp. 55–66.

225a. STOKVIS, A. M. H. J.   Manuel d'histoire, de généalogie, et de chronologie de tous les états du globe, depuis les temps les plus reculés jusqu'à nos jours.   3 vols.   Leyden, 1888–93.

Vol. ii. ch. iii.   Great Britain and Ireland.

225b. WORDSWORTH, CHRISTOPHER.   The ancient kalendar of the university of Oxford.   *Oxford Hist. Soc.*   Oxford, 1904.

§ 6. PALÆOGRAPHY AND DIPLOMATICS.

a. Manuals and Treatises, Nos. 226–50.
b. Facsimiles, Nos. 251–66.

Palæography is the study of the handwriting of former ages. Diplomatics is the study of the construction or constituent parts of records whereby we are enabled to determine their age and authenticity or historical value. 'Le paléographe,' says Léon Gautier, 'étudie le corps des chartes, le diplomatiste en étudie l'âme.' Mabillon was the founder of the science of diplomatics ; and the greatest English diplomatist was George Hickes, whose monumental work (No. 234), as well as the whole subject of diplomatics, has been sadly neglected in England. In general, Hickes accepts the critical canons laid down by Mabillon, but combats some of the latter's views. Madox, Kemble, and Hardy (Nos. 238, 1419, 2108) contributed to our knowledge of charters ; and recently scholars like Round, Maitland, Miss Bateson, and Stevenson have begun to deal with records in a thoroughly scientific manner.

The list given below is fairly complete as regards the books produced in England, but comprises only a selection of the best continental works. For additions to this list, see Giry, Manuel, 37–50 ; E. D. Grand, Leçon d'Ouverture du Cours de Paléographie (Montpellier, 1890), 15–24 ; Prou, Manuel, 3–12 ; Thompson, Introduction, 571–83 (poorly arranged) ; and the periodical reports of Bresslau, Wattenbach, and Tangl in the Jahresberichte (No. 22) since 1879. A good short account of the literature will be found in Wattenbach's Schriftwesen, 1–39. For useful bibliographies, see Bulletin of the John Rylands Library (Manchester, 1903), i. 67–79 ; and M. F. Moore's Two Select Bibliographies of Mediæval Historical Study (London, 1912), 29–70.

The best general work on palæography is Wattenbach's

Fig. 35. GROSS, C., *The Sources and Literature of English History.*
(Copyright: Longmans.)

books". Its compiler says: "Worthless and obsolete treatises are omitted, except in the case of a few recent works which are mentioned merely in order that the student may be warned to shun them". He claims "it is better to give an inadequate commentary than to allow students to grope in utter darkness".

Gross is divided into four major sections, general authorities, the Germanic origins of the English, the Anglo-Saxon, and the mediaeval periods. The general authorities section includes chapters on method, bibliography, periodicals, auxiliaries, archives and libraries, printed sources and modern writers. "Auxiliaries" also includes dictionaries of various languages, palaeography, seals, biography, topography, numismatics, chronology, archaeology, costume, armour and weapons. The influence of Gross on the American Historical Association's *Guide* is obvious. The "printed sources" section is specially valuable including not only official series recorded in the recent sectional lists of Her Majesty's Stationery Office, and society publications recorded by Mullins (see pp. 95–7) but "collections privately edited". Under "chroniclers" details are given of appropriate volumes in the well-known nineteenth-century Bohn's library, Migne's *Patrologia* (soon to be reprinted), and Pertz' *Monumenta Germaniae historica*. These massive sets cover most of the material listed. Though full bibliographical information cannot always be given, a reference is usually made to a source for it. The section on modern writers is perhaps most noteworthy for its classified arrangement; the local history section, arranged by counties, is well balanced. There are some useful appendices, though these are superseded to a large extent. A new edition of Gross, edited by E. B. Graves, is in preparation.

How does (Fig. 36) C. Read, *Bibliography of British History: Tudor Period, 1485–1603* (2nd edition, Clarendon Press, Oxford, 1959), measure up to Gross? The idea of a general bibliography of modern British history probably originated in 1903, and five years later a joint Anglo–American Committee was set up. World War I intervened before publication could commence, and in 1923 the formal Anglo–American Committee was dissolved, but the historians who had taken over from the original collaborators decided

4618 NASH, THOMAS. Nashes Lenten stuff . . . of Great Yarmouth in Norfolk. Lond. 1599; repr. in *Harl. Mis.* (281), vi, 143–81.
Relates to the herring fishing.

4619 RECORDS OF THE CITY OF NORWICH. By William Hudson and J. C. Tingey. 2 vols. Norwich, 1906–[10].
Valuable, but chiefly medieval. Cf. also *Catalogue of the records of the city of Norwich*, by W. Hudson and J. C. Tingey, Norwich, 1898; and W. Hudson, *Sketch of the commercial history of Norwich till . . . the time of Q. Elizabeth*, *Proc. Hug. Soc. of London*, ii (1887–8), 519–24.

4620 RECORDS OF THE GILD OF ST. GEORGE in Norwich, 1389–1547: a transcript. By Mary Grace. *Norfolk Rec. Soc.* ix (1937).
Tudor period is covered pp. 78–157.

4621 A REGISTER OF THE FREEMEN OF NORWICH, 1548–1713. By Percy Millican. Norwich, 1934.
A register devoted to obscure names.

4622 RICHARDS, WILLIAM. The history of Lynn. 2 vols. Lynn, 1812.

4623 RYE, WALTER. Depositions taken before the mayor and aldermen of Norwich. Norwich, 1905.
Cf. also idem, *Extracts concerning musters in the sixteenth century*, Norfolk and Norwich Arch. Soc., 1847; *Norwich pageants, extracts from the grocer's book*, Norwich, 1856.

4624 PALMER, C. J. The history of Great Yarmouth. Great Yarmouth, 1856.
Valuable.

4625 SWINDEN, HENRY. History and antiquities of Great Yarmouth. Norwich, 1772.
The best history of Yarmouth.

(5) *Other Works*

4626 BURSTALL, E. B. The Pastons and their manor of Binham. *Norfolk Arch.* xxx (1952), 101–29.

4627 COZENS-HARDY, B. The Norwich Chapelfield house estate since 1545 and some of its owners and occupiers. *Norfolk Arch.* xxvii (1941), 351–84.

4628 COZENS-HARDY, B. Presents to the Sheriff of Norfolk, 1600–1603. *Norfolk Arch.* xxvi (1941), 52–58.

4629 EXTRACTS FROM THE TWO EARLIEST MINUTE BOOKS of the Dean and chapter of Norwich cathedral, 1566–1649. By J. F. Williams and B. Cozens-Hardy. *Norfolk Rec. Soc.* xxiv (1953).

4630 GRACE, MARY. The chamberlains and treasurers of the city of Norwich, 1293–1835. *Norfolk Arch.* xxv (1935), 181–201.

4631 INVENTORIES OF NORFOLK CHURCH GOODS (1552). By H. B. Walters. *Norfolk Arch.* xxvi, 1938 (1938), 245–70; xxvii, 1939 (1941), 97–144; xxvii, 1940 (1941), 263–89; xxvii, 1941 (1941), 385–416; xxviii, 1942

Fig. 36. CONYERS READ, *Bibliography of British History: Tudor Period.* (Copyright: Clarendon Press.)

independently to allocate the Tudor period to American scholars and the Stuart period to English historians, but in practice scholars from each nation assisted with each volume. Conyers Read is generally more detailed than Gross, and includes books, pamphlets, essays and items in journals and transactions of societies. Scotland, Ireland and Wales are fully covered; only the last two are covered in part in Gross. The second edition of Conyers Read covers titles published up to the end of 1956. There are more sections than in Gross, covering political, constitutional, ecclesiastical, economic and social history; there are lengthy chapters on the history of law, political theory, discovery, and military and naval history. Local history is very well covered, Norfolk having thirty-six items compared with Gross's twelve. Conyers Read is continued by Godfrey Davies, *Bibliography of British History, Stuart Period, 1603–1714* (1928); and S. Pargellis and D. J. Medley, *Bibliography of British History, the Eighteenth Century, 1714–1789* (1951), planned on the same lines. Not in this series but worthy of attention is C. L. Grose, *A Select Bibliography of British History, 1660–1760* (1939). There are brief bibliographies in the Historical Association's *Helps for Students of History Series* covering 1485–1939 and the period since 1926, and also English constitutional history. In the Library Association's County Libraries Section's *Readers' Guides* are volumes on *Medieval, Tudor and Stuart, Hanoverian* and *Victorian Britain*. E. S. Upton has produced a *Guide to Sources of English History from 1603 to 1660 in Early Reports of the Royal Commission on Historical Manuscripts* (2nd edition, Scarecrow, New York, 1964).

The above bibliographies set out to record all or a good portion of the material in the fields they cover, but there are many publications which give the picture of development, year by year. (Fig. 37), Library Association, *British Humanities Index* (quarterly, with annual cumulations), is the best known of these. Of its nature, a great deal of the material indexed is historical. This work commenced in 1915 as the *Subject Index to Periodicals*; the years 1923–5 were never published. The scope and method of arrangement of this invaluable bibliography has changed several times over the years,

Newspapers: Germany (F.R.)
See also:
'Spiegel, Der'
Newspapers: Great Britain
Issues of press freedom brough.' iome...to the house that Jack built. Norman Shrapnel. Guardian, (12 Mar 63) p.16
Journalism H and C. T. S. Matthews.' Spectator, (1 Mar 63) p.260-2
The real Vassall scandal. Time and Tide, (14/20 Mar 63) p.15
Reflections on the press. R. H. S. Crossman. Guardian, (22 Mar 63) p.24
See also:
Gossip Columns
'Sunday Telegraph'
Newspapers: Greece
Press under pressure. Economist, 206 (2 Mar 63) p.792
Newspapers: United States
New York newspapers may try to do without printers. Times, (4 Jan 63) p.7
The New York newspaper strike. Alistair Cooke. Listener, 69 (17 Jan 63) p.111
Printers win in New York press strike. Alistair Cooke. Guardian, (9 Mar 63) p.7
Publishers see no cause for alarm over U.S. press. Times, (15 Mar 63) p.10
Settlement in New York newspaper strike: stoppage cost $100m. in three months. Times, (9 Mar 63) p.7
60-day strike costs New York newspapers $70m. Times, (7 Feb 63) p.12
Threat to extend New York newspaper strike. Times, (15 Feb 63) p.7
When new news is bad news... New York stopgap. Alistair Cooke. Guardian, (7 Jan 63) p.1
Nigeria: Antiquities
A munificent gift for the British Museum: the ivory double gong from Benin. Illustrated London News, 242 (23 Feb 63) p.271. il.
Nigeria: History
See also:
Lagos: History
Nile, Upper
The Anglo-German agreement of 1890 and the Upper Nile. G. N. Sanderson. English Historical R., 78 (Jan 63) p.49-72
Nishapur Pottery. See Pottery, Persian
Nkrumah, Kwame
Is Dr. Nkrumah changing course? E. G. Butterworth. Guardian, (25 Jan 63) p.10
Noise
Town planning and noise abatement: development of a general theory. Hans Bernhard Reichow. Architects' J., 137 (13 Feb 63) p.357-60. il.
Non-Combatants
Non-combatants—do they exist? Reginald Hargreaves. Quarterly R., 301 (Jan 63) p.67-76
Nonnus
Nonniana. M. L. West. Classical Q., 12 (Nov 62) p.223-34
Norfolk: Unemployment
Unemployment in villages masked by migration. Times, (18 Feb 63) p.5
Norfolk Broads
Control of the Norfolk Broads. David Fairhall. Guardian, (2 Mar 63) p.6
'Time running out' for Norfolk Broads. Guardian, (14 Mar 63) p.4

Norman Antiquities
· See also:
Pottery, Saxo-Norman
Norman Charters. See Charters
Normandy, Battle of. See World War II, 1939-1945
North Atlantic Treaty Organization
Against a nuclear NATO. Richard Scott. Guardian, (13 Feb 63) p.18
Multibafflement. Economist, 206 (2 Mar 63) p.775-6
NATO and nuclear independence. Leonard Beaton. Guardian, (6 Feb 63) p.10
North Borneo. See Borneo, North
Northamptonshire
See also:
Althorp Park
Corby
North-East England
The agony of Andy Capp. Richard West. New Statesman, 65 (8 Feb 63) p.178-80
New image of the north-east. Times, (25 Jan 63) p.11
North-East England: Social Life
Beyond the curtain. New Society, (21 Feb 63) p.24
Northern Ireland
The six counties of Ulster. Sir Shane Leslie. Month, 29 (Jan 63) p.16-19
United Ulstermen. Andrew Boyd. Spectator, (15 Feb 63) p.185
Which foot do you dig with? H. Montgomery Hyde. Spectator, (18 Jan 63) p.73-4
See also:
Belfast: Planning
Northumberland
See also:
Cresswell Tower
Northumberland: History
See also:
Berwick-upon-Tweed: History
Border Country
North-West England
The future development of the north-west. P. J. O. Self and Wyndham Thomas. Town and Country Planning, 31. (Jan 63) p.55-62
Remedies for unemployment. 4. The north-west. Peter Jenkins. Guardian, (8 Feb 63) p.6
Northwick Park
Ancient art at Northwick. I. Vases. R. A. Higgins. Apollo, 77 (Feb 63) p.96-101. il.
Novels. See Fiction
Nubia: History
The lure of Africa. 3. Egypt, Nubia and Darfur. Robin Hallett. Geographical Mag., 35 (Mar 63) p.666-74. il.
Nuclear Disarmament. See Disarmament
Nuclear Energy Industry
Nuclear power will be needed in a hurry. 1. Prospects for British and American industry. Times, (21 Jan 63) p.14; 2. The role of the breeder reactor. (22 Jan 63) p.16
Nuclear Tests
'Don't put spokes in the wheels.' (Abridged from
· *Pravda*). Viktor Mayevsky. Guardian, (30 Jan 63) p.16
Political obstacles to a test ban. Wayland Young. Guardian, (12 Mar 63) p.8
Nuclear Warfare
American doubts on limiting nuclear war: opposing strengths leading to a stalemate. Times, (4 Feb 63) p.9

Fig. 37. *British Humanities Index.* Quarterly part. (Copyright: Library Association.)

but has always been useful for archaeological and historical material;
it covers local antiquarian societies and all the better known general
journals. An earlier period is covered by W. F. Poole's *Index to
Periodical Literature* (Houghton, Boston), which with its supplements
covers 1802–1906. Confined to history and archaeology is G. L.
Gomme's *Index of Archaeological Papers, 1665–1890* (Constable,
1907). At the beginning is given a very comprehensive list of the
periodicals indexed which include such fringe material as the
Philological Society's *Transactions*, the Hampshire Field Club's
publications and the *Folklore Journal*. Unfortunately, this work
has no subject index. Subject indexes are, however, given each
year for the annual continuations to it, published by the Congress
of Archaeological Societies in union with the Society of Antiquaries, covering the period to 1910. Imperfect as this work is, it
is the only one confined to Britain until 1934 when Milne (see
below, Fig. 39) commences. Much of the missing ground is
covered by (Fig. 38) E. L. C. Mullins, *Texts and Calendars; an
Analytical Guide to Serial Publications* (Royal Historical Society,
1958), which deals with most of the main national and local historical
and archaeological societies from their foundation to 1957; it does
not, however, analyse the contents of periodicals such as *History*
and the *English Historical Review*. Mullins has sections on official
bodies such as the Record Commissioners, the Public Record
Office and the Irish Record Office; national societies (British
Academy, British Record Society, etc.); English local and Welsh
societies. "Four types of serial publications containing record
material are outside its limits. The first is parish register series;
the second is series in which the record volumes are outnumbered
by volumes of transactions or by non-record material or by material
more closely akin to some other branch of learning than to history;
the third is series devoted wholly or predominantly to the facsimile
reproduction of maps and texts; the fourth is series of documents
from their own archives published by local authorities" (preface).
Even with these limitations, Mullins is very valuable, giving more
detail, in many cases, than the publishers themselves give.

The most detailed annual bibliography on British history ever

with an appendix, containing the visitation of a part of Cheshire in the year 1533, made by William Fellows, Lancaster herald, for Thomas Benolte, Clarenceux king of arms, and a fragment of the visitation of the city of Chester in the year 1591, made by Thomas Chalenor, deputy to the Office of Arms. Edited by John Paul Rylands. 1882.

19. The visitation of Bedfordshire, annis domini 1566, 1582, and 1634, made by William Harvey, esq., Clarencieulx king of arms, Robert Cooke, esq., Clarencieulx king of arms, and George Owen, esq., York herald, as deputy for Sir Richard St. George, kt., Clarencieulx king of arms; together with additional pedigrees, chiefly from Harleian ms. 1531, and an appendix containing a list of Bedfordshire knights and gentry taken from Lansdowne ms. 887. Edited by Frederic Augustus Blades. 1884.   23.19

> With names and arms of Bedfordshire knights *temp.* Edw. I, and a return of county gentry for 12 Hen. VI.

20. The visitation of the county of Dorset, taken in the year 1623, by Henry St. George, Richmond herald, and Sampson Lennard, Bluemantle pursuivant, marshals and deputies to William Camden, Clarenceux king of arms. Edited by John Paul Rylands. 1885.   23.20

21. The visitation of the county of Gloucester, taken in the year 1623, by Henry Chitty and John Phillipot as deputies to William Camden, Clarenceux king of arms; with pedigrees from the heralds' visitation of 1569 and 1582-3, and sundry miscellaneous pedigrees. Edited by Sir John Maclean and W. C. Heane. 1885.   23.21

22. The visitations of Hertfordshire, made by Robert Cooke, esq., Clarencieux, in 1572, and Sir Richard St. George, kt., Clarencieux, in 1634, with Hertfordshire pedigrees from Harleian mss. 6147 and 1546. Edited by Walter C. Metcalfe. 1886.   23.22

23. Allegations for marriage licences issued by the dean and chapter of Westminster, 1558 to 1699; also, for those issued by the vicar-general of the archbishop of Canterbury, 1660 to 1679. Extracted by Joseph Lemuel Chester and edited by Geo. J. Armytage. 1886.   23.23

> Contd. in 23.33, 34 below, both of which contain licences omitted from this vol.

24. Allegations for marriage licences issued from the faculty office of the archbishop of Canterbury, London, 1543 to 1869. Extracted by Joseph Lemuel Chester and edited by Geo. J. Armytage. 1886.   23.24

N   181

Fig. 38. MULLINS, E. L. C., *Texts and Calendars*. (Copyright: Royal Historical Society.)

attempted began in 1937. Entitled *Writings on British History*, it was made possible by a bequest to the Royal Historical Society of the well-known historian, Sir George Prothero. The preface to the first volume says "one of the tools most conspicuously lacking in the equipment of English historical studies is an annual list. . . . The second edition (1915) of C. Gross, *Sources and Literature of English History from the Earliest Times to About 1485* is now more than twenty years old. The bibliographies of Tudor and Stuart history, published by the Society in conjunction with the American Historical Association, and the bibliography of eighteenth-century history now in course of preparation, afford a more up-to-date guide for students of modern British history; but no provision has yet been made for the nineteenth century, and these bibliographies are in any case designed as guides to the principal authorities and not as exhaustive lists of writings published within a given period. The last section of the *Jahresberichte der Geschichtwissenschaft* which related to English history appeared in 1913 and dealt with work on modern history published between 1901 and 1905. The *Annual Bulletin of Historical Literature*, issued by the Historical Association, and the *International Bibliography of Historical Sciences*, are, of set purpose, highly selective". (Fig. 39) A. T. Milne (editor), *Writings on British History* (Cape, 1934–, In progress, Irregular), sets out to fill the gap.

It comprehends all periods from Anglo-Saxon times to 1914, though Roman Britain is excluded. The bibliography aims at completeness, though the British Empire (later Commonwealth) is treated in outline. Many hundreds of British and foreign periodicals of standing have been searched, but not general weekly magazines. The main division of the work is into general works and period histories; the general section includes such divisions as archives, constitutional, social, economic, educational, maritime and ecclesiastical history. Collected biography is also included. There are lengthy sections devoted to English local history, and all these divisions are repeated on a smaller scale in the separate sections of part II, period histories. Unfortunately, this splendidly detailed bibliography, which is certainly not too full for the

WEST (G. B.). Billingsgate. *London Soc. Jour.*, no. 197 (July 1934) 100-07. 996

WHITAKER-WILSON (CECIL). Whitehall Palace. Muller, 1934. 175 pp., 997
illus., plan. [*Rev.* T.L.S., 1735 (2 May 1935) 290].

YEANDLE (WALTER HAROLD). A corner of Finsbury. An account of the 998
history of the parish and church of St. Clement, City Road. W. Knott, 1934.
[145] pp., illus. [*Rev.* T.L.S., 1704 (27 Sept. 1934) 660].

NORFOLK

ANDERSON (G. H.). The town hall of Lynn and its treasures. King's Lynn: 999
King's Lynn Corp., 1934. 16 pp., illus.

BRIGGS (OLIVE VERNON). Some painted screens of Norfolk. *Roy. Inst. Brit.* 1000
Architects Jour., 3rd ser., XLI no. 19 (8 Sept. 1934) 997-1015.

DICKINSON (ROBERT ERIC). The town plans of East Anglia. *Geography*, XIX 1001
pt. 1 (March 1934) 37-50.

DORLING (EDWARD EARLE). Notes on the medieval heraldry remaining in the 1002
cathedral church of Norwich. *Friends Norwich Cath. Ann. Rept. for* 1933
(1934) 8-24.

FENN (ERIC ALFRED HUMPHERY). The origin of the inland waterways of East 1003
Anglia. Blakes, 1934. 16 pp.

GILLETT (HENRY MARTIN). Walsingham and its shrine. Preface by F. C. 1004
Devas, S. J. Burns, Oates & W., 1934. 94 pp., illus., appendices, bibliog.

GRACE (MARY). The chamberlains and treasurers of the city of Norwich, 1293- 1005
1835. *Norfolk Archaeol.*, XXV pt. 2 (1934) 181-201.

GRANT (A. ROWLAND H.). Church of St. Mary Magdalene, Sandringham; 1006
with notes on more recent gifts to the church, by Arthur R. Fuller. King's
Lynn: West Norfolk & King's Lynn Newspaper Co. (printers), 1934. 19 pp.,
illus.

HOLMES (HENRY N.). Progress in the conditions of employment in Norwich. 1007
Jour. State Medicine, XLII no. 7 (July 1934) 373-90. [Historical sketch since
16th century].

LONG (SYDNEY H.). Preservation of Kett's Oak. *Norfolk Naturalists Soc.* 1008
Trans. for 1933, XIII pt. 4 (1934) 356-57. [On the Norwich-Wymondham road].

MILLICAN (PERCY), *ed.* The register of the freemen of Norwich, 1548-1713. 1009
A transcript. With an introduction, an appendix to those freemen whose
apprenticeship indentures are enrolled in the City Records, and indexes of
names and places. Norwich: Jarrolds (by authority of the Norwich Corporation), 1934. xxiv, 306 pp. [*Rev.* Amer. Hist. Rev., XLI (Jan. 1936) 373-74;
E.H.R., LI (April 1936) 382-83; T.L.S., 1711 (15 Nov. 1934) 798].

MORTIMER (C. G.). Our Lady of Walsingham. Catholic Truth Society, 1934. 1010
27 pp., plan.

MOTTRAM (RALPH HALE). The contribution of a provincial centre (Norwich) 1011
to English letters. *Essays by Divers Hands*, new ser., XIII (1934) 41-55.

Fig. 39. MILNE, A. T., *Writings on British History*. (Copyright:
Jonathan Cape.)

specialized work on a small field now attempted by many amateurs and young scholars, has so far not proceeded beyond 1945 (last volumes published 1960). The *Archaeological Bulletin for the British Isles* (1940–9) continued as *Archaeological Bibliography for Great Britain and Ireland* (1950–, In progress) covers some archaeological material not dealt with by Milne; its scope is the earliest times to A.D. 1600. It is produced by the Council for British Archaeology.

There are three standard comprehensive series covering English history; Longmans' *Political History of England* (1905–15); Methuen's *History of England* (1910–34); and *The Oxford History of England* (1936–65, General editor Sir G. Clark), all multi-volumed series obtainable in most libraries. We propose to deal only with the Oxford history, and (Fig. 40) E. F. Jacob, *The Fifteenth Century, 1399–1485* (Clarendon Press, Oxford, 1961) is a typical volume. Jacob definitely sets out to introduce the newer approaches to history of the last forty years. His preface mentions in particular the influence of private as distinct from the public records; study of the greater landed families, research into the personnel of Parliament, fresh information on the financial activities of Government, and increased emphasis on social, legal and economic history. There are chapters headed: "the trader and the countryman", "the towns", "the peaceful arts", not paralleled in the two older series, though Trevelyan's *England under the Stuarts* in the Methuen series remains a classic. The *Oxford History of England* is scarcely for the general reader, and its scale determines that it must largely be based on (cited) secondary authorities. A. J. P. Taylor's *England since 1914* (1965) is more readable, if more controversial than earlier volumes. Nevertheless, the series is essential for any preliminary study of a period, preceding a more detailed line of research. A brief dictionary is S. H. Steinberg's *New Dictionary of British History* (Arnold, 1963); this does not completely supersede the older work by Sir S. Low and F. S. Pulling, *Dictionary of British History* (Cassell, 1928). The volumes of the Royal Commission on Historical Monuments (three series) for England, Scotland and Wales will be dealt with under local history. Among periodicals and serials, the *English Historical Review*, *History*, the *Historical Journal*, *History Today*, the

with the siege of Troy'.[1] Bankes, a baron of the Exchequer, could possess the *Florarium Bartholomei* by the Austin canon John of Mirfield, Sir Thomas Berkeley a glossed psalter and the *Legenda sanctorum* in English, and Sir Gerard Braybroke service-books and works of devotion. But the noble laity generally went in for history (The Trojan Legend, the Brute Chronicle, and various *gesta regum*), books of courtesy, and treatises describing what a person of coat armour should know. The *Book of Hawk-ing, Hunting and the Blazing of Arms*, commonly called the *Boke of St. Albans*, was published by the St. Albans schoolmaster (as Wynkyn de Worde called him) just after Bosworth. He had been printing *apud villam sancti Albani* since 1480; and Wynkyn de Worde thought it worth printing again (with an addition on angling). It is a compilation devoted to the pursuits and interests of a *generosus*, in this case a country gentleman. The longest treatise in the *Boke*, which was alleged to have been put together by Mistress Juliana Bernes or Barnes, is the *Liber Armorum*, derived from the *De officio militari* of Nicholas of Upton, canon of Salisbury, and the English *Book of the Lineage of Coat Armour*, a fifteenth-century compilation. There is no need to dwell upon the importance of heraldry as a subject of polite study and speculation in the fifteenth century. If to the minds of Malory and Caxton (who printed a translation of the *Ordeyne de Chevalerie*) chivalry had a moral value for its inculcation of the free and knightly attributes, heraldry was the formal way of displaying the gentle lineage which, to contemporary minds, disposed a man towards virtue. The origins of coat armour, according to the *Boke of St. Albans*, were to be found in the siege of Troy, where 'in *Gestis Troianorum* it telleth what the first beginning of the Law of Arms was'. This existed before any law in the world save the law of nature: but even before the siege of Troy knighthood existed and an even greater institution: 'Know ye that these two orders were, first wedlock, and then knighthood.' The treatise goes as far as to claim that Christ was a gentleman and bore coat armour of ancestors: the four evangelists had gentle ancestry, sprung as they were from Judas Maccabaeus; but after his death, his kin 'fell to labours and were called no gentlemen'. The four doctors of Holy Church, however, were 'gentlemen of blood and coat armour'.

[1] *Reg. Chichele*, iii. 46, 48.

Fig. 40. *The Oxford History of England.* JACOB, E. F., *The Fifteenth Century, 1399–1485.* (Copyright: Clarendon Press.)

Transactions of the Ancient Monuments Society, Antiquaries' Journal, Antiquity, Archaeologia, the *Journal of the British Archaeological Association,* the *Journal of Industrial Archaeology,* the *Bulletin of the Institute of Historical Research,* the *Classical Quarterly,* the *Classical Review,* the *Journal of Egyptian Archaeology,* the *Journal of Hellenic Studies, Medium Aevum,* and the *Transactions of the Royal Historical Society,* should be noted.

Sara E. Harcup has produced *Historical Archaeological and Kindred Societies in the British Isles,* Institute of Historical Research, 1965, with alphabetical and topographical sequences, and a select list of subjects.

We must now consider other parts of the British Isles:

Scotland

MEIKLE, H. W. and others, *Scotland: a Select Bibliography,* Cambridge Univ. Press, 1950. A shorter guide is J. D. Mackie's *Scottish History,* National Book League, 1956.

TERRY, C. S., *A Catalogue of the Publications of Scottish Historical and Kindred Clubs and Societies, 1780–1908,* Maclehose, Glasgow, 1909. This is continued by C. Matheson's *Catalogue of the Publications of Historical and Kindred Clubs and Societies, 1908–27,* Milne and Hutchinson, Aberdeen, 1928. This includes a subject index to Terry's work. The Library Association guide (County Libraries Section) on the *Face of Scotland,* 2nd edition, 1964, is the most up-to-date short work.

P. HUME BROWN'S *History of Scotland* (3 vols., Cambridge Univ. Press, 1899–1909) remains the best standard history, but ends at 1843. W. C. Dickinson and G. S. Pryde have published *A New History of Scotland* (2 vols., Nelson, 1961–2), which deals more fully with economic affairs, and continues the story to the present day.

Scottish Historical Review (periodical).

Ireland

MACALISTER, R. A. S., *The Archaeology of Ireland,* 2nd edition, Methuen, 1949.

CURTIS, E., *A History of Ireland*, 6th edition, Methuen, 1950.

Bibliographies of Ireland include the National Library of Ireland *Bibliography of Irish History, 1870–1921* (2 vols., Stationery Office, Dublin, 1936–40) and C. Maxwell, *A Short Bibliography of Irish History* (Historical Association, 1921). See also A. R. Eager (above, p. 86).

T. P. O'Neill has produced *Sources of Irish Local History* (Library Association of Ireland, Dublin, 1958).

Irish Historical Studies (periodical).

Wales

LLOYD, J. E., *A History of Wales*, 3rd edition, 2 vols., Longmans, 1949.

JENKINS, R. T., and REES, W. (editors), *A Bibliography of the History of Wales*, 2nd edition, Wales Univ. Press, Cardiff, 1962.

LIBRARY ASSOCIATION, COUNTY LIBRARIES SECTION, *The Face of Wales*, Library Association, 1958.

UNITED KINGDOM: HISTORY. LOCAL

We must now give some attention to local history, and reference has already been made to Hoskins' *Local History in England*.[1] Still further reference to local matters will be made when we come to study source materials (Chapter 6). An excellent general book is J. L. Hobbs' *Local History and the Library* (Deutsch, 1962), and there are three useful short lists. The National Council of Social Service, *A Selection of Books on English Local History* (N.C.S.S., 1949) is arranged by counties with normally some half dozen titles to a county; no annotations are given. The Library Association, County Libraries Section, *Readers' Guide to Books on the Sources of Local History* (2nd edition, L.A., 1959) is somewhat fuller, and less usefully, perhaps, is arranged by topics such as castles, church bells, fairs and markets, genealogy, etc. Most useful of the three i (Fig. 41) Historical Association, *English Local History Handli*

[1] See page 4 and also F. Celoria, *Teach Yourself Local History*, E.U.P., 195

(3rd edition, the Association, 1965), also arranged by subject, but much fuller (1500 items). The last four sections, for example, are XXIII dialect, XXIV local worthies, XXV miscellaneous (medicine, plagues and epidemics, fires, freemasonry, floods, law and lawyers, music, etc.), XXVI societies concerned with local history. The "worthies" section includes notes on locating portraits as well as biographies. The advice given to would-be local historians in the preface to this pamphlet cannot be bettered. "Time will be saved, and much useless labour and speculation will be avoided, if the enquirer, before beginning any local investigation, will consult the *Victoria County History* and the earlier standard county histories for his particular locality, as well as the transactions of his county archaeological or record society. It should be mentioned, however, that caution is needed in using printed county histories. They vary greatly in value and some of the volumes of the *Victoria County History* produced up to 1914 and even later require scrutiny wherever no exact reference to an original document is given. It is always advisable to verify all references if possible, as errors often creep in although authors and editors may have exercised great care. He should also ascertain whether the Historical Monuments Commission or the English Place-name Society has issued volumes dealing with his county. In all cases he will be well advised to consult the local librarian and county archivist and the curator of his local museum; but he will be foolish to persist in ploughing a lonely furrow when this is not necessary; and, if his interest and researches are likely to become a life-long activity . . . he should seek membership of his local archaeological society, and join a local branch of the Historical Association"(description and Fig. 41 from the second edition, 1952).

Sara Harcup's work (p. 101, above) supplements *Scientific and Learned Societies of Great Britain* (6th edition, 1962), recording 116 historical, etc., societies, but most of them are local, dealing with special sections of history, or ancillary studies. The major national societies are the British Archaeological Association (founded 1843), Historical Association (1906), Prehistoric Society (1908), Royal Archaeological Institute (1843), Royal Historical Society (nine-

65

MISCELLANEOUS—(cont.)

G. GOODWIN. Art. in *Archæologia*, vol. xxx, 1841, and also *Sessional Papers of R.I.B.A.* 1868-9.

G. F. FORT. *Historical Treatise on Early Builders' Marks* (Philadelphia, Pa.). 1885.

R. H. C. DAVIS. *Masons' Marks in Oxfordshire and the Cotswolds* (in 84th *Report* of Oxfordshire Archl. Soc.) 1938-9. An important local study.

5. Storms and Floods.

C. E. P. BROOKS and J. GLASSPOOLE. *British Floods and Droughts.* 1928.

C. C. CLARKE. *Hundred Wonders of the World.* 1822. Gives information as to earthquakes, etc.

6. Law and Lawyers.

See also VI above.

W. BLACKSTONE. *Commentaries on the Laws of England.* (Many edns. since 1765.)

SIR W. HOLDSWORTH. *History of English Law,* 1927; and *Some Makers of English Law,* 1938; also XVII, 1, above.

SIR J. F. STEPHEN. *History of the Criminal Law.* 3 vols. 1883.

L. RADZINOWICZ. *A History of English Criminal Law and its Administration from 1750.* Vol. I. 1948.

H. POTTER. *Historical Introduction to English Law.* 1932.

H. POTTER. *A Short Outline of English Legal History.* 1945.

T. F. T. PLUCKNETT. *Concise History of the Common Law.* 4th edn. 1948.

R. L. HENRY. *Contracts in the Local Courts of Medieval England.* 1929.

E. DE HAAS. *Antiquities of Bail.* 1940.

A. PULLING. *Order of the Coif.* 1884.

W. J. LOFTIE. *Inns of Court and Chancery.* 1895.

G. PITT-LEWIS. *History of the Temple.* 1898.

SIR F. D. MACKINNON. *Law and Lawyers.* (Art. in *Johnson's England.* vol. ii, pp. 287 ff.) 1933.

7. Music.

See also above XIII, 23, Hymnody, and XIII, 24, Parish Music, etc.

Oxford History of Music. 8 vols. 2nd edn., 1929-34.

J. PULVER. *Biographical Dictionary of Old English Music.* 1927.

C. V. STANFORD and C. FORSYTH. *History of Music.* 1916.

E. WALKER. *History of Music in England.* 2nd edn., 1924.

E. H. FELLOWES. *English Madrigal Composers.* 1921. *William Byrd.* 2nd edn., 1948. *Orlando Gibbons.* 1925.

Fig. 41. *The English Local History Handlist.* (Copyright: Historical Association.)

teenth century) and Society of Antiquaries of London (1707). *Introducing Local History*, National Council of Social Service, and its *Supplement*, 1964, give much useful information on local history, and a list of organizations concerned with it. The Workers' Educational Association, local education authorities, the extra-mural departments of universities, political parties (particularly the Co-operative Wholesale Society) are other bodies concerned to a considerable degree with national and local history. The Standing Conference for Local History (a branch of the N.C.S.S.) holds an annual conference and affiliates most other British national organizations concerned with local history, and numerous County Local History Committees. The Universities of Hull, Leicester, Manchester, Southampton and University College, London, all have teaching posts in local history.

Of the three lengthy works mentioned in the *Handlist* that aim to cover all Britain by localities, the *Victoria County History* is by far the most important from our point of view. Commenced in 1899, over 100 vols. have been produced. It is clear from an examination of Doubleday and Page, *Guide to the Victoria County History* (*c.* 1904), that times have changed. There is much emphasis on ecclesiastical history, agriculture and the manor. Under the section "sport", hunting, racing, polo and shooting have the most elaborate instructions; there is no consideration of today's mass amusements nor even of music or the theatre. "Local celebrities", it is suggested, should include "painters, designers, architects, carvers, writers, scientists, the founders of public works"—no word here of industrialists, trade unionists, comedians or professional footballers or cricketers. The *Guide* is a very thorough document, but in its reference to original sources says little of local sources compared with the very thorough treatment accorded to the materials in the Public Record Office and the British Museum.

(Fig. 42), *Victoria County History, A History of the County of Cambridge and the Isle of Ely;* Vol. III, *The City and University of Cambridge* (edited by J. P. C. Roach, Oxford Univ. Press, 1959) may serve as an excellent recent example of the "new model" *V.C.H.* Banking, public health, industries, the theatre are but

THE CITY OF CAMBRIDGE

CAMBRIDGE, the county town, and since 1951 a city, owes its position to the crossing of two natural lines of communication. The Cam, constituting a river route from south-west to north-east, was a main artery for traffic through the Fenland until the railway period;[1] as the Recorder of Cambridge said in his speech to James I in 1615, 'This river, with navigation to the sea, is the life of traffic to this town and county.'[2] It was the chalk and gravel ridge that determined the line of the road which continued the Worsted Street to Huntingdon. Known in the Middle Ages as Stoneway or Huntingdon Way,[3] it crossed the river by 'the one bridge in England which gives name to a county'.[4] Roads from St. Neots and Ely join the Huntingdon Road west of the bridge, and to the east roads from Newmarket, Bishop's Stortford, Ware, and Baldock converge on the city.

To the end of the 18th century the built-up area of Cambridge was concentrated round the castle site north-west of the bridge and the market-place south-east of it, roughly 1 mile long and $\frac{1}{2}$ mile broad, surrounded by the town fields which stretched east and west for $3\frac{1}{2}$ miles. Outlying settlements at Barnwell downstream and Newnham upstream were only absorbed by the expansion of the 19th century which, beginning along the Newmarket Road, extended the built-up areas southwards and northwards both sides of the river until the houses of Cambridge in 1951 extended $2\frac{1}{2}$ miles south-east of the bridge and a mile to the north. In 1912 and 1935 the Borough boundaries were successively extended to include the whole of Chesterton and Cherry Hinton and parts of Impington and Milton, Fen Ditton, Great Shelford, Trumpington, and Grantchester.[5] The remains of the medieval town fields are to be seen south-west of the Huntingdon Road and in the various 'pieces' and college playing fields. 'Medieval Cambridge is largely separated from the expanding Cambridge of today by a ring of open land formed by the Commons and the Backs.'[6]

It was counted a day's journey from London to Cambridge in the 14th century,[7] and in 1702 a coach took 15 hours.[8] The first coach ran from Cambridge to London in 1653.[9] From 1663 onwards turnpike trusts were improving communications,[10] and between 1724 and 1797 a series of Acts for improving the road between Cambridge and London and other main roads was passed.[11] By the second half of the century there was a daily coach service to London, with others running to Birmingham, Norwich, Yarmouth, and all the chief centres of East Anglia.[12] In 1837 ten different coaches left Cambridge for London every week day, and two for Oxford.[13] The last stage coach left Cambridge in 1849.[14] The first milestones in England since the Roman occupation were erected along the London road by Trinity Hall in 1729 and bore the college arms; the first, at Trumpington Ford, was over 12 ft. high.[15] There was also a regular boat service from

[1] H. C. Darby, *The Cambridge Region*, 162.
[2] Cooper, *Annals*, iii. 70.
[3] *P.N. Cambs.* (E.P.N.S.), 30–31.
[4] Maitland, *Township and Borough*, 37.
[5] See maps in Darby, *Cambridge Region*, 178–9, and W. Holford and H. M. Wright, *Cambridge Planning Proposals* (Cambridge, 1950).
[6] J. B. Mitchell in Darby, *Cambridge Region*, 180. This is clearly illustrated in the photograph reproduced below, plate facing p. 287.
[7] Parliamentary writs *de expensis*.

[8] J. E. B. Mayor, *Cambridge under Queen Anne*, 115.
[9] Cooper, *Annals*, iii. 454.
[10] A. Gray, *Town of Cambridge*, 140; *V.C.H. Cambs.* ii. 85.
[11] Cooper, *Annals*, iv. 182, 186, 207, 365, 460.
[12] Ibid. 273. 331. By 1776 the journey to town could be done in 8 hours, and by 1788 there was a daily return service: *Cambridge Chronicle*.
[13] *The Cambridge Guide* (1837), 266–71.
[14] A. Gray, *Town of Cambridge*, 185.
[15] Ed. Conybeare, *Highways and Byways in Cambs.* 160; *Hist. of Cambs.* 235.

Fig. 42. *The Victoria County History*. (Copyright: Victoria County Histories, R. B. Pugh, Esq.)

four of the topics treated which were not envisaged in the original plan, and the volume is splendidly printed and copiously illustrated whilst retaining the original half-title design of the older *V.C.H.* volumes. In the section on individual areas below, it will be indicated whether a *V.C.H.* is in existence or not. There is certainly no substitute for this work. The Historical Monuments Commission production is neither so vast in scale nor so useful to the historian, but we may look at the volumes for Cambridge for comparative purposes. (Fig. 43), *Royal Commission on Historical Monuments, England; An Inventory of the Historical Monuments in the City of Cambridge* (2 vols., H.M.S.O., 1959). Although full of the history of individual monuments, the great feature of this work is the splendid series of detailed photographs of every aspect of Cambridge buildings, both ecclesiastical and secular. Brasses, staircases, bookcases, doors, screens are all here in profusion, and there are colour reproductions of some of the glass in King's College. For the first time in this series, buildings in the first half of the nineteenth century have been included in the survey. Compared with the hundred or so extant volumes of the *V.C.H.*, only twenty-three of the *English Monuments* volumes have been published. By contrast the volumes of the English Place-name Society, still in progress on a county basis, are of less general value to the historian. Another county series, the *County Archaeologies* (Methuen, 1930–7), attained only 8 vols., but Nikolaus Pevsner's *Buildings of England* (Penguin, 1951–, In progress; topographical with some historical matter) is rapidly covering the country.

There are several general bibliographies of English local history, though it is difficult to separate them into topography and history. We may instance such valuable works as the pre-war Kelly's county directories, with their long historical introductions. Unfortunately, these are never likely to be reprinted or continued. The pioneer work of this type, still valuable, is S. Lewis' *Topographical Dictionary of England* (7th edition, 4 vols., Lewis, 1848–9). The Library Association *British Humanities Index, Regional Lists*, 1954– (annual), which now cover Scotland (in one issue) as well as the individual English counties, are the fullest current lists, and with this indication of a change in the climate of opinion there was difficulty in obtaining money for the completion of Gibbs' scheme and although trenches for the foundations of his W. range were opened they were never used; in 1727 an injunction was granted to stop the new work. Reasons were adduced against building on a public way (North School Street) and so near that part of the Caius boundary, but there is little doubt that the possible screening of King's College Chapel was a material consideration. The Court did not find for the plaintiffs but the work was never recommenced.

In 1738 a move was made to obtain the land for the S. range, balancing the Senate House, but acquisition was not completed until 1769. In the meantime plans were

was linked to the Senate House by a low screen-wall, which was subsequently demolished. Towards the end of the century both Brettingham, 1785, and Soane, 1791, prepared plans for a S. range to complete the lay-out, but after 1797 the proposal for the new building seems to have been abandoned.

The Senate House is one of the most important of James Gibbs' works. If his original scheme had been completed it would have resulted in a group of some of the most distinguished classical buildings of the period in England. Designed as a flanking block to a building that was to close the E. to W. vista, it says much for Gibbs' adherence here to classical rule, and the unity of composition in part as well as in whole, that the present

The SENATE HOUSE

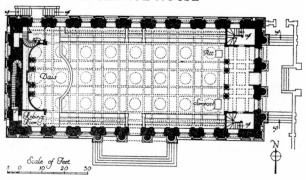

prepared by Burrough and published by James Essex for rebuilding the E. range of the Schools to provide room for the Royal Library on the first floor; the new front was to be in advance of the ends of the N. and S. ranges, of the Divinity and Law Schools, and in style to continue the elevational treatment of the Senate House. The Chancellor, the Duke of Newcastle, put forward another design, by Stephen Wright, which although in much the same position on plan differed in articulation and style. Wright included in his design a S. range to balance the Senate House.

Wright's scheme was chosen and work on the Library range was begun in 1754 and completed in 1758 at a cost of £10,506 (see SCHOOLS BUILDING, *East Range*); the S. range was never built. The completed building

unattached building is regarded as a noble and complete entity.

Architectural Description—The Senate House is rectangular on plan and stands on a plain low podium with steps up to centrepieces on the S. and E. The S. front (Plate 69) is of nine bays. The three central bays are divided and flanked by fluted attached Corinthian columns supporting a pedimented entablature with an ornamental cartouche flanked by palms etc. in the tympanum and surmounted by three vases; the entablature is carried round the building. The side bays are divided by plain Corinthian pilasters, coupled at the angles of the building; above the entablature is a balustraded parapet with pedestal blocks. The windows of the lower range, one in each bay except in the centre, have square heads, moulded architraves, console-brackets below the sills and straight and curved pedi-

Fig. 43. *The Royal Commission on Historical Monuments, England.*
(Copyright H.M.S.O.)

since 1955 have included books as well as periodical articles relating to a particular locality. Even so, the *East Anglian Bibliography* (1960–, In progress) proves how much more can be done to list items which escape the copyright net, by working in a particular area. This appears quarterly. A similar work is the *North Midland Bibliography* (1963–, In progress). Both these works are published by branches of the (British) Library Association. Stoke-on-Trent Public Libraries is now bringing out *Current Bibliography of Published Material Relating to North Staffs. and South Cheshire* (vols. 1–, 1964–, In progress).

The pioneer works by Gough, Upcott and Anderson,[1] dealing mainly with topography, fall outside the scope of this particular volume in the *How to Find Out* series, but (Fig. 44) A. L. Humphreys, *Handbook to County Bibliography* (the author, 1917), is invaluable up to the time of its compilation. Recent efforts have been directed towards the bibliography of individual counties, and it is somewhat surprising that no one has attempted to bring out an up-to-date edition of Humphreys. There are two sequences in the book, pp. 1–311, and 315–45, both arranged by English, Irish, Scottish and Welsh counties, in two alphabetical sequences, London being treated as a county for this purpose. There follow 22 pp. of lists of general English works, and shorter similar sections on Ireland, Scotland and Wales. There is a detailed index of authors, personal names, places and subjects. The English general section is in no discernible order, but leads off (see reproduction) with Anderson and Gough (Upcott is fourth), so presumably this is an order of merit. The county lists are similarly arranged. The Leicestershire list, for example, begins with a bibliography published by Leicester Public Libraries and follows, with Nichols, the old standard county history. In using Humphreys it must be noted that works are included only for their bibliographical value, however intrinsically useful they may be otherwise. The only mention of the *Victoria County Histories* is, therefore of Doubleday and Page's *Guide*

---

[1] Gough, R., *British Topography*, 1780. Upcott, W., *A Bibliographical Account of the Principal Works Relating to English Topography*, 3 vols., 1818. Anderson, J. P., *The Book of British Topography*, 1881.

ENGLAND.

[GENERAL WORKS.]

[The List of Books and References in this Section attempts only to give a few of the leading well known Guides. Its chief purpose is to direct attention to many of the less-known bibliographies, indexes, etc.]

Anderson (John Parker). The Book of British Topography. A Classified Catal. of the Topog. Works in the Lib. of the Brit. Mus. relating to Great Britain & Irel. 1881. A New edition in preparation.

Gough (Richard). British Topography, or, an Hist. Account of what has been done for illustrating the Topog. Antiquities of Gt. Brit. & Irel. 2 vols. London, 1780.

For an account of Gough's own copy, in 5 vols., at the Bodleian Lib., Oxford, which he had prepared for a Third edn., see Macray's 'Annals,' 1890, p. 289.

Bandinel (Bulkeley). A Catal. of the Books relating to Brit. Topog., etc., bequeathed to the Bodl. Lib. in 1799, by Richard Gough. Oxford, 1814.

Upcott (William). A Biblio. Account of the principal Works relating to English Topography. 3 vols. London, 1818.

Spalding (John Tricks). A Biblio. Account of the Works relating to English Topography in the Lib. of John Tricks Spalding, Nottingham. 5 vols. Exeter, 1912-13. Privately printed.

Hotten (John Camden). A Hand-book to the Topog. and Family Hist. of Engl. & Wales. London, n.d.

Smith (Alfred Russell). A Catal. of Ten Thousand Tracts and Fifty Thousand Prints and Drawings, illustrating the Topography & Antiquities of England, Wales, Scotland, and Ireland. Collected by William Upcott and John Russell Smith. London, 1878.

Daniell (Walter V.) and Nield (Frederick J.). Manual of Brit. Topography. A Catal. of County and Local Histories, etc. London, 1909.

Sonnenschein (William Swan). The Best Books. 3rd edn. London, 1912. Pt. II. (includes Topography).

Hoare (Sir R. C.). A Catal. of Books relating to the Hist. & Topog. of Engl., Wales, Scot., & Irel., at Stourhead, Wilts. 1815. 25 copies only printed.

—— **Catal. of the Hoare Lib. at Stourhead, co. Wilts.,** compiled by J. Bowyer Nichols. London, 1840.

Catal. of the Library in the Public Record Office, and Supplement. [Compiled by T. Craib.] Third Edition. London, 1902, 1909.

List of Topographical Works relating to Great Britain and Ireland, printed for official use, by the Library of the Public Record Office. 1907.

List of Works relating to British Genealogy and Local History. (*Bulletin of the New York Public Lib.*, vol. xiv. 1910.) Also issued separately.

Fig. 44. HUMPHREYS, A. L., *Handbook to County Bibliography.*
(Copyright: the author.)

(see above p. 105). There are three and a half pages on the county of
Leicester in general including the county town (in certain counties,
Norfolk and Northumberland for example, there is a separate entry
for the main town). As well as recording monographs with
bibliographies, Humphreys gives analytical entries for the local
archaeological society's transactions, and for other works. After
the main section there are page references to the appropriate sections
of Anderson, Upcott, Gough, etc.—a very useful feature. There
follows a series of references arranged under localities—only six
for the whole of Leicestershire. Here one wonders if the same
standards have been applied, for there is only one reference to the
second town, Loughborough; three to Market Harborough and
one to Melton Mowbray. The addenda gives a further four
Leicestershire titles.

We will conclude this section by listing some of the main county
bibliographies and comprehensive works; it will only be possible
to mention one or two titles for each county represented—many
counties, alas, have not yet achieved a bibliography, and some have
no old county history. Further details must be sought in Humphreys,
Minto and Walford (see p. 21). *The Amateur Historian* (N.C.S.S.,
quarterly) is the most useful periodical for English local history.
Before embarking on our list we may quote Humphreys' criticisms
in his preface of 1917, happily now partially out of date:

"In surveying what has already been done for various counties
bibliographically, one is obliged to regard what still remains to be
accomplished. Certain counties have had the good fortune to
find their bibliographers, while other counties, possessed of a
wealth of topographical material, have not succeeded in securing
one. As far back as 1837 the bibliography of the county of Kent
was undertaken by that fine old pioneer, John Russell Smith,
his book, *Bibliotheca Cantiana*, one of the first and one of the best, is
excellent up to the time when it was issued.

"London has yet to find its bibliographers. The duty of compiling
a bibliography of London belongs to the Corporation, which,
with all its wealth, has never issued a satisfactory catalogue of its
possessions in the Guildhall Library, nor has it ever issued a perio-

dical bulletin of bibliographical information, as is being done by all good libraries in America and by many here. The counties of Bedfordshire, Berkshire, Derbyshire, Hertfordshire, Leicestershire and Shropshire are a few instances only of counties which have great claims bibliographically, but so far no one has been forthcoming to undertake the work required. Welsh and Irish counties are almost all untouched. In Scotland a band of zealous and capable bibliographers is producing good work."

Libellous as this possibly now is in relation to some of the counties mentioned (see below), its general sense remains as true as ever. High printing costs and the tediousness of much bibliographical work will ensure, unfortunately, that the gaps in some counties' bibliography will remain. Many of those listed below are mere author lists, or deficient in major bibliographical particulars. At the present time the boundaries of many counties are being changed by the Local Government Boundary Commission, but only in London is the process complete. Charles Gross' *A Bibliography of British Municipal History* (2nd edition, Leicester University Press, 1965), is to be continued by G. H. Martin.

London

LIBRARY ASSOCIATION. REFERENCE AND SPECIAL SECTION, *The County of London; a select book list*, L.A., 1959. L.C.C. Library, *Members' Library Catalogue*, Vol. 1, *London, History and Topography*, 1939, is fuller within its limits.

LONDON COUNTY COUNCIL AND LONDON SURVEY COMMITTEE, *The Survey of London*, L.C.C., vols. 1–, 1900–, In progress. About 30 vols. published. Arranged by parishes. *Sir* W. Besant's earlier survey (10 vols., 1902–12) is arranged by periods. Several of the old Metropolitan Boroughs merged in 1965 into the new London Boroughs, and one extinguished County Council (Middlesex), have brought out useful brochure histories.

V.C.H., 1 vol., 1909.

Hist. Mon. Comm., 5 vols., 1924–8.

Bedfordshire

CONISBEE, L. R., *A Bedfordshire Bibliography*, Beds. Historical Record Society, Bedford, 1962.

MACKLIN, H. W., *Bedfordshire and Huntingdonshire*, Methuen, 1917.

FISHER, T., *Collections Historical Genealogical and Topographical for Bedfordshire*, Nichols, 1812–36. Plates with insubstantial text.

V.C.H., 3 vols. and index, 1904–14.

Berkshire

READING PUBLIC LIBRARIES, *Local Collection Catalogue of Books and Maps*, Central Library, Reading, 1958.

ASHMOLE, E., *The History and Antiquities of Berkshire*, Carnan, Reading, 1736. C. Coates began additions to this work in 1812.

V.C.H., 4 vols. and index, 1906–27.

Buckinghamshire

GOUGH, H., *Bibliotheca Buckinghamiensis*, De Fraine, Aylesbury, 1890.

LIPSCOMB, G., *The History and Antiquities of the County of Buckingham*, 4 vols., Robins, 1847.

V.C.H., 4 vols. and index, 1905–28.

Hist. Mon. Comm., 2 vols., 1912–13.

Cambridge and the Isle of Ely

GIFFORD, P. R. (editor), *Cambridgeshire; an Annotated List of the Books, Maps, Prints (etc.)* . . . *in the Cambridgeshire County Library Local History Collection*, Cambs. Ed. Committee, Cambridge, 1961. Full catalogue of all books printed in Cambridge and Cambridgeshire by R. Bowes, 1894. *Hereward's Isle* (4th edition, 1962) is a catalogue of books in the Isle of Ely County Library.

CARTER, E., *History of the County of Cambridge*, Bentley, 1819.

V.C.H., 4 vols. and index, 1938–, In progress.
Hist. Mon. Comm., 2 vols., 1959.

Cheshire

COOKE, J. H., *Bibliotheca Cestriensis*, Mackie, Warrington, 1904.
ORMEROD, G., *The History of the County Palatine and City of Chester*, 2nd edition, 3 vols., Routledge, 1882.

Cornwall

BOASE, G. C., and COURTNEY, W. P., *Bibliotheca Cornubiensis*, 3 vols., Longmans, 1874–82. Supplemented by Boase, G. C. *Collectanea Cornubiensis*, 1890.
POLWHELE, R., *History of Cornwall*, 5 vols. in 1, Cadell & Davis, Falmouth,1803–6.
V.C.H., 1 vol. (and one incomplete), 1906–24.

Cumberland

HUTCHINSON, W., *The History of the County of Cumberland*, 2 vols., Jollie, Carlisle, 1794. See also under Durham (Donkin) and Westmorland (below).
V.C.H., 2 vols., 1901–5.

Derbyshire

DERBY PUBLIC LIBRARIES, *Derbyshire; a Select Catalogue of Books About the County*, Public Libraries, Derby, 1930.
PILKINGTON, J., *View of the Present State of Derbyshire*, 2 vols., Drewry, Derby, 1789.
V.C.H., 2 vols., 1905–7.

Devonshire

DAVIDSON, J., *Bibliotheca Devoniensis*, Roberts, Exeter, 1852. *Supplement*, 1862.

POLWHELE, R., *The History of Devonshire*, 3 vols., Cadell, Exeter, 1797–1806.

V.C.H., 1 vol., 1906.

Dorset

DOUCH, R. A., *A Handbook of Local History: Dorset*, Univ. of Bristol, Bristol, 1962. *Supplement*, 1962.

HUTCHINS, J., *The History and Antiquities of the County of Dorset*, 4 vols., Nichols, 1861–73.

V.C.H., 1 vol., 1908.

Hist. Mon. Comm., 1 vol., 1952.

Durham

DONKIN, W. C., *An Outline Bibliography of the Northern Region*, King's College, Newcastle, 1956. Covers also Cumberland, Northumberland, Westmorland and Yorkshire (North Riding).

SURTEES, R., *The History and Antiquities of the County Palatine of Durham*, 4 vols., Nichols, 1816–40.

V.C.H., 3 vols., 1905–28.

Essex

WARD, G. A. (comp.), *Essex Local History; a Short Guide to Books and Manuscripts*, National Register of Archives (Essex), Brentwood, 1950.

MORANT, P., *History and Antiquities of the County of Essex*, 2 vols., Virtue, 1836.

V.C.H., 5 vols. and bibliography, 1903–66. The bibliography volume in the *V.C.H.* (1959), is very comprehensive.

Hist. Mon. Comm., 4 vols., 1916–23.

Gloucestershire and Bristol

GLOUCESTER PUBLIC LIBRARY, *Catalogue of the Gloucestershire Collection*, Public Library, Glouceser, 1928.

On Bristol, see E. R. N. Mathews, *Bristol Bibliography*, 1916.

RUDDER, S., *A New History of Gloucestershire*, the author, Cirencester, 1799.

V.C.H., 2 vols., 1907–65.

Hampshire and the Isle of Wight

GILBERT, H. M. and GODWIN, G. N., *Bibliotheca Hantoniensis*, Ye Olde Boke Shoppe, Southampton, 1891. *Supplement* (by Wilson), 1898.

WOODWARD, B. B. and others, *A General History of Hampshire*, 3 vols., Virtue, 1861–9.

V.C.H., 5 vols. and index, 1900–14.

Herefordshire

ALLEN, J. (comp.), *Bibliotheca Herefordiensis*, Allen, Hereford, 1821. The Herefordshire County Library has published a *Select List* of books in the local collection (1955).

DUNCUMB, J. and others, *Collections Towards the History and Antiquities of the County of Hereford*, 8 vols., Murray, 1804–1915. Different portions were by J. Duncumb, W. H. Cooke, M. S. Watkins and J. H. Matthews.

V.C.H., 1 vol., 1908.

Hist. Mon. Comm., 3 vols., 1931–4.

Hertfordshire

HERTFORDSHIRE COUNTY MUSEUM, *Catalogue of the "Lewis Evans" Collection of Books and Pamphlets Relating to Hertfordshire*, 2 parts, County Museum, St. Albans, 1906–8. There is also a modern guide to contents of periodicals and transactions (1959) by the Herts. Local History Council, compiled by M. F. Thwaite.

CHAUNCY, Sir H., *The Historical Antiquities of Hertfordshire*, 2 vols., Griffin, Bishop's Stortford, 1826.

V.C.H., 4 vols. and index, 1902–23.
Hist. Mon. Comm., 1 vol., 1910.

Huntingdonshire

HUNTINGDON COUNTY LIBRARY, *Catalogue of the Local History Collection*, 2nd edition, County Library, Huntingdon, 1958.
For general work, see under Bedfordshire (above—Macklin). This county is not covered by the L.A. *Regional Lists* (above, pp. 107–8).
V.C.H., 3 vols. and index, 1926–38.
Hist. Mon. Comm., 1 vol. (1926).

Kent

HASTED, E., *The Historical and Topographical Survey of the County of Kent*, 2nd edition, 13 vols., Bristow, Canterbury, 1797–1801. Additional vol. by H. H. Drake, 1886.
V.C.H., 3 vols., 1908–32.

Lancashire

FISHWICK, H., *The Lancashire Library; a Bibliographical Account of Books on Topography, Biography, History . . . Relating to the County Palatine*, Pearse, Warrington, 1875. A full Lancashire bibliography is in preparation. There are bibliographies of Wigan by H. T. Folkard, and of Bolton by A. Sparke.
BAINES, E., *The History of the County Palatine and Duchy of Lancaster*, 3rd edition, 5 vols., Heywood, Manchester, 1883–93.
V.C.H., 7 vols., 1906–14.
There is a regional work on the Furness area (West, T., *The Antiquities of Furness*, 1805).

Leicestershire

LEE, J. M., *Leicestershire History; a Handlist to Printed Sources in the Libraries of Leicester*, University of Leicester, 1958.

NICHOLS, J., *The History and Antiquities of the County of Leicester*, 4 vols. in 8, Nichols, 1795–1815.

V.C.H., 5 vols., 1907–64.

Lincolnshire

LINCOLN PUBLIC LIBRARY, *Bibliotheca Lincolniensis; a Catalogue of the Books, Pamphlets, etc., Relating to the City and County of Lincoln*, Morton, Lincoln, 1904. A select list was issued by the Lincolnshire Local History Society (2nd edition, 1949).

ALLEN, T., *The History of the County of Lincoln*, 2 vols., Saunders, Lincoln, 1833–4.

V.C.H., 1 vol., 1906.

Middlesex

ROBBINS, R. M., *Middlesex*, Collins, 1953. The first volume in the *New Survey of England* series, of which only Cornwall has additionally appeared.

V.C.H., 2 vols., 1911–62.

Hist. Mon. Comm., 1 vol. (1937).

Norfolk

QUINTON, J. (comp.), *Bibliotheca Norfolciensis; a Catalogue of Writings of Norfolk Men and of Works Relating to the County of Norfolk*, Colman, Norwich, 1896.

BLOMEFIELD, F. and PARKIN, C., *An Essay Towards a Topographical History of the County of Norfolk*, 2nd edition, 11 vols., Miller, 1805–10. Index by J. N. Chadwick, 1862.

The East Anglian Bibliography, 1960–, In progress, lists current material, including Suffolk and Cambridgeshire items.

V.C.H., 2 vols., 1901–6.

Northamptonshire

TAYLOR, J., *Bibliotheca Northantonensis*, 1800–83, Taylor, Northampton, 1884.

BRIDGES, J., *The History and Antiquities of Northamptonshire*, 2 vols., Payne, Oxford, 1791.

V.C.H., 4 vols., 1902–37.

Northumberland

NEWCASTLE UPON TYNE PUBLIC LIBRARIES COMMITTEE, LOCAL CATALOGUE, Reid, Newcastle, 1932.

TAYLOR, H. A., *Northumberland History; a brief Guide to Records and Aids in Newcastle upon Tyne*, Newcastle and Northumberland Councils, 1963.

NORTHUMBERLAND COUNTY HISTORY COMMITTEE, *A History of Northumberland*, 15 vols., Reid, Newcastle, 1893–1940. Continues John Hodgson's *History of Northumberland*, 7 vols., 1820–58.

Nottinghamshire

BRISCOE, J. P., *Nottinghamshire Collection: List of Books in the Nottingham Free Public Libraries*, The Libraries, Nottingham, 1890. The County Library local collection was catalogued in 1953.

THOROTON, R., *History of Nottinghamshire*, 3rd edition, 3 vols., White, 1797.

V.C.H., 2 vols., 1906–10.

Oxfordshire

As (Fig. 45) E. H. Cordeaux and D. H. Merry, *A Bibliography of Printed Works Relating to Oxfordshire* (Oxford Univ. Press, 1955) is considered among the very best of the county bibliographies,

841. BALLARD, A., The assize of bread in Oxfordshire in the nineteenth century. (Rept., Oxf. archaeol. soc., 1906, p. 22-25.)   R. Top. 330

842. Social and economic history. (Victoria county history, 1907, vol. 2, p. 165-224.)   R. 9, 41 s

843. E. J. Brooks & sons register of furnished and unfurnished residences, and of . . . estates [&c.] to let or for sale. [Including city and county.] 1909, 1913.   G.A. Oxon c. 256 (4, 5)

844. A rural community council in being. An account of some work in Oxfordshire villages. Banbury, 1929, 8°. 36 pp.   O.P.L.

845. THOMPSON, F., An Oxfordshire hamlet in the 'eighties. (National review, 1937, Aug., p. 222-28.)   Per. 22775 d. 14

846. Oxfordshire federation of women's institutes. Old times exhibition, 27-30 April, 1937. (Oxf.), 1937. 8°. 16 pp.   177 d. 92 (8)

847. Oxfordshire rural community council. Village life in Oxfordshire, a report. Oxf., (1937), 8°. 12 pp.   O.C.R.L.

848. BUXTON, L. H. D., TREVOR, J. C., and BLACKWOOD, B., Measurements of Oxfordshire villagers. (Journ., Roy. anthrop. inst., vol. 69, 1939, p. 1-10.)   Soc. 247115 d. 98

849. HIGGINS, C., Social life in Georgian days in Berkshire and Oxfordshire. (Country Life, 1940, vol. 87, p. 92-97.)   Per. 384 b. 6

850. Oxford univ., agric. econ. research inst. Country planning, a study of local problems [in N. Oxfordshire]. Lond., 1944, 8°. 288 pp.   2479115 c. 22

851. THOMPSON, F., Lark Rise to Candleford, a trilogy. [Orig. publ. as Lark Rise; Candleford Green; Over to Candleford. Reminiscences of North Oxfordshire village life in the late 19th century.] Lond., &c., 1945, 8°. 556 pp.   247126 c. 229

852. GREEN, DAVID, Country neighbours. 1st ed. [Reminiscences, mainly about the Evenlode country.] Lond., 1948, 8°. 203 pp.   G.A. Oxon 8° 1215

853. THOMPSON, F., Still glides the stream. [A description of life in a North Oxfordshire village at the end of the 19th century.] Lond., &c., 1948, 8°. 233 pp.   247126 e. 238

854. ALLEN, A. B., Rural education. 2 vols. [Vol. 1 consisting mainly of general material about village customs &c.] Lond., (1950), 8°.   2621 c. 397

See 2830 [Hearth-blowers, Henley, 1947].

Fig. 45. CORDEAUX and MERRY, *A Bibliography of Oxfordshire*. (Copyright: the authors.)

we will use it as an example of the species, though it will already
be obvious that the guides to individual counties differ in almost
every conceivable respect—age, typography, inclusiveness (both
in the number of titles and in the fullness of descriptions), arrangement (author, subject, classified, or a combination), etc. Some
purport to be the catalogues of particular private or public libraries
—and are necessarily incomplete on the day of publication. Many
contain inaccuracies, not only because they are often compiled by
enthusiastic amateurs (with plenty of knowledge about their
county's local history but none about the principles of cataloguing),
but also because the works they describe are very scarce indeed,
and exist, if at all, in confusing variants. One list may give a title
as being an article in a local or general historical periodical; another
may be recording the same item in the form of an offprint, and
not mention its provenance. Today, fortunately, offprints usually
bear some indication of their origin. Another pitfall for the local
historian is the existence of ordinary paper, large paper, and extra-
illustrated copies of certain books, particularly in the eighteenth
and nineteenth centuries; such differences may well lead to some
inexperienced researcher looking for a "missing" illustration that
never existed in the copy of the book in the edition that he is using.
As in all the works discussed in this book, a good bibliography is
to be preferred to an indifferent one, but in local history it may be
said that even a fragmentary list provides a better starting point
than nothing at all. One would not recommend a fresh biographer
of, let us say, Wellington or Palmerston, to read every previous
life; there would be no harm in his doing this, but he would be
more likely to use his time valuably in studying state papers that
had not previously been used (original source materials will be
dealt with in Chapter 6). On the other hand, the field of local
history studies is often so narrow that it is desirable to read every-
thing previously published however fragmentary or inaccurate.

What are the particular merits of Cordeaux and Merry? It is
well printed and defines its terms clearly—i.e. it excludes the city
and the university. It also gives locations in the Bodleian (Oxford
University) and other important libraries, including the British

Museum. It does not set out to record books by Oxfordshire authors, not otherwise having an Oxfordshire interest, but "in addition to complete publications, any works containing a topographical division have been listed, but national gazetteers and similar works, arranged alphabetically, have been ignored. The *Transactions* and *Journals* of archaeological and historical societies, both national and regional, have been analysed. In addition, most of the better known periodicals, relating to the various aspects of the classification scheme, and such publications as *Country Life* and the *Gentleman's Magazine*, have been dealt with in detail. Many isolated entries from other periodicals, not otherwise examined, have been included. No attempt, however, has been made to analyse newspapers; and maps, prints, plans and drawings have normally been excluded. Auction catalogues of real estate have received a formal entry under each place involved. A number of Bodleian 'scrap' collections (picture postcards, societies' circulars, advertisements and the like) have also been incorporated: although trivial in themselves, as collections they have a definite value. In some cases it has not been possible to compile a complete entry. This applies particularly to school and parish magazines, and the papers of local societies. It was felt, however, that the practical value of identifying them, even by an incomplete entry, outweighed any other consideration". This statement of objects admirably summarizes the pitfalls and gaps that await any student of local history anywhere. Cordeaux and Merry do not give very full title entries (for example the publisher is not given), but their subject arrangement is admirably clear; there are ample cross-references, and every entry is numbered. The section *Social History*, illustrated in Fig. 45, is broken down further on into cultural societies and libraries, freemasons, friendly societies, political societies, savings associations, temperance societies and women's institutes. There is a large section on individual localities, and newspapers and directories are included in the general section. The university and city, excluded by Cordeaux and Merry, are included in F. Madan, *Oxford Books*, 3 vols., Clarendon Press, Oxford, 1895–1931. The standard old book on the University, biographical and historical, is A. Wood, *Athenae Oxonienses* (2 vols., 1691-2).

V.C.H., 7 vols., 1907-, In progress.
Hist. Mon. Comm., 1 vol., 1939.

Rutland

BLORE, T., *The History and Antiquities of the County of Rutland*, Newcomb, Stamford, 1811.
V.C.H., 2 vols. and index, 1908-36.

Shropshire

LLOYD, E., *Antiquities of Shropshire*, Eddowes, Shrewsbury, 1844. A brief illustrated list was published by the Shrewsbury and Shropshire Libraries in 1950.
V.C.H., 1 vol., 1906.

Somerset

GREEN, E., *Bibliotheca Somersetiensis*, 3 vols., Barnicott and Pearce, Taunton, 1902.
See also *Bristol Bibliography* (under Gloucestershire).
COLLINSON, J. and RACK, E., *The History and Antiquities of the County of Somerset*, 3 vols., Cruttwell, Bath, 1791.
V.C.H., 2 vols., 1906-11.

Staffordshire

SIMMS, R., *Bibliotheca Staffordiensis*, Lomax, Lichfield, 1894. A brief illustrated list was published by Stafford Public Library in 1953.
SHAW, S., *The History and Antiquities of Staffordshire*, 2 vols., Nichols, 1798-1801.
V.C.H., 4 vols., 1908-, In progress.

Suffolk

SUCKLING, A., *History and Antiquities of the County of Suffolk*, 2 vols.,
Weale, 1846–8. Index, 1952.

V.C.H., 2 vols., 1907–11.

Surrey

MINET PUBLIC LIBRARY, *Catalogue of the Collection of Works Relating
to the County of Surrey*, University Press, Aberdeen, 1901.
Supplement, 1923. The Guildford Public Libraries published a
brief list in 1957, and Lambeth produced *A Short Guide to the
Surrey Collection*, 1965.

MANNING, O. and BRAY, W., *The History and Antiquities of the County
of Surrey*, 3 vols., Nichols, 1804–14.

V.C.H., 4 vols. and index, 1902–14.

Sussex

EASTBOURNE PUBLIC LIBRARIES, *Catalogue of the Local Collection*,
The Libraries, Eastbourne, 1956.

HORSFIELD, T. W., *The History, Antiquities and Topography of the
County of Sussex*, 2 vols., Baxter, Lewes, 1835.

V.C.H., 6 vols., 1905–, In progress.

Warwickshire

BIRMINGHAM PUBLIC LIBRARIES, *Catalogue of the Birmingham Collection*, Reference Library, Birmingham, 1918. *Supplement*, 1931.

WILSON, R. E., *A Hand-List of Books Relating to the County of
Warwickshire*, Wilson, Birmingham, 1955.

(Fig. 46), Dugdale, *Sir* W., *Antiquities of Warwickshire*, 2nd edition,
2 vols., Osborn & Longman, 1730. (A third edition of 1765 is
considered inferior to this edition.) Dugdale may serve as the
pattern of the old county histories, which exist for most of the
counties of England (though not often elsewhere in Great Britain).
It may be wondered why they still retain their value in the face of
the *V.C.H.*, individual monographs, and fresh methods of scientific

GHTLOW HUNDRED.   135

on defended * him from the
' Godeva, [otherwise called
tba] a most beautifull and
one Thorold Shiriff of Lin-
nd founder d of Spalding
stock e and lineage of Tho-
ity in the time of Kenulph
Countess Godeva, bearing
ion to this place, often
ier f Husband, that for the
blessed Virgin, he would
us servitude whereunto it
uking her for importuning
iconsistent with his profit,
hould thenceforth forbear
she, out of her womanish
solicit him; insomuch that
would ride on Horseback
the town to the other h, in
ople, he would grant her
he returned, But will you
And he replying, yes; the
ppointed day got on Horse-
hair loose, so that it co-
t the Legs, and thus per-
turned with joy to her Hus-
granted to the Inhabitants
[from servitude, evil Cu-
i servitute & malis Custumis,
rvallensis i] which immunity
re been kind of a manumis-
vile tenure, whereby they
iad under this great Earl,
from all manner of Toll,
ihton k affirms: In memory
f him and his said Lady
vindow of Trinity Church
R. 2. time, and his right
er with these words writ-

County: and departing n this life in a good old
age, at his house in Bromley, [otherwise Bromleage] 2 Cal. Sept. 1057. (13. Edw. Conf.) was
honourably interred o in the Monastery here at
Coventre, before mentioned, unto which he bequeathed p it, with a great quantity of Gold and
Silver. By some Authors he is called Comes Lei-
cestrie; but 'tis plain, by what I have already
cited, that it should be Cestrie q.

And now before I proceed, I have a word more
to say of the noble Countess Godeva; which is,
that besides her devout advancement of that pi-
ous work of his, in founding this magnificent Monastery (for my Author r says it was instigante
uxore sua Godeva) omnem thesaurum (saith another f) eidem Ecclesiæ contulit, &c. She gave her
whole treasure thereto, and sent for skilfull Gold-
smiths; who, with all the Gold and Silver she
had, made Crosses, Images of Saints, and other
curious ornaments, which she devoutly disposed
thereto. Neither did her zeal to God's service and
honour rest there; for, over and above all this, she
built s the monastery of Stow near Lincoln, de-
dicating it to the blessed Virgin; and endow'd u in
with the Lordships of Newark, Flatburgh, and
Hartinewelle, giving possession of them by a fair
Jewell, and rich Bracelets curiously wrought, as
her Charter imports; whereunto were witnesses
K. Edw. the Conf. himself, Aldred Archb. of
York, Wlfwi B. of Dorchester, E. Leofrik, her
husband, with divers more great Earls and others.

But I am not certain of the time when she dy-
ed; neither do the particular of all the lands, which
the Earl her husband and she had, any where appear, inasmuch as there are but part of them pointed at in Domesday Book. Those in this County, which that Record mentions to have been held
by her in Edw. the Conf. time, were Coventre,
Alpath, Atherston, Barthill and Ansty, Kines-
bury, Ansty and Folkhull, Salford and Bick-
mersh. w all which, except the two last, were fer-

Fig. 46. DUGDALE's *Warwickshire*. (Copyright: Longmans.)

and historical investigation. Certainly these works have retained far more of a value in local history than similar old works in general history. This is, perhaps, on account of the large numbers of contemporary illustrations and maps they mostly contain, which depict places at particular times; perhaps, despite their "class" bias by modern standards, and complete absence of treatment of economic conditions, for their tremendous topographical detail. Dugdale is among the better of the county histories, especially the second edition, revised by William Thomas (2 vols., 1730). Following a typical red and black title page is a dedication to "the gentry of Warwickshire" and another to the Bishop of Worcester. The preface claims that the author "spent the chiefest of my time for much more than twenty years, diligently searching into the vast treasuries of publique records". Arrangement is by the *Hundred*, the main local division of counties in England before the new arrangements of the later nineteenth century. The work is mostly concerned with the descent of individual manors, and there is much information on families. The treatment of Coventry covers both history and topography in great detail, and there are interesting "prospects", as well as some portraits, views of seats, etc. It is fair to say that, where there is an old county history, it must be the starting point for almost all subsequent work.

V.C.H., 6 vols. and index, 1904–, In progress.

Westmorland

WHELLAN, W., *The History and Topography of the Counties of Cumberland and Westmorland*, Whellan, Pontefract, 1860.
Hist. Mon. Comm., 1 vol., 1936.

Wiltshire

GODDARD, E. H. (comp.), *Wiltshire Bibliography*, Wilts. Education Committee, Trowbridge, 1929.
HOARE, *Sir* R. C., *The Ancient History of Wiltshire*, 2 vols., W. Muller and others, 1812–21.

V.C.H., 8 vols., 1953–, In progress.

Worcestershire

BURTON, J. R. and PEARSON, F. S., *Bibliography of Worcestershire*, 3 parts, Parker, Oxford, 1898–1907.

NASH, T., *Collections for the History of Worcestershire*, 2 vols., White, 1781–99.

V.C.H., 4 vols. and index, 1901–26.

Yorkshire

YORKSHIRE ARCHAEOLOGICAL SOCIETY, *Catalogue of the Printed Books*, 2 vols., the Society, Wakefield, 1935–6. There are individual lists on Leeds, Sheffield, etc.

ALLEN, T., *A New and Complete History of the County of York*, 6 vols., Hinton, 1828–31.

V.C.H., General, 3 vols. and index, 1907–25.

V.C.H., N. Riding, 2 vols. and index, 1914–25.

V.C.H., City of York, 1 vol., 1961.

Hist. Mon. Comm., 1 vol., 1964.

There are regional works by G. Poulson on Holderness, J. D. Whitaker on Craven and Richmondshire, and J. Hunter on Hallamshire, etc.

Isle of Man

CUBBON, W. (comp.), *A Bibliographical Account of Works Relating to the Isle of Man*, 2 vols., Oxford Univ. Press, 1933–9.

TRAIN, J., *An Historical and Statistical Account of the Isle of Man*, 2 vols., Quiggin, Douglas, 1845.

Channel Islands

ANSTED, D. T. and LATHAM, R. G., *The Channel Islands*, 3rd edition, Allen, 1893.

Scotland

MITCHELL, *Sir* A. and CASH, C. G., *A Contribution to the Bibliography of Scottish Topography*, 2 vols., Edinburgh Univ. Press, 1917.

HANCOCK, P. D. (comp.), *A Bibliography of Works Relating to Scotland, 1916–50*, 2 vols., Edinburgh Univ. Press, 1960.

Hist. Mon. Comm., Berwick (1909), Caithness (1911), Dumfriesshire (1920), East Lothian (1924), Edinburgh (1951), Fife, Kinross and Clackmannan (1933), Galloway, 2 vols. (1912–14), Midlothian and West Lothian (1929), Orkney and Shetland, 3 vols. (1946), Outer Hebrides (1928), Roxburghshire, 2 vols. (1956), Sutherland (1911), Selkirk (1957), Stirlingshire, 2 vols. (1963).

Wales and Monmouthshire

DENBIGHSHIRE COUNTY LIBRARY, *Bibliography of the County*, 3 vols., and *Supplement*, County Library, Ruthin, 1935–59.

FLINT COUNTY LIBRARY, *Bibliography of the County of Flint*, part 1, *Biographical Sources*, Flint County Library, 1953.

BRADNEY, J. A., *The History of Monmouthshire*, 4 vols., Hughes and Clarke, 1907–29.

Hist. Mon. Comm., Montgomery (1911), Flint (1912), Radnor (1913), Denbigh (1914), Carmarthen (1917), Merioneth (1921), Pembroke (1925), Anglesey (1937), Caernarvonshire, 3 vols. (1956–64).

Ireland

O'NEILL, T. P., *Sources of Irish Local History*, Library Association of Ireland, Dublin, 1958. See also A. R. Eager (above p. 86).

THE BRITISH COMMONWEALTH

Although the British Empire may have been dissolved, and the British Commonwealth be a somewhat nebulous entity, we may fitly conclude this chapter with some account of general works dealing with it, leaving individual parts of it to be treated along with independent states in the next chapter. Apart from Russia and most of South America, there is not a large land area anywhere in the world that is not concerned at some point in its development with the history of the British Empire, and with the governmental policy known as colonialism. The views of the newly independent territories as to their history differ widely from those of their former administrators so that in studying the colonial history of any nation one must take into account the background of the writer; it is almost impossible to write unbiased colonial history, and the subject is one which excites great political and racial feeling. The best introductory bibliography is, perhaps, W. P. Morrell, *British Overseas Expansion and the History of the Commonwealth* (Historical Association, 1961), a revision of earlier bibliographies. Like the Historical Association publication already illustrated (Fig. 20), it is selective, but clear and authoritative. The value of this and the other Historical Association bibliographies referred to in this book cannot be over-estimated; their level is right for the student with some general historical knowledge beginning to specialize on a particular topic. The arrangement is an "imperialistic" one, the first British Empire (the present U.S.A., etc.) being followed by Canada, Australia, New Zealand and (the now republican) South Africa. Asia, the Caribbean and the Pacific Islands follow. There is a section on British Imperial policy and slavery; atlases and the now independent Middle East states conclude the main headings. A. R. Hewitt's *Guide to Resources for Commonwealth Studies in London* (Athlone Press, 1957), dealing very considerably with manuscript materials, will be considered at p. 221, but the great Royal Empire Society's *Subject Catalogue* (4 vols., Royal Empire Society, 1930–7) cannot be omitted in any treatment of bibliographies of printed material (the biography catalogue has already been discussed above, pp. 83–4). Not only does it treat the pre-war history of the Empire both generally (Vol. 1) and by areas, but it also includes references to numerous articles, individual parts of collected volumes, etc., as well as to published works. Comprehensive works on the Empire as a whole include the *Cambridge History of the British Empire* (8 vols. in 9, Cambridge Univ. Press, 1929–59) not only the fullest treatment of the subject but valuable as are the other Cambridge histories for its lengthy bibliographies, and W. K. Hancock's *Survey of British Commonwealth Affairs* (2 vols., Oxford Univ. Press, 1937–42). For economic history the fullest work is L. C. A. and C. M. Knowles' *Economic Development of the British Overseas Empire* (3 vols., Routledge, 1924–36).

CHAPTER 4

Individual Countries

INTRODUCTION

It may be said that one of the more original aims of this book is to lessen the disparity in difficulty between readers who have and have not access to old-established libraries and comprehensive bookshops. Many of the works mentioned in the first three chapters are by no means common, but at least there are plenty of substitute works dealing with the particular aspects of biography and history covered—and in a book so much of whose scope consists in the listing of bibliographies there is little excuse for the student who does not do a little investigation for himself. It is a different story when we wish to investigate, let us say, Mexico, Monaco or Vietnam. There may have been a bibliography or a recent comprehensive work, but it is perhaps unavailable, or in a language we cannot read. We must then fall back on the lessons already learned —if there is no specific guide, then consult a universal one or a general encyclopaedia; if not those, then one of the general guides described in Chapter 1. Recall Chandler's opening sentence (*How to Find Out*, p. 1): "Information for an educational project, a doctoral dissertation, an industrial investigation or a general inquiry may be obtained from one of the following sources:

1. Books.
2. Articles in encyclopedias, handbooks, etc.
3. Yearbooks.
4. Periodicals.
5. Newspapers.

6. Documents.
7. Local Experts and Consultants.
8. National Experts and Consultants.
9. International Experts and Consultants.

"For some types of inquiry, only one of the above sources needs to be consulted. For many inquiries, all the above sources must be explored." In considering historical works, remember the inevitability of bias, and do not embark on a detailed study of some far distant place unless you are prepared either to go there, or to read very widely about it.

We have already stated (above, p. 6) that general bibliographies, either of authors or subjects, find no place in this book, though for countries where bibliographies of history are few or scarce, we are driven back on them, with more excuse, perhaps, as all that is past is history. If, therefore, we are really unable to find what we require we may derive some information from (Fig. 47) R. L. Collison's *Bibliographical Services Throughout the World, 1950–59* (UNESCO, Paris, 1961), which at the least may provide an address to which further inquiries may be directed. It is, unfortunately, like most works depending on contributions from a wide range of sources, very uneven in its different parts, as shown by the treatment accorded to Haiti and Holy See on the page reproduced.

This chapter sets out to give for the five continents and their constituent countries, examples of retrospective and current bibliographies of biography and history together with a few comprehensive works. The countries most closely connected with the Anglo-Saxon tradition—the U.S.A., the older Commonwealth countries, and also the nearer European civilizations, are given fullest treatment. For the countries not adequately represented and for further comment, one must have recourse to Walford, Winchell or one of the great general encyclopaedias.

AFRICA

One cannot keep pace with the changing political divisions of Africa, and so any Who's Who becomes quickly out of date.

REPUBLIC OF GUINEA

See Republic of Dahomey, page 59.

HAITI

There is no National Commission for Bibliography or similar body to supervise the bibliographical work in Haiti.

Library co-operation exists on an informal day-to-day basis only. There are no union catalogues of books, no union lists of serials, and no bibliographical centre.

Legal deposit of printed material is not compulsory in Haiti and there is consequently no national current bibliography. In 1951 the National Correspondent published his *Dictionnaire de bibliographie haïtienne* (Washington, Scarecrow Press. x + 1052 p.), and this has been kept up to date on cards with the object of publishing supplements locally.

There are no indexes to the contents of periodicals, and the nearest approach to a current bibliography of a special subject has been Maurice A. Lubin's *Productions haïtiennes de 1942 à 1952* (Port-au-Prince, the author, 1952, 27 p.). The only other bibliographical publication of note issued during the period has been R. Piquion's *Archives* (Port-au-Prince, Ed. Deschamps, 1954, 33 p.).

No training in bibliography, or librarianship, is available in Haiti.

HOLY SEE

The work of the Holy See in the bibliographical field is well known and, during the period under review, several important contributions to research and scholarship have been published, notably:

Catalogo delle pubblicazioni periodiche esistenti in varie biblioteche di Roma e Firenze. 1955. xiii + 495 p.

Le pitture geografiche murali della terza loggia e di altre sale vaticane. 1955. viii + 42 p.

DEVREESSE, Robert. *Les manuscrits grecs de l'Italie méridionale: histoire, classement, paléographie.* 1955. 67 p.

PRATESI, Alessandro. *Carte latine di abbazie calabresi provenlienti da l'archivio Aldobrandini.* 1958. iv + 584 p.

Codices Vaticana latini: codices 1135-1266; recensuit M.-H. Laurent, 1958. (8), 555 p.

78

Fig. 47. COLLISON, R. L., *Bibliographical Services Throughout the World.* (Copyright: UNESCO.)

R. Segal, *Political Africa; a Who's Who of Personalities and Parties* (Stevens, 1961), is necessarily already out of date, but gives information not available elsewhere; *The Central and East African Who's Who* (the Publishers, Salisbury, 1956), is a somewhat older survey of parts of the region; both these, of course, are from the European viewpoint. There is an old good German encyclopaedia, H. Schnee's *Deutsches Kolonial-Lexikon* (Quelle, Leipzig, *c.* 1920), which deals very fully with the former German African colonies; the Belgian viewpoint is given in M. L. Bevel's *Le dictionnaire colonial* (2 parts, Guyot, Brussels, 1950–1). Recent happenings are covered in *Africa, a handbook*, 2nd edition C. Legum (*Handbooks to the Modern World*) Blond, 1966. *African Abstracts* (Int. African Institute, London, vols. 1–, 1950–) is supported by UNESCO; it analyses some sixty current periodicals. Turning to "straight" bibliographies, a good select list is the United States Library of Congress, European Affairs Division, *Introduction to Africa; a Selective Guide* (University Press of Washington, Washington, 1952). The Library of Congress has also published in Washington *Africa South of the Sahara, 1951–57* (1957), and *North and Northeast Africa, 1951–57* (1957), both edited by Helen F. Conover, which supplement the 1952 *Introduction to Africa*; A. M. L. Robinson, *A Bibliography of African Bibliographies Covering Territories South of the Sahara* (4th edition, South African Public Library, Cape Town, 1961); France, État-Major de l'armée, *L'Afrique française du nord* (4 vols., Imprimerie Nationale, Paris, 1930–5); and E. Lewin, *Annotated Bibliography of Recent Publications on Africa South of the Sahara* (Royal Empire Society, 1943), give three different nationalistic approaches, and Mary Holdsworth has published *Soviet African Studies, 1918–1959* (Royal Institute of International Affairs, 1961 (continuation by the Central Asian Research Centre, 1959–61, London, 1963)).

French interests are covered by the *Encyclopédie coloniale et maritime* (Éditions de l'Empire Française, Paris, 1947–, In progress) and from the same publisher, *Encyclopédie de l'Afrique française* (1953–, In progress). P. Carson has produced *Materials for West African History in the Archives of Belgium and Holland* (Athlone Press,

1962). Lastly, we may refer to a periodical, *Revue encyclopédique de l'Afrique, politique, economique, sociale, culturelle et scientifique*, a monthly dealing with the former French Africa.

The African races themselves have so far produced little history, though they are certainly not satisfied with its presentation by Europeans. In October 1964, Mr. Mboya, Kenya's Minister of Justice, said that a number of "valueless" European history books would have to be burnt because Kenya schools had taught a "European version of history" in the past. There were graduates in Kenya who knew nothing of African customs. The Ghana Academy of Sciences is preparing the *Encyclopaedia Africana* (10 vols.), which will no doubt present an African view.

Algeria

FRANCE, MINISTÈRE DU SAHARA, *Essai de bibliographie du Sahara français et des regions avoisinantes*, 2nd edition, Arts et Métiers Graphiques, Paris, 1960.

Central African Republic

INTERNATIONAL AFRICAN INSTITUTE, *Select Annotated Bibliography of Tropical Africa*, Twentieth Century Fund, New York, 1956.

Like other works relating to this region of constantly changing political boundaries, these deal with a wide area.

Congo

ARTIGUE, P., *Qui sont les leaders congolais?*, 2nd edition, Edition Europe–Afrique, Brussels, 1961.

INSTITUT ROYAL COLONIAL BELGE, *Biographie coloniale belge*, Academie Royale, Brussels, vols. 1–, In progress. A serial work, with cumulative indexes in the later vols.

Encyclopédie du Congo Belge, 3 vols., Éditions Bieleveld, Brussels, 1950–3.

HEYSE, T. and BERLAGE, J. (editors), *Documentation générale sur le Congo et le Ruanda-Urundi*, Campenhout, Brussels, 1958–60. See also under Belgium.

Egypt

DAWSON, WARREN R., *Who Was Who in Egyptology; a Biographical Index of Egyptologists*, Egypt Exploration Society, 1951.

Who's Who in the U.A.R. and the Near East, 24th edition, the publishers, Cairo, 1959. Arab bias and coverage.

VANDIER, J. V., *Manuel d'archéologie égyptienne*, Picard, Paris, 1952–, In progress.

POSENER, G., *Dictionnaire de la civilisation égyptienne*, Hazan, Paris, 1959. English translation 1962.

JANSSEN, S. M. A. (comp.), *Annual Egyptological Bibliography*, Brill, Leyden, vols. 1–, 1948–, In progress.

Ethiopia

FUMAGALLI, G., *Bibliographia etiopica*, Hoepli, Milan, 1893. Continuation by S. Zanutto, 1929–32.

Ghana

CARDINALL, A. W., *Bibliography of the Gold Coast*, Government Press, Accra, 1932.

JOHNSON, A. F., *A Bibliography of Ghana*, Longmans, London, 1963.

Libya

HILL, R. W., *A Bibliography of Libya*, Durham Colleges, Durham, 1959.

Madagascar

GRANDIDIER, G. and JOUCLA, E., *Bibliographie de Madagascar*, 3 vols., Société d'éditions géographiques, Paris, 1905–57. Covers earliest times to 1955.

Malawi

See Nyasaland and Rhodesia.

Mauritius

Dictionnaire de biographie mauricienne, Société de l'histoire de l'Île, Port Louis, 1941–, In progress. Excludes living persons.

TOUSSAINT, A. and ADOLPHE, H., *Bibliography of Mauritius, 1502–1954*, Government of Mauritius, Port Louis, 1956. Annual supplements published.

Morocco

CENIVAL, P. DE and others, *Bibliographie marocaine, 1923–33*, Larose, Paris, 1937. Continued in periodical *Hespéris*.

Nigeria

Who's Who in Nigeria, Nigerian Printing Co., Lagos, 1956.

HARRIS, W. J. (comp.), *Books about Nigeria*, 5th edition, University Press, Ibadan, 1963.

Nyasaland and Rhodesia

Who's Who of Southern Africa, Wooton & Gibson, Johannesburg, 1963. Irregular. Includes also the former Federation of Rhodesia (Zambia), Nyasaland (Malawi) and Central and East Africa.

CENTRAL AFRICAN FEDERATION, *A Select Bibliography of Recent Publications*, 1960.

Sierra Leone

LUKE, *Sir* H., *Bibliography of Sierra Leone*, 2nd edition, Oxford Univ. Press, 1925.

South Africa

Who's Who of Southern Africa, Wooton and Gibson, Johannesburg, 1963. Irregular.

ROSENTHAL, E. (comp.), *Encyclopaedia of Southern Africa*, 3rd edition, Warne, 1965. Deals also with the Central African Federation, S.W. Africa, Mozambique and the High Commission Territories. Current coloured personnel are excluded.

NICHOLSON, G., *German Settlers in South Africa; a Bibliography*, the University, Cape Town, 1962.

(Fig. 48), Mendelssohn, S., *Mendelssohn's South African Bibliography*, 2 vols., Routledge, 1910. Primarily based on a comprehensive library, and by far the fullest South African bibliography. There are proposals to bring it up to date. For later works, general bibliographies must be consulted as for works in Afrikaans (Nienaber, P. J., *Bibliographie van Afrikanse Boeke*, Voortrekkerpers bpk, Johannesburg, 1943).

Sudan

HILL, R. L., *A Biographical Dictionary of the Anglo-Egyptian Sudan*, Clarendon Press, Oxford, 1951.

HILL, R. L., *A Bibliography of the Anglo-Egyptian Sudan*, Oxford Univ. Press, 1939.

NASRI, A. EL N. H., *A Bibliography of the Sudan, 1938–1958*, University College, 1960. Typescript. Continues Hill.

Swaziland

ARNHEIM, J. (comp.), *Swaziland, a bibliography*, School of Librarianship, Capetown, 1963.

or " rising," of 1881, is exceedingly limited, and the author considered that it was advisable that an account of the earlier war should be published in view of the grave state of affairs in South Africa. Mr. Haggard maintained that, " Difficult as it is to make the fact understood among a proportion of the home electorate and publicists, it cannot be stated too often or too clearly that this war which is to come is a war that was forced upon us by the Boers in their blind ignorance and conceit. The mass of them believe . . . that they are a match for the British Empire."

*HAGGARD, H. RIDER : She. A History of Adventure. By H. Rider Haggard. . . . With thirty-two illustrations by Maurice Griffenhagen and Charles H. M. Kerr. Longmans, Green & Co. London, New York, and Bombay. 310 pp. Cr. 8vo. 1900.

The beauty of the plot, and the originality of the character of the heroine, with her wondrous charm of power and loveliness, together with the intense interest with which the development of the story is invested, have made this romance one of the most popular of Mr. Haggard's novels. The scene, like many other tales by this author, is laid in Central South-East Africa, but the language of Ayesha's subjects is represented as being Arabic, and the poetic declamations which form a feature of the work are in the style adopted by the ancient Arabs. The first edition was dedicated to Mr. Andrew Lang and published in 1886, since when many editions have been issued, and a dramatised version has been put on the stage.

*HAGGARD, H. RIDER : The Witch's Head. By H. Rider Haggard. . . . With sixteen full-page illustrations by Charles Kerr. Reproduced by Boussod, Valadon et Cie., of Paris. New impression. Longmans, Green & Co., London, New York, and Bombay. viii + 344 pp. Cr. 8vo. 1900.

A tale of fighting and hunting in the Transvaal and Zululand at the time of the first annexation of the South African Republic and the war with Cetywayo.

*HAGGARD, H. RIDER : Swallow. A Tale of the Great Trek. By H. Rider Haggard. New impression, reissue. Longmans, Green and Co. London, New York, and Bombay. viii + 348 pp. Cr. 8vo. 1901.

The author has been very skilful in the delineation of the complex and curious character of the Boers in the interior, the inbred hatred they possessed for the British, their constant brooding over real and fancied grievances, and the mixture of cunning and piety which appears to have been so ingrained in their nature. The evil results of the admixture of black blood into the sturdy Boer race are well exemplified in the character of " Swart Piet," a by no means impossible or even improbable sketch, whilst the occult knowledge and prescience represented in the person of the witch-doctor-chieftainess throw some light on the superstitions and methods of thought of the aboriginal natives.

*HAGGARD, H. RIDER : Black Heart and White Heart, and other Stories. By H. Rider Haggard. Reissue. Longmans, Green and Co. London, New York, and Bombay. xii + 414 pp. Cr. 8vo. 1903.

This volume was first printed in May 1900, and the first story is an exciting tale of Zululand in the time of Cetywayo. " Elissa ; or, The Doom of Zimbabwe " is a romance having for its scene the mysterious ruins in

Fig. 48. MENDELSSOHN, S., *Mendelssohn's South Africa Bibliography*.
(Copyright: Routledge.)

Tanganyika. Tanzania

Handbook of Tanganyika, 2nd edition, Government Printer, Dar es Salaam, 1958. Has bibliography.

Zambia

See Nyasaland and Rhodesia.

AMERICA

Whereas North America mainly follows the Anglo-Saxon tradition, the influence of such important minorities as the Red Indians, the Maya and the French Canadians should not be overlooked. In South America, tradition is mainly Spanish or Portuguese. Like Africa, the American continent has important racial problems, with the culture of the Negro population as yet inadequately reflected in the literature. In this section we shall deliberately give the fullest coverage to the United States. Firstly, however, we must look at those works which deal with more than one nationality, and which must often be substituted for the unwritten or unavailable national bibliography, etc., of biography or history. Not a great deal has been published on the American continent as a whole, though one comprehensive work, not unnaturally, is Mexican: the Instituto Panamericano de geografia e historia's *Program of the History of America* (18 vols., the Institute, Mexico City, 1953). Archaeology is covered by *Abstracts of New World Archaeology* (vol. 1–, 1960–, In progress), beginning in 1959. This is published in Washington by the Society for American Archaeology, but covers the individual countries of South America as well. Two comprehensive library catalogues are the New York Public Library's *Dictionary Catalog of the History of the Americas* (28 vols., Hall, Boston, 1961), and the Newberry Library, Chicago *Catalog of the Edward E. Ayer Collection of Americana and American Indians* (8 vols., Hall, Boston, 1961). The second catalogue is stronger on early items; the first on entries for articles in periodicals. Note also J. Sabin's *Bibliotheca Americana* (29 vols., Sabin, New York,

1928–36), and C. Leclerc's *Bibliotheca Americana* (Maisonneuve, Paris, 1878, with supplements; reissued 1961).

Antarctica as a whole is covered by R. D. Hayton's *National Interests in Antarctica; an Annotated Bibliography* (Government Printing Office, Washington, 1959). This is an annotated list which deals with history and associated subjects. There is a comprehensive *Who's Who in Latin America* (3rd edition, 7 parts, Marquis, Chicago, *c.* 1945–51), but as this is arranged by individual countries, several alphabets have to be checked if the country of origin of the biographee is not known. It contains some 8000 lives covering twenty republics. Most of the works on groups of countries relate to Latin America, and there is an *Encyclopédie de l'Amerique latine, politique, economique, culturelle* (Presses universitaires de France, Paris, 1954), though this is not in systematic order, and is unindexed. Historiography is covered by A. C. Wilgus' *Histories and Historians of Hispanic America* (Wilson, New York, 1942). An excellent brief bibliography for English-speaking readers is R. A. Humphrey's *Latin American History* (Oxford Univ. Press, 1958). Even shorter is S. Pendle's *South America* (National Book League, 1957). There is an annual *Handbook of Latin American Studies* (University of Florida Press, Gainesville, vols. 1–, 1936–); this is annotated and deals with the "fringe" subjects of anthropology, international relations, labour and social welfare, law and sociology, as well as history. Recent volumes include special articles. More specialized is H. Kantor's *Bibliography of Unpublished Doctoral Dissertations and Masters' Theses Dealing with the Governments, Politics, and International Relations of Latin America* (American Political Science Association, Gainesville, Florida, 1953). More up to date than Humphreys, but less accurate, is a select guide by S. A. Bayitch, *Latin America; a Bibliographical Guide* (University of Miami, Coral Gables, Florida, 1961). The Soviet viewpoint is given in L. Okinshevich and C. J. Gorokhoff's *Latin America in Soviet Writings, 1945–1958* (University of California, Los Angeles, 1959), and there is a classified abstracting service, *Latin America in Periodical Literature* (vols. 1–, 1962–, In progress), from the same publishers. About 125 abstracts are given in each monthly issue,

English, Spanish, and Portuguese language magazines being covered. Finally, before turning to individual countries we may mention the forthcoming publication of *The Catalogue of the Hispanic Society of America* (10 vols., Hall, Boston). This library contains more than 100,000 volumes, including early printed items. One Who's Who covers many areas for which no separate guide exists. It is the *Pan-Pacific Who's Who, 1940–1* (Honolulu Star-bulletin, Hawaii, 1940). It covers Alaska, British Columbia, California, Canal Zone, Hawaii and Oregon.

Argentina

UDAONDO, E., *Diccionario biográfico colonial argentino*, Huarpes, Buenos Aires, 1945.

UDAONDO, E., *Diccionario biográfico argentino*, Casa edition, Buenos Aires, 1938. The first work covers the period up to 1810, the second the following period.

PARKER, W. B., *Argentines of Today*, 2 vols., Hispanic Society of America, Buenos Aires, 1920.

Quién es quién en la Argentina, 6th edition, Kraft, Buenos Aires, 1955.

Gran enciclopedia Argentina, Ediar, Buenos Aires, vols. 1–, 1956–, In progress.

CARBIA, R. D., *Historia critica de la historio grafía argentina*, Imp. Lopez, Buenos Aires, 1939.

Diccionario historico argentino, 6 vols., Ediciones Historicas Argentinas, Buenos Aires, 1953–4.

Bolivia

PARKER, W. B., *Bolivians of Today*, 2nd edition, Hispanic Society of America, 1922.

Quien es quien en Bolivia, the publishers, La Paz, 1942.

Brazil

SEGADAS MACHADO-GUIMARAES, A. DE., *Diccionario bio-bibliográphico Brasiliero*, the author, Rio de Janeiro, 1938.

Quem é Quem no Brasil, Sociedade Brasiliera, São Paulo, 1955.

Teixeira de Oliveira, J., *Diccionario brasileiro de batas históricas*, edited by Pan-Americana, Rio de Janeiro, 1944.

Borba de Moraes, R., *Manual bibliográfico de estudos brasileiros*, Souza, Rio de Janiero, 1949. Continued by *Serie bibliográfica de estudos brasileiros*, 1954–, In progress.

Brazil, Comissão de Estudo dos Textos da Historia do Brazil, *Bibliografia de História do Brasil, 1943–*, Imp. Nac., Rio de Janeiro, 1944–, In progress.

Pierson, D., *Survey of the Literature on Brazil of Sociological Significance published up to 1940*, Harvard Univ. Press, Cambridge, Massachusetts, 1945.

British Guiana

Delgh, C. N. and Roth, V., *Who is Who in British Guiana*, Daily Chronicle, Georgetown, 1945–8.

Canada

Wallace, W. S., *The Dictionary of Canadian Biography*, 2nd edition, 2 vols., Macmillan Co., Toronto, 1945.

Standard Dictionary of Canadian Biography; the Canadian Who Was Who, 2 vols., Trans Canada Press, Toronto, 1934–8.

Les biographies françaises d'Amerique, Journalistes Associés, Sherbrooke, 1950.

Who's Who in Canada, International Press, Toronto, 1910–, Irregular.

Newfoundland Who's Who, the publishers, St. John's, 1952.

Burpee, L. J. S., *Oxford Encyclopaedia of Canadian History*, Clarendon Press, Oxford, 1926.

Staton, F. M. and Tremaine, M. (editors), *A Bibliography of Canadiana, being items in the Public Library of Toronto*, Public Library, Toronto, 1934. *Supplement*, 1959.

LeJeune, L., *Dictionnaire général de biographie, histoire, littérature . . . du Canada*, 2 vols., Université d'Ottawa, Ottawa, 1931.

WRONG, G. M. and others, *Review of Historical Publications Relating to Canada, 1896–1918*, 22 vols., Briggs, University of Toronto, 1897–1919. Continued in *Canadian Historical Review*, the principal Canadian periodical.

GAGNON, P., *Essai de bibliographie canadienne*, 2 vols., l'auteur, Quebec, 1895–1913.

GARIGUE, P., *A Bibliographical Introduction to the Study of French Canada*, McGill University, Montreal, 1956.

PEEL, B. B., *A Bibliography of the Prairie Provinces to 1953*, University of Toronto Press, Toronto, 1956.

Encyclopedia of Canada, University Associates of Canada, Toronto, 1935–7.

GAMEAU, F. X., *Histoire du Canada*, 5th edition, 2 vols., Alean, Paris, 1913–20.

Caribbean Islands

See also Cuba and Puerto Rica.

RAGATZ, L. J., *A Guide for the Study of British Caribbean History, 1763–1834*, Government Printing Office, Washington, 1932.

Who's Who, Jamaica, British West Indies, 8th edition, Who's Who, Kingston, 1954.

British Caribbean; Who, What, Why? Bell and Bain, Glasgow, 1955–6. Irregular.

HISS, P. H., *A Selective Guide to the English Literature on the Netherlands West Indies; with a Supplement on British Guiana*, Netherlands Information Bureau, New York, 1943.

NEW YORK PUBLIC LIBRARY, *List of Works Relating to the West Indies*, the Library, New York, 1912.

REID, C. F., *Bibliography of the Virgin Islands of the United States*, Wilson, New York, 1941.

BENJAMINS, H. D. and SNELLEMAN, J. F., *Encyclopaedie van Nederlandsch West Indie*, Nijhoff, s' Gravenhage, 1914–17.

Chile

FIGUEROA, V., *Diccionario historico, biográfico y bibliográfico de Chile, 1800–1930*, 5 vols. in 4, Balcells, Santiago, 1925–31.

Diccionario Biográfico de Chile, La Nacion, Santiago, 1940.

PARKER, W. B., *Chileans of To-day*, Putnam, New York, 1920.

ANRIQUE REYES, N. and SILVA ARRIGADA, L. I., *Ensayo de una bibliográfia histórica i jeográfica de Chile*, Imp. Barcelona, Santiago, 1902.

Colombia

ASPINA, J., *Diccionario biográfico y bibliográfico de Colombia*, 3 vols., De Cromos, Bogota, 1927–39.

Quién es quién en Venezuela, Panama, Ecuador, Colombia, Perry, Bogota, 1952.

GIRALDO JARAMILLO, G., *Bibliográfia de bibliográfia colombianas*, 2nd edition, Instituto Caro y Cuervo, Bogota, 1960.

Costa Rica

LINES, J. A., *Bibliográfia antropológica aborigen de Costa Rica*, the publishers, San José, 1943.

Cuba

PERAZA SARAUSA, F., *Diccionario biográfico cubano*, the publishers, Havana, vols. 1–, 1951–, Irregular.

Cuba en la mano; enciclopedia popular ilustrada, the publishers, Havana, 1940.

HAVANA. BIBLIOTECA NACIONAL, *Impresos relativos a Cuba editadas en las Estados unidos de Norte américa*, Ministerio de Educación, Havana, 1956.

Ecuador

PEREZ MARCHANT, BRAULIO, *Diccionario biográfico del Ecuador*, Escuela de Artes y Oficios, Quito, 1928.

French Guiana

ABONNE, E. and others, *Bibliographie de la Guyane française*, Editions Larose, Paris, vol. 1–, 1957–, In progress.

Guiana

See British Guiana and French Guiana.

Martinique

GAZIN, J., *Elements de bibliographie générale methodique et historique de la martinique*, Impr. Antillaire, Fort-de-France, 1926.

Mexico

MESTRE CHIGLIAZZA, M., *Efemérides biográficas*, Porrua, Mexico City, 1945.

PERAL, M. A., *Diccionario biográfico mexicano*, 2 vols. and appendix, edited by P.A.C., Ed. P.A.C., Mexico City, *c.* 1944.

LEDUC, A. and others, *Diccionario de geografia, historia y biográfia mexicanas*, Bouret, Mexico City, 1910.

GONZALEZ, L., *Fuentes de la historia contemporánea de Mexico*, El Colegio de Mexico, Mexico City, vols. 1–, 1961–, In progress. Projected to cover 1910–40.

CALIFORNIA STATE LIBRARY, SACRAMENTO, *Catalogue of Mexican Pamphlets in the Sutro Collection*, and supplements. 14 parts, California State Library, San Francisco, 1939–41.

VALLE, R. H., *Bibliografía Maya*, D.F., Mexico City, 1937–41.

RAMOS, R., *Bibliografía de la historia de Mexico*, Instituto Panamericano de Geografia e Historica, Mexico City, 1956.

KIBBE, P. R., *A Guide to Mexican History*, Minutiae Mexicana, Mexico City, 1964.

Paraguay

PARKER, W. B., *Paraguayans of To-day*, 2nd edition, Hispanic Society of America, 1921.

Quien es quien en le Paraguay? the publishers, Buenos Aires, vols. 1–, 1945–, Irregular.

Peru

MENDIBURU, M. DE, *Diccionario histórico biográfico del Perú*, 2nd edition, 11 vols., Enrique Palacios, Lima, 1931–5. Appendices have appeared.

PARKER, W. B., *Peruvians of To-day*, the author, Lima, 1919.

TAURO, A., *Bibliografía peruana de historia, 1940–53*, Talleres graficos, Lima, 1953.

Puerto Rico

Quién es quién en Puerto Rico, Imp. Venezuela, San Juan, 1947.

Salvador

GARCIA, M. A., *Diccionario Histórico-Enciclopédico de la República de El Salvador*, La Luz, San Salvador, vols. 1–, 1927–, In progress.

U.S.A.

Despite the great amount of United Kingdom material dealing with the origins of the U.S.A., a vast amount of publishing has been done in the United States itself. The American people are extremely interested in their history, and particularly in their forebears who emigrated to what is now the U.S.A. There is usually a distinct difference of appearance between works of English and American origin, but many masterly works of scholarship have emanated from across the Atlantic; two especially we have mentioned, viz. Howe (pp. 49–51), and some of the comprehensive British period bibliographies (pp. 72–3). Generally, American scholars have more resources at their disposal than their British colleagues, such as travel allowances, greater sabbatical leave,

6

more generous reproduction techniques, so that the best American scholarship is now acquiring the reputation for thoroughness that used to be accorded to teutonic scholarship. (Fig. 49), American Council of Learned Societies, *Dictionary of American Biography* (20 vols., index, and 2 supplements, Scribner, New York, 1928–58) is similar in standard to the (English) *Dictionary of National Biography*. Its scope is not confined to citizens of the United States by birth or naturalization, but "three other restrictions were adopted: first, that no living persons should have biographies in the Dictionary; second, that no persons who had not lived in territory now known as the United States should be eligible; and third, that no British officers serving in America after the colonies had declared their independence should appear in the dictionary". The bibliographies are probably fuller than in the English work, as greater resources, provided originally by the *New York Times*, were at the editors' disposal.   "Actions, however beneficent or honourable, which are accompanied or are capable of accomplishment by many thousands of persons are actions of mediocrity, and lack the dimension which justifies the biographer's notice. The fact that a man is a devoted husband and father, an efficient school-master, an exemplary parish priest, gives him in itself no claim to biographic commemoration".   The dictionary with its two supplements includes nearly 15,000 articles of persons who died before 1940. More statement of opinion is allowed than in the *Dictionary of National Biography*; "the articles should be based as largely as possible on original sources; should be the product of fresh work; should eschew rhetoric, sentiment, and colouring matter generally, yet include careful characterization; should be free from the influence of partisan, local or family possessions" . . . and generally this aim has been achieved. An unusual feature is a series of six indexes of (a) contributors, (b) biographees with contributors' names, (c) birth places, (d) schools and colleges, (e) occupations, and (f) topics discussed in the lives. J. G. E. Hopkins has edited a *Concise Dictionary of American Biography* (Oxford Univ. Press, 1964), on the model of the *Concise National Cyclopaedia of American Biography* (White, New York, vols. 1–, 1892–, In progress), a

the Medical and Chirurgical Faculty of Maryland at Baltimore, the state medical society which Archer helped to found in 1799. He was on its examining board and a member of the executive committee. In 1801 he was a presidential elector and served as a representative in Congress from that date until 1807. He contributed a few papers to the *Medical Repository* of New York and introduced senega as a remedy in the treatment of croup. His health began to fail at the time of the completion of his service in Congress; he had a partial paralysis and gave up active pursuits. He died suddenly, probably from another cerebral hemorrhage, while sitting in his chair at his home in Harford County.

Archer was married in 1766 to a daughter of Thomas Harris, of the family that founded Harrisburg, Pa., by whom he had ten children, of whom five studied medicine. Several portraits of him are extant; one in the court-house at Belair, Harford County, Md., a second in the hall of the Medical and Chirurgical Faculty at Baltimore, and a third in the State House at Annapolis, Md.

[The chief sources of information are the *Medic. Annals of Md.* (1903); articles by Eugene F. Cordell in the *Johns Hopkins Hospital Bull.* (1899 and 1902); J. Carson, *Hist. of the Medic. Dept. of the Univ. of Pa.* (1869); *Biog. Cong. Dir. 1744–1911* (1913); *Am. Archives,* ser. 4, vol. I, p. 403; vol. IV, p. 737; ser. 5, vol. II, p. 637.]

W. L. B.

ARCHER, SAMUEL (1771–Apr. 14, 1839), merchant, philanthropist, was born near the village of Columbus, Burlington County, N. J., and went to Philadelphia about 1794. In 1797 he married Elizabeth West, who was a member of the Society of Friends, and nine years his senior. The same year he began business in Philadelphia under the firm name of Archer & Newbold, described in the Philadelphia Directory as merchants. The following year he was engaged in the retail dry-goods trade, but in another twelvemonth was in the importing business. In 1804 he took in Robert L. Pittfield, an accountant, as partner, and the firm name was changed to Samuel Archer & Company, which, a few years later, became Archer & Bispham, Stacy B. Bispham entering the firm as the successor of Pittfield, who retired. Between the years 1800 and 1812, the greater part of the business in importations from India and China was transacted through Philadelphia and Archer's firm was among the largest importers of muslins from the East Indies. These goods were not then manufactured in this country. The house was also noted as an extensive importer of Chinese manufactures, but a great deal of Archer's business was in textiles of Brit-

ish make. So large a buyer was he and so scrupulous in all his business dealings, that it was currently said his credit in Europe was unlimited. "The business for the house in that day was immense, having reached in a single year over two million of dollars in amount" (Simpson, p. 20). In 1810–11 Archer made a visit to Europe to purchase goods. The War of 1812, which began soon after his return home, cut off the bulk of the foreign trade of the house, but after hostilities had ceased, with rare courage and business sagacity, he began to export to China American-made fabrics, the manufacture of which was just beginning here. He is credited with having been the first American merchant to export extensively American-made cotton goods to Asia. While fortune smiled upon many of his daring enterprises, it also, occasionally, frowned upon him, and he suffered several serious reverses, owing, it is said, to his generous disposition to place too much confidence in some concerns and men with whom he engaged in business. He took an active interest in the financial institutions of his adopted city, and was one of the original managers of the Philadelphia Saving Fund Society (1816), the first of its kind in the United States; and the same year he was elected a director of the Insurance Company of North America, the first marine insurance company organized in this country. In 1817 he was one of four wealthy men who presented a lot on which was erected the Philadelphia Orphan Asylum; his partner at that time, Robert Ralston, was another of the quartet. William D. Lewis, who furnished the sketch of his life which appeared in Simpson's book, wrote of him (p. 21) that he "held a prominent place among the enterprising merchants of our city for near half a century. When basking in the sunshine of great riches and prosperity, he possessed much simplicity of manners and an utter absence of all display. . . . Charity, benevolence, and uprightness seemed to be the natural qualities of his character exhibited through life." His portrait, painted by Anna C. Peale, and engraved by Samuel Sartain, pictures him in the quiet simplicity of the Quakers, whose ideals he made his own, although he was not a member of that religious society at the time of his marriage. He was buried, however, in a Friends' burial-ground in Philadelphia.

[Henry Simpson, *Lives of Eminent Philadelphians Now Deceased* (1859), portr.; Abraham Ritter, *Phila. and Her Merchants* (1860), p. 145; Jas. M. Willcox, *A Hist. of the Phila. Saving Fund Soc.* (1916); T. H. Montgomery, *A Hist. of the Insurance Company of North America* (1885). Manuscript records of the Society of Friends in Philadelphia are authority for some of the statements made.]

J. J.

Fig. 49. *The Dictionary of American Biography.* (Copyright: Scribner.)

rather unsystematic work, due to its various sequences. The coverage is much wider than that of the *D.A.B.*, but few bibliographies are given, and the lives are of journalistic origin in most cases. Over 40 vols. have appeared, and some have been revised, but the loose-leaf index volume is a valuable key to the whole work. The third large American retrospective biographical work is *Appleton's Cyclopaedia of American Biography* (7 vols., Appleton, New York, 1888–1900). About 18,000 lives are covered, and occasional illustrations (facsimile signatures, portraits) are given, as in the *National Cyclopaedia*.

Who's Who in America (Marquis, Chicago, vols. 1–, 1899–, biennial), includes persons selected because of their special prominence, or distinction, or those included arbitrarily because of their official position or public standing. Prominent non-Americans are included. Close on 50,000 entries are included in this enormous double-columned volume, which is based mainly on information supplied by the biographee. Not all entries are carried forward, but it is not necessary to retain the first 26 vols. as the deaths of persons in them are covered in 3 vols. of *Who Was Who in America*, by the same publishers, Vol. 1, 1897–1942; Vol. 2, 1943–50; Vol. 3, 1951–60. There is also a historical volume covering the years 1607–1896, but this is of course not based on personal entries. Contrary to the corresponding English work, the current volumes are brought up to date by monthly (recently quarterly) supplements; there is also a ten-year cumulative index.

Other biographical works of note include:

> MATTHEWS, W. (comp.), *American Diaries*, University of California Press, Berkeley, 1945. This covers printed diaries, 1629–1860.
>
> CATTELL, J., *Directory of American Scholars*, 3rd edition, Bowker, New York, 1957.
>
> *Who's Who in Colored America*, Burckel, New York, 1950.
>
> KAPLAN, L. and others, *Bibliography of American Autobiographies*, University of Wisconsin, Madison, 1961. Arranged by authors with subject index of biographees. Excludes diaries.

UNITED STATES LIBRARY OF CONGRESS, *Biographical Sources for the United States*, 1961. Analyses 163 collective biographies.
Who's Who of American Women, Marquis, Chicago, vols. 1–, 1958–, biennial.

Many works on regional and local biography in the United States have been published, including the following:

Who's Who in the East, Vol. 1, Marquis, Chicago, 1942–3–, 1943–, Irregular.

Who's Who in the Midwest, and *Who's Who in the South and South-west*, by the same publisher, are on similar lines. Marquis also publish *Who's Who in New England*, and *Who's Who in the West* (includes also W. Canada), at irregular intervals. These works contain far more entries relating to their areas than the parent *Who's Who in America*.

Who's Who in New York (City and State), 12th edition, Lewis, New York, 1952.

Tewkesbury's Who's Who in Alaska, Tewkesbury, Juneau, vols. 1–, 1947–, Irregular.

There are various retrospective bibliographies of the history of the United States, but first we may look at a bibliography of bibliographies, H. P. Beers' *Bibliographies in American History* (Wilson, New York, 1942), which includes over 11,000 bibliographies, both separately published and those included in other works. Political, diplomatic, local and other special aspects of American history are included. There are several lists of American historical societies, the most useful being C. Crittenden, and Doris Godard, *Historical Societies in the United States and Canada* (The American Association for State and Local History, Washington, 1944), which lists 904 national and local societies. L. W. Dunlap's *American Historical Societies, 1790–1860* (the author, Madison, Wisconsin, 1944) gives great detail on the sixty-five societies covered. More recent is the American Association for State and Local History, *Directory of Historical Societies and Agencies in the United States and Canada* (the publishers, Ohio, Columbia, 1956), but it gives little more than directory information. A useful though rather dated analysis of the publications of American historical societies is A. P. C. Griffin's *Bibliography of American Historical Societies* (Government Printing Office, Washington, 1907). This is arranged by societies, covers both the U.S.A. and Canada, and is continued in the relevant section of *Writings on American History* (see below). W. B. Kuehl has published *Dissertations in history; an index to dissertations in American Universities, 1873–1960*, Kentucky Univ. Press, Lexington, 1965.

The fullest American retrospective bibliography is probably J. Sabin, *Dictionary of Books Relating to America* (29 vols., Sabin, New York, 1868–92). This is an author list, covering some 190,000 references. Reviews are cited. Probably more useful and manageable is J. N. Larned's *The Literature of American History; a Bibliographical Guide* (American Library Association, Boston, 1902), which has critical annotations. E. Channing and others, *Guide to the Study and Reading of American History* (Ginn, Boston, 1912) is a classified bibliography with author, title and subject indexes. It is supplemented by the *Harvard Guide to American History* (Harvard Univ. Press, Cambridge, Massachusetts, 1954). The standard of inclusion does not equal that adopted by Channing. We may note some other useful guides in this section:

> UNITED STATES LIBRARY OF CONGRESS, *A Guide to the Study of the United States of America*, Government Printing Office, Washington, 1960, which has 1241 annotated items on history, though it deals with all subjects. It is particularly good on local and regional history.
>
> CARMAN, H. J. and THOMPSON, A. W., *A Guide to the Principal Sources for American Civilization, 1800–1900, in the City of New York: Printed Materials*, Columbia Univ. Press, New York, 1962. This continues Greene, E. B. and Morris, R. B., *A Guide to the Principal Sources for Early American history (1600–1800) in the City of New York*, 2nd edition, Columbia Univ. Press, New York, 1953.
>
> AMERICAN STUDIES ASSOCIATION. Committee on Microfilm

Bibliography. *Bibliography of American Culture, 1493–1875*, University Microfilms, Michigan, 1957. This is useful for overseas libraries as it includes 5000 titles on microfilm and 1500 titles reprinted in the twentieth century.

SPANGLER, E. (editor), *Bibliography of Negro History; Selected and Annotated Entries*, Ross and Haines, Minneapolis, 1963.

There is an excellent current bibliography, *Writings on American History*, which has covered most years since 1902 since its foundation in 1905, though it has had a chequered history under various publishers. From Vol. 13 (1918), it has been published as Vol. 2 of the annual report of the American Historical Association. Until 1935, it included all books and articles, wherever published, containing anything of value on the history of the United States and British North America, and all books published in the United States or Europe on Latin America or the Pacific Islands. From 1936 the United States only and its outlying possessions have been covered. The arrangement is classified, with author, title and subject index. Like its English counterpart, the publication appears some years after the years it records, but no volumes have yet appeared covering the years 1941–7. An index to the years 1902–40 appeared in 1956, and it contained some headings not covered in the individual annual indexes. At present the main work is published by the Library of Congress at Washington. A new work of a similar type is E. H. Boehm (editor), *America, History and Life* (American Bibliographical Center, Santa Barbara, 1964–, In progress), which abstracts 500 Canadian and United States publications.

An important work of historiography is H. H. Bellot, *American History and American Historians* (Oklahoma Press, Norman, 1952), covering American historians of the period 1890–1940. There are numerous standard histories of varying ages and lengths, one of the best known being C. A. and M. R. Beard's *The Rise of American Civilization* (2 vols., Macmillan, New York, 1929). Valuable sets include the *American Nation Series* (28 vols., Harper, New York, 1904–18), and the *Pageant of America* (15 vols., Yale Univ. Press, New Haven, 1925–9). (Fig. 50), *The New American Nation Series* (Harper,

United States Magazine and Democratic Review
United States Telegraph
Washington *Globe*
Washington *Union*

Published Correspondence, Diaries, and Memoirs

Indispensable for any serious study of the period are John Spencer Bassett (ed.), *Correspondence of Andrew Jackson* (7 vols., Washington, 1926–35); John Bassett Moore (ed.), *The Works of James Buchanan* (12 vols., Philadelphia, 1908–11); Calvin Colton (ed.), *The Private Correspondence of Henry Clay* (Boston, 1856), and *The Works of Henry Clay* (10 vols., New York, 1904); Worthington C. Ford (ed.), *The Writings of John Quincy Adams* (7 vols., New York, 1913–17); J. Franklin Jameson (ed.), "Correspondence of John C. Calhoun," American Historical Association, *Annual Report*, 1899 (Washington, 1900), II; Reginald C. McGrane (ed.), *The Correspondence of Nicholas Biddle . . . 1807–1844* (Boston, 1919); Gaillard Hunt (ed.), *The Writings of James Madison* (9 vols., New York, 1900–10); Luther Hamilton (ed.), *Memoirs, Speeches, and Writings of Robert Rantoul, Jr.* (Boston, 1854); Daniel Webster, *Writings and Speeches* (18 vols., Boston, 1903); James D. Richardson, *A Compilation of the Messages and Papers of the Presidents* (11 vols., New York, 1910); Richard K. Crallé (ed.), *The Works of John C. Calhoun* (6 vols., Charleston and New York, 1851–56).

Among the memoirs, diaries, and autobiographies of the period, the following were useful: Charles Francis Adams (ed.), *Memoirs of John Quincy Adams* (12 vols., Philadelphia, 1874–77), is full of acidulous criticism and useful information. It is indispensable for a study of the period. Thomas Hart Benton's *Thirty Years View* (2 vols., New York, 1854), cannot be overlooked, although it is sometimes inaccurate and prejudiced. William A. Butler's *A Retrospect of Forty Years* (New York, 1911) is sprightly. James A. Hamilton, *Reminiscences* (New York, 1869), is helpful, especially on the political side, while Ben: Perley Poore's *Reminiscences* (2 vols., Philadelphia, 1886), and Margaret E. Smith, *The First Forty Years of Washington Society*, ed. Gaillard Hunt (New York, 1906), give important information about the society of the nation's capital. Nathan Sargent's *Public Men and Events* (2 vols., Philadelphia, 1875) is Whiggish in tone, but perceptive. Winfield Scott, *Memoirs of Lieutenant-General Scott, LL. D.* (2 vols., New York, 1864), reveals both the strength and the weaknesses of this rather extraordinary man. Henry B. Stanton's *Random Recollections* (New York, 1886) must not be overlooked, and of course the same is true of Martin Van Buren's *Autobiography*, ed. John C. Fitzpatrick, American Historical Association, *Annual Report*, 1918 (Washington, 1920), an analysis which portrays the ex-President's point of view on the political struggles of the period.

Fig. 50. *The New American Nation Series* (volume by G. G. Van Deusen). (Copyright: Harper & Row.)

New York, 1954–), "from the days of discovery to the mid-twentieth century has been launched to take the place of the famous but now out-dated American Nation series. As the scope of history broadened to embrace science, technology, religion, popular culture, public administration and similar subjects, and as new evidence about the past accumulated, it became clear that it was time for a fresh and judicious appraisal of the whole of the American past. To this end the *New American Nation Series* is dedicated. Designed for the general reader as well as the scholar, the forty-odd volumes of the series are written by leading historians of this generation who have here combined to make a new and, it is hoped, significant contribution to the understanding of American history." Of a handy size, the volumes contain footnotes, and a detailed list of sources. *The Life History of the United States* (Time Incorporated, New York, 1963–, In progress), has a brief text but makes fully effective use of the most modern techniques of colour and monochrome illustration. There is a *Dictionary of American History* (2nd edition, 5 vols., and supplement, Scribner, New York, 1944–61), which takes a comprehensive view of history but whose articles are short, though bibliographies are given. W. Andrews has edited a *Concise Dictionary of American History* (Scribner, New York, 1962). As well as the general encyclopaedias there is the so-called *Encyclopaedia of American history* (edited by R. B. Morris and H. S. Commanger, 2nd edition, Harper, New York, 1961). This is merely an annalistic work not giving judgements or bibliographies. *Harper's Encyclopaedia of United States History from 458 A.D. to 1912* (10 vols., Harper, New York, 1912), is, by contrast, a true encyclopaedia. The *American Historical Review* is the leading periodical, and there is a *Union List of American Historical Periodicals in United Kingdom Libraries* (Institute of Historical Research, 1959).

The existence of the American Association for State and Local History as the publisher of some of the works referred to above is evidence of the place of local studies in American life. For most states the starting point is the appropriate volume in the American Guide series amongst which we may cite (Fig. 51) Writers' Program of the Work Projects Administration, *Pennsylvania; a*

gions where the railroad had not yet penetrated. A dirge was sung for the Conestoga wagon, one stanza of which ran:

> Oh, it's once I made money by driving my team,
> But now all is hauled on the railroad by steam,
> May the Devil catch the man that invented the plan,
> For it ruined us wagoners and every other man.

Meanwhile Harrisburg had been linked to Lancaster by rail. While the present Pennsylvania Railroad occupies much of the Philadelphia-Columbia Railroad right of way from Philadelphia to Lancaster, the right of way from Lancaster to Harrisburg is entirely that of the old Harrisburg, Portsmouth, Mount Joy & Lancaster road. The Lehigh Valley Railroad, incorporated originally in 1846 as the Delaware, Lehigh, Schuylkill & Susquehanna, was begun in 1851 and completed in 1855; connections were established with Philadelphia, New York, New Jersey, and points west. The Philadelphia & Reading Railroad had opened a line between the two cities in 1842, and the Philadelphia, Germantown & Norristown Railroad had begun operation in 1831.

Among the first railroads to cross Pennsylvania's border was the Cumberland Valley, which made its first run in 1837, carrying passengers from Carlisle to Chambersburg. In 1856 the line was extended to Hagerstown, Maryland. This railroad employed the first sleeping-car used on any railroad in the United States, and probably in the world. This was a passenger car with two thirds of its space devoted to berths. Later an entire car, the Carlisle, was put into service for sleeping purposes.

In 1852 the Erie & North East Railroad Company completed a road from Erie to the New York State line, using a six-foot gauge. In the same year the Franklin Canal Company opened a railroad line from Erie west to the Ohio State Line, connecting with another road extending to Cleveland. This line to the west used a gauge of four feet ten inches, so that travelers were compelled to change trains at Erie. The transfer was a serious inconvenience, and in 1853 the Erie & North East Company entered into a contract with the New York Central Railroad, which was building a road from Buffalo to the Pennsylvania line, whereby the former road was to change its gauge to four feet ten inches, making a uniform gauge from Buffalo to Cleveland. The Erie people, seeing their city becoming a way station instead of remaining the lake terminus of the New York & Erie Railroad, rebelled on December 9, 1853; mobs bombarded railroad officials with rotten eggs, tore down bridges, ripped up tracks, and rioted generally until Federal intervention put an end to the disorder, commonly referred to as the 'Peanut War.'

Fig. 51. *The American Guide Series* (volume on Pennsylvania). (Copyright: Oxford Univ. Press, New York.)

Guide to the Keystone State (Oxford Univ. Press, New York, 1940). Of the 660 lavishly illustrated pages, pp. 3–346 contain much historical material. Part I, "the General Background", covers such topics as the Indians, history, ethnic groups, farms, religion, education, literature, music, etc. Part II on "Cities and Towns" includes much historical material. There is a useful chronology (8 pp.), so that although these works are primarily topographical, a good half of each volume has historical material within it. A complete list of the series, many of which are now, unfortunately, difficult to obtain, is given in E. A. Baer, *Titles in Series* (Vol. 1, Scarecrow Press, Washington, 1953, items 492–660).

The following regional items should be noted:

LOGASA, H., *Regional United States; a Subject List*, Faxon, Boston, 1942.

PETERSON, C. S., *Consolidated Bibliography of County Histories in Fifty States*, 2nd edition, the author, Baltimore, 1963. Aims to list all histories of at least 100 pp.

SMITH, C. W., *Pacific Northwest Americana; a Checklist of Books and Pamphlets Relating to the History of the Pacific Northwest*, 3rd edition, Binfords & Mort, Portland, 1950.

DOBIE, J. F., *Guide to Life and Literature of the Southwest*, Southern Methodist Press, Dallas, 1952.

KURTZ, K., *Literature of the American Southwest*, Occidental College, Los Angeles, 1956.

WALLACE, W. S., *Bibliography of Published Bibliographies on the History of the Eleven Western States, 1941–1947*, Historical Society of New Mexico, Albuquerque, 1953.

CALIFORNIA LIBRARY ASSOCIATION, *California Local History; a Centennial Bibliography*, Stanford Univ. Press, Stanford, 1950.

KANSAS STATE HISTORICAL SOCIETY, *Comprehensive Index, 1875–1930, to Collections, Biennial Reports and Publications of the Kansas State Historical Society*, the Society, Topeka, 1959.

GREENLY, A. H., *A Selective Bibliography of Important Books,*

Pamphlets and Broadsides Relating to Michigan History, Stinehour Press, Lunenburg, 1958.

BLEGEN, T. C. and NYDAHL, T. L., *Minnesota History*, Minnesota Univ. Press, Minneapolis, 1960.

EIBERSON, H., *Sources for the Study of the New York Area*, City College Press, New York, 1960.

Dr. Leo Hershkowitz, Professor of Political Science, Queens College of New York, says New York history has been strangely neglected. "American colonial historiography, like Caesar's Gaul, is divided into three parts—New England, South, and West. The first and most formidable of these is symbolized by the eternal Puritan serving as moralist and mentor for the nation. This New England legend, of which Massachusetts is the center, is known to every schoolboy. Salem, Bunker Hill, and Paul Revere are national images. The Southern legend emphasizing Virginia is just a little less important. Written large in American history are Jamestown, Patrick Henry, and the House of Burgesses, not to mention the Father of his country and the whole Virginia dynasty. Daniel Boone and the frontier are part of the seedbed of Democracy. Hollywood and television have ensured that the richness of Western experience will not be forgotten.

"Somehow overlooked in this description of history is an area of the country whose contributions deserve considerable attention. The so-called middle colonies have been largely forgotten and New York in particular has been passed over. In almost any American history it occupies proportionately the least space and is treated in broad and unsympathetic terms.

"New York's image emerges as a Washington Irving buffoon. There is scarcely a single historian writing in New York who has achieved national prominence. There is no New York school of history."

THORNTON, M. L., *A Bibliography of North Carolina, 1589–1956*, North Carolina Press, Chapel Hill, 1958.

CORNING, H. M., *Dictionary of Oregon History*, Binfords and Mort, Portland, 1956.

PENNSYLVANIA. HISTORICAL AND MUSEUM COMMISSION, *Bibliography of Pennsylvania History*, 2nd edition, the Commission, Harrisburg, 1957.

TURNBULL, R. J., *Bibliography of South Carolina, 1563–1950*, 6 vols., University of Virginia Press, Charlottesville, 1956–60.

Handbook of Texas, 2 vols., Texas State Historical Association, 1952.

STREETER, T. W., *Bibliography of Texas, 1795–1845*, 3 vols., Harvard Univ. Press, Cambridge, Massachusetts, 1955–60.

SHETLER, C., *Guide to the Study of West Virginia History*, West Virginia Univ. Library, Morgantown, 1960.

Uruguay

PARKER, W. B., *Uruguayans of To-day*, Hispanic Society of America, New York, 1921.

SCARONE, A., *Uruguayos contemporáneos*, Barreiro y Ramos, Montevideo, 1937.

ARAŪJO, O., *Diccionario popular de historia de la república o del Uruguay*, 3 vols., Dornaleche y Reyes, Montevideo, 1901–3.

Venezuela

Quién as quién en Venezula, Panama, Ecuador, Colombia, Perry, Bogota, 1952.

SILVA UZCÁTEGUI, R. D., *Enciclopedia Larense; geografia, historia, cultura y lenguaje del estado Lara*, 2 vols., Impresores Unidos, Caracas, 1941.

ASIA

This continent is little more than a geographical expression ranging from Moslem traditions in the West to Oriental works in pictographic languages on the Pacific shore. Western influences, however, have left their mark, particularly in Ceylon, India, Jordan and Pakistan. There is an *Asia Who's Who* (Pan-Asia Newspaper Alliance, Hong Kong, 1957–, Irregular). Historiography is covered by London University, School of Oriental and African Studies, *Historical Writing on the Peoples of Asia* (Oxford Univ. Press, vols. 1–, 1961–), a serial publication. The following purport to cover the whole of Asia:

> WINT, GUY (editor), ASIA (*Handbooks to the Modern World*), Blond, 1966.
>
> ROYAL ASIATIC SOCIETY OF GREAT BRITAIN AND IRELAND, *Catalogue of Printed Books Published before 1932 in the Library*, the Society, 1940.
>
> UNIVERSITY OF LONDON, *Library Catalogue of the School of Oriental and African Studies*, Facsimile reprint, Boston, 1963.
>
> *Asien-Bibliographie*, Asien-Bücherei, Frankfurt/Hessen, vols. 1–, 1949–, quarterly. Covers German publications and periodical articles.
>
> *Bibliography of Asian Studies, 1956–*, In *Journal of Asian Studies*, 1957–, annual.
>
> AMERICAN ORIENTAL SOCIETY, *Catalog of the Library*, Yale Univ. Press, New Haven, 1930.

Somewhat wider in scope is P. K. Garde's *Directory of Reference Works Published in Asia* (UNESCO, Paris, 1956). Of the separate parts of Asia, the Far East has most literature available, not unnaturally, in view of the political interests there. German, Polish, and Russian language items are given, as well as those in English.

> U.S. LIBRARY OF CONGRESS, Orientalia division, *Southern Asia Publications in Western Languages*, the Library, Washington, vols. 1–, 1952–, quarterly. Deals with Western language material.
>
> WILSON, P., *South Asia; a Selected Bibliography on India, Pakistan, Ceylon*, American Institute of Pacific Relations, New York, 1957.
>
> PHILIP, C. H., *Handbook of Oriental History*, Royal Historical Society, 1951.
>
> EMBREE, J. F., *Southeast Asia: a Selected Bibliography*, American Institute of Pacific Relations, New York, 1955.

IRIKURA, J. K., *Southeast Asia: Selected Annotated Bibliography of Japanese Publications*, Yale Univ., New Haven, 1956.

Orientalische Bibliographie, 1887–1911, 1926, vols. 1–26, Reuther, Berlin, 1888–1928. This is a German annual bibliography.

MARBURG WESTDEUTSCHE BIBLIOTHEK, *Orient-Literatur in Deutschland und Österreich, 1945–50*, Lahn, Marburg, 1950–, In progress.

Bibliografia Jugo-Vostochnoi Azii, Institut Narodov Azii, Moscow, 1960. Contains Russian items from pre-revolutionary times to 1958.

VANDEN BERGHE, L. and VAN PROOSDIJ, B. A., *Bibliographie Analytique de l'Assyriologie et de l'Archeologie du Proche-Orient*, Brill, Leyden, vols. 1–, 1956–, In progress.

PANSTWOWE WYDAWN, W., POLSKA AKADEMIA NAUK, KOMITET ORIENTALISTYCZNY, *Bibliografia Polskich prac Orientalistycznych, 1945–55*, Warsaw, 1957.

Indo-China is now known as Laos and Vietnam but the older bibliographies on the area are still valuable—P. Boudet and R. Bourgeois' *Bibliographie de l'Indochine française, 1913–26* (Impr. d'extrême-Orient, Hanoi, 1929), and H. Cordier's *Bibliotheca Indosinica; Dictionnaire bibliographique des ouvrages relatifs à la penninsule Indochinoise* (4 vols. and index, Leroux, Paris, 1912–32); *Northeastern Asia, a Selected Bibliography* (2 vols., University of California Press, Berkeley, 1939), covers 14,000 titles including 10,000 in Chinese, Japanese, Korean and Russian.

On Central Asia there is the Central Asian Research Centre's *Bibliography of Recent Soviet Source Material on Soviet Central Asia and the Borderlands* (the Centre, No. 1–, 1957–), and on the Southwest, Henry Field's *Bibliography on Southwestern Asia* (3 vols., Miami Univ. Press, Coral Gables, 1953–6). Islamic aspects are covered by J. D. Pearson and J. F. Ashton's *Index Islamicus* (1906–55, Heffer, Cambridge, 1958).

Afghanistan

AKRAM, M., *Bibliographie analytique de l'Afghanistan*, Vol. 1 (all published), Centre de Documentation Universitaire, Paris, 1947.

WILBER, D. N., *Annotated Bibliography of Afghanistan*, Human Relations Area Files, New Haven, 1956.

Arabia

MACRO, E. (comp.), *Bibliography of the Arabian Peninsula*, Miami Univ. Press, Coral Gables, 1958.

U.S. LIBRARY OF CONGRESS, *The Arabian Peninsula*, the Library, Washington, 1951.

Burma

NEW YORK UNIVERSITY, Burma Research Project, *Annotated Bibliography of Burma*, Human Relations Area Files, New Haven, 1956.

NEW YORK UNIVERSITY, Burma Research Project, *Japanese and Chinese Language Sources on Burma; an Annotated Bibliography*, Human Relations Area Files, New Haven, 1957.

Ceylon

WILSON, P., *South Asia; a selected Bibliography on India, Pakistan, Ceylon*, American Institute of Pacific Relations, New York, 1957.

China

U.S. LIBRARY OF CONGRESS. Asiatic Division. *Eminent Chinese of the Ching period (1644–1912)*, 2 vols., Government Printing Office, Washington, 1943–4.

Who's Who in China; Biographies of Chinese Leaders, Chinese Weekly Review, Shanghai, vols. 1–, 1918–.

PERLEBERG, M., *Who's Who in Modern China*, Ye olde Printerie, Hong Kong, 1954. Covers the period from 1912 to 1953.

HAN, YU-SHAN, *Elements of Chinese Historiography*, Hawley, Hollywood, 1955.

LUST, J., *Index Sinicus: a Catalogue of Articles Relating to China in Periodicals and other Collective Publications, 1920–1955*, Heffer, Cambridge, 1964.

U.S. LIBRARY OF CONGRESS, *Manchuria, an Annotated Bibliography*, the Library, Washington, 1951. In numerous languages.

CORDIER, H., *Bibliotheca Sinica*, 4 vols., Guilmoto, Paris, 1904–8. *Supplement*, 1922–4. In French. Author index, 1953.

FAIRBANK, J. K. and LUI KWANG-CHING, *Modern China; a Bibliographical Guide to Chinese Works, 1898–1937*, Harvard Univ. Press, Cambridge, Massachusetts, 1950. Fairbank (with M. Banno) has also compiled a bibliography of Japanese studies of modern China (Charles E. Tuttle Co., Tokyo, 1955).

GARDNER, C. S., *A Union List of Selected Western Books on China in American Libraries*, 2nd edition, American Council of Learned Societies, Washington, 1938.

SKACHKOV, P. E., *Bibliografiia Kitaia*, Izd-vo Vostochnoi Lit-ry, Moscow, 1960. This covers Russian language material, 1730–1957.

Hong Kong

Hong Kong Who's Who, 1958–60, Luzzatto, Hong Kong, 1959.

India

BUCKLAND, C. E., *Dictionary of Indian Biography*, Sonnenschein, 1906.

THE TIMES OF INDIA, *Directory and Year Book*, Allen & Unwin, 1964, Irregular. Includes "Who's Who".

The Cambridge History of India, 7 vols., Cambridge Univ. Press, 1922–, In progress.

PHILIPS, C. H. (editor), *Historians of India, Pakistan and Ceylon*, Oxford Univ. Press, 1961.

Fig. 52. GREAT BRITAIN, INDIA OFFICE, *Catalogue of the Library of the India Office*, 2 vols., Eyre & Spottiswoode, 1888–1914.

BRITISH COUNCIL, *British Books on India*, British Council, 1961.

Bibliografiia Indii, Akademiia Nauk SSSR, Moscow, 1959.

Annual bibliography of Indian Archaeology, Kern Institute, Leiden, vols. 1–, 1926–, In progress.

CHAUDHURI, S., *Bibliography of Indological Studies from 1953*, Asiatic Society, Calcutta, 1958–, annual.

SHARMA, J. S., *Indian National Congress; a Descriptive Bibliography of India's Struggle for Freedom*, Chaud, Delhi, 1959.

MAHAR, J. H., *India; a Critical Bibliography*, Arizona Univ. Press, Tucson, 1964.

Indonesia

Encyclopaedie van Nederlandsch-Indië, vols. 1–9, Incomplete, Nijhoff, The Hague, 1917–40.

KENNEDY, R., *Bibliography of Indonesian Peoples and Cultures*, 2nd edition, 2 vols., Human Relations Area Files, New York, 1963.

Repertorium op de literatuur betreffende de Nederlandsche Koloniën, 1 vol. and 8 suppls., Nijhoff, The Hague, 1895–1935.

U.S. LIBRARY OF CONGRESS, *Netherlands East Indies; a Bibliography of Books Published after 1930, and Periodical Articles after 1932 Available in U.S. Libraries*, the Library, Washington, 1945.

Iran

SABA, M., *Bibliographie française de l'Iran*, 2nd edition, the author, Teheran, 1951. Covers French books, from 1560 onwards.

WILSON, Sir A. T., *Bibliography of Persia*, Clarendon Press, Oxford, 1930.

U.S. LIBRARY OF CONGRESS, *Iran; a Selected and Annotated Bibliography*, the Library, Washington, 1951. *Supplement*, 1958.

HANDLEY-TAYLOR, G., *Bibliography of Iran*, Dictionary of International Biography Co., 1964.

16   ARCHÆOLOGY.

Clercq, M. de. Antiquités Assyriennes. Folio. In progress.
Paris, 1885, &c.
Clermont-Ganneau, C. Recueil d'Archéologie Orientale. Tome I.
Paris, 1885.
Cole, H. H. Preservation of National Monuments. Reports I. to III.
Calcutta, 1882–85.
——. Preservation of National Monuments. 10 parts.
Folio. ——, 1884–85.
Conder, C. R. Altaic Hieroglyphs and Hittite Inscriptions.
London, 1887.
Corpus Inscriptionum Græcarum Græciæ Septentrionalis. Ed.
G. Dittenberger. Vol. I.   *Berolini,* 1892.
Cousens, H. Archæological Survey of Western India. No. 12. The
Caves at Nadsur and Karsambla.   *Bombay,* 1891.
——. Notes on the Buildings and other Antiquarian Remains at
Bijapur.   Folio. *Bombay,* 1890.
——. Bijapur.   *Poona,* 1889.
——. List of Photographic Negatives of Ancient Buildings, &c. of
Bombay.   *Poona,* 1888.
Crawley-Boevey, A. W. Scheme for the Protection and Conservation
of Antient Buildings in and around the City of Ahmedabad.
Bombay, 1886.
Creighton, H. The Ruins of Gour described and represented in
Eighteen Views.   4to. *London,* 1817.
Cunningham, Maj.-Gen. Sir A. Mahabodhi.   *London,* 1892.
Delattre, A. J. L'Assyriologie depuis onze ans.   *Paris,* 1891.
Delitzsch, E., and Haupt, P. Beiträge zur Entzifferung und Erklärung
der Kappadokischen Keilschrifttafeln.   *Leipzig,* 1893.
Donner, O. Wörterverzeichniss zu den Inscriptions de L'Jenissei. ·
Helsingfors, 1892.
Epigraphia Indica and Record of the Archæological Survey of India.
Edited by J. Burgess. In progress.   *Calcutta,* 1888.
Euting, Julius. Sinäitische Inschriften.   *Berlin,* 1891.
——. Nabatäische Inschriften aus Arabien.   4to. *Berlin,* 1885.
Fleet, J. F. Corpus Inscriptionum Indicarum. Vol. III. Inscriptions
of the Early Gupta Kings.   4to. *Calcutta,* 1888.
Friedrich, Thomas. Kabiren und Keilinschriften.   *Leipzig,* 1894.
Führer, A. List of Photographic Negatives of Monumental Antiquities
in the N.W.P. and Oudh.   ——, 1889.
Grœneveldt, W. T., und Brander, F. L. A. Catalogus der Archeo-
logische Verzameling v. h. Bataviaasch Genootschap v. Kunsten.
Batavia, 1887.
Halévy, J. Les Deux Inscriptions Hétéennes de Zindjîrlî.
Paris, 1894.
Hilprecht, H. V. The Babylonian Expedition of the University of
Pennsylvania. In progress.   *Philadelphia,* 1893.
Hirschfeld, G. Die Felsenreliefs in Kleinasien und das Volk der
Hittiter.   4to. *Berlin,* 1887.
Huth, Dr. Georg. Die Inschrift von Karakorum.   *Berlin,* 1892.
Inscriptions de l'Orkhon, publiées par la Société Finno-Ougrienne.
Helsingfors, 1892.
—— de l'Jénissei.   Folio. *Helsingfors,* 1889.
Kaibel, G. Inscriptiones Græcæ, Siciliæ, et Italiæ.   *Berolini,* 1890.

Fig. 52. INDIA OFFICE, *Catalogue of the Library.*

Israel

Near and Middle East Who's Who, the publishers, Jerusalem, vols. 1–, 1945–. This volume deals with Israel (Palestine) and Jordan (Trans-Jordan).

THOMSEN, P., *Die Palastina-Literatur*, 5 vols., Hinrich, Leipzig, 1911–38. This covers books and periodicals in many languages.

MAYER, L. A., *Bibliography of the Samaritans*, Brill, Leyden, 1964.

LUKE, H. C. and KEITH-ROACH, E., *The Handbook of Palestine and Trans-Jordan*, 2nd edition, Macmillan, 1930.

Who's Who in Israel, Marnutt, Tel Aviv, vols. 1–, 1952–, Irregular.

Japan

Who's Who of Contemporary Japan, Japanese Political Economy Research Institute, Tokyo, 1963.

Japan Biographical Encyclopaedia and Who's Who, Japan Biographical Research Department, Tokyo, 1961.

BORTON, H. and others, *A Selected List of Books and Articles on Japan in English, French and German*, Harvard Univ. Press, Cambridge, Massachusetts, 1954.

CORDIER, H., *Bibliotheca Japonica*, Leroux, Paris, 1912.

Bibliografiia Japonii, Izd-vo Vostochnoi Lit-ry, Moscow, 1960.

HALL, J. W., *Japanese History: a Guide to Japanese Reference and Research Materials*, Michigan Univ. Press, Michigan, 1954.

Japan Bibliographic Annual, Hokuseido Press, Tokyo, 1956–, annual.

SAKAMAKI, S., *Ryukyu: a Bibliographical Guide to Okinowan Studies*, Hawaii Univ. Press, Honolulu, 1963.

Jordan

See also Israel.

PATAI, R., *Jordan, Lebanon and Syria; an Annotated Bibliography*, Human Relations Area Files, New Haven, 1957.

Korea

UNESCO Korean Survey, Dong-a Publishing Co., Seoul, 1960. Includes bibliographies.

HARVARD UNIVERSITY, *A Classified Catalogue of Korean Books in the Harvard-Yenching Institute Library at Harvard University*, The University, Cambridge, Massachusetts, 1962.

CALIFORNIA UNIVERSITY, Institute of East Asiatic Studies, *Korean Studies Guide*, California Univ. Press, Los Angeles, 1954. *Russian Supplement*, 1958.

U.S. LIBRARY OF CONGRESS, *Korea; an Annotated Bibliography of Publications in Western Languages*, the Library, Washington, 1950. There are other bibliographies from the same source on works in Far Eastern (1950), and Russian (1950) languages.

Lebanon

See Jordan.

Malaya and Singapore

The Leaders of Malaya and Who's Who, Morais, Kuala Lumpur, 1963.

CHEESEMAN, H. A. R., *Bibliography of Malaya, being a Classified List of Books wholly or partly in English relating to the Federation of Malaya and Singapore*, Longmans, 1959.

Pakistan

Biographical Encyclopaedia of Pakistan, 1960–1, 2nd edition, International publishers, Lahore, 1960.

The Indian and Pakistan Year Book and Who's Who, The Times of India, Bombay, vols. 37–, 1951–, In progress. First volume to include Pakistan.

GHANI, A. R., *Pakistan; a Select Bibliography*, University Institute of Chemistry, Lahore, 1951.

ABERNETHY, G. L., *Pakistan; a Selected Annotated Bibliography*, 2nd edition, American Institute of Pacific Relations, New York, 1960.

Palestine

See Israel.

Persia

See Iran.

Philippines

MANUEL, E. A., *Dictionary of Philippine Biography*, Filipiana Publishers, Quezon City, vols. 1–, 1955–, In progress.

Who's Who in the Philippines, McCullough, Manila, vols. 1–, 1937–, In progress.

CHICAGO UNIVERSITY, *Selected Bibliography of the Philippines*, Human Relations Area Files, New Haven, 1956.

NEWBERRY LIBRARY, *A Catalogue of Printed Materials relating to the Philippine Islands, 1519–1900*, the Library, Chicago, 1959.

Siam

See Thailand.

Syria (and U.A.R.)

See also Egypt.

MASSON, P., *Éléments d'une bibliographie française de la Syrie*, Barlatier, Marseilles, 1919.

Thailand

BANGKOK, CHULALONGKORN UNIVERSITY, *Bibliography of Material about Thailand in Western Languages*, the University, Bangkok, 1960.

MASON, J. B. and PARISH, H. C., *Thailand Bibliography*, University of Florida Libraries, Gainesville, 1958.

Turkey

Who's who in Turkey, Oktay, Ankara, Vol. 1–, 1958–, Irregular.

Türkiye teracimi ahval ansiklopedisi; encyclopédie biographique de Turquie, Hamit Matbaasi, Stamboul, 1932, Vol. 3 (only). In Turkish and French.

AKADEMIIA NAUK SSSR, INSTITUT VOSTOKOVEDENIIA. *Bibliografiia Turtsii, 1917–58*, Izd-vo Vostochnoi Lit-ry, Moscow, 1959.

BIRGE, J. K., *A Guide to Turkish Area Study*, American Council of Learned Societies, Washington, 1949.

MIKHOV, N. V., *Bibliographie des articles de périodiques allemands, anglais, français et italiens sur la Turquie et la Bulgarie*, Imp. de la Cour, Sofia, 1938. Covers articles published mainly between 1715 and 1880.

U.S.S.R.

See Europe.

Vietnam

MICHIGAN STATE UNIVERSITY OF AGRICULTURE AND APPLIED SCIENCE, *What to read on Vietnam*, 2nd edition, Institute of Pacific Relations, New York, 1960.

AUSTRALASIA

Australasia is the most recently discovered of the five continents. None the less, there is considerable interest in its early history and biography as far back as the seventeenth century. The continent has a fairly full-scale encyclopaedia to itself, and Ferguson's bibliography ranks with the most detailed and precise in existence. The scholarship is not entirely of Anglo-Saxon origin, although Australia and New Zealand naturally present the most titles, with treatment of their aboriginal civilizations in rather a minor key. Curiously, there is little regional historical bibliography in Australia. There is French, Dutch and German work to be recorded (New Caledonian titles are exclusively the work of a Frenchman). The growing strategic American interest in Oceania is shown by the considerable work of the Library of Congress staffs in this area.

Australia

(Fig. 53) *The Australian Encyclopaedia*, 2nd edition, 10 vols., Angus & Robertson, Sydney, 1958.

SERLE, P., *Dictionary of Australian Biography*, 2 vols., Angus & Robertson, Sydney, 1949.

Who's Who in Australia, Colorgravure publications, Melbourne, vols. 1–, 1906–, Irregular.

SPENCE, S. A., *A Bibliography of Selected Early Books and Pamphlets relating to Australia, 1610–1880*, the author, Mitcham, 1952. *Supplement, 1881–1900*, 1955.

FERGUSON, J. A., *Bibliography of Australia*, Angus and Robertson, Sydney, vols. 1–, 1941–. Five volumes have so far appeared. Locations are given for Australian libraries and the British Museum. Period covered is 1784–1901.

POLITZER, L. L., *Bibliography of Dutch Literature on Australia*, the author, Melbourne, 1953. The same author has produced bibliographies of French (1952) and German (1952) literature on Australia.

New Caledonia

O'REILLY, P., *Calédoniéns; répertoire biobibliographique de la Nouvelle-Calédonie*, Musée de l'Homme, Paris, 1953.

O'REILLY, P., *Bibliographie méthodique analytique et critique de la Nouvelle-Calédonie*, Musée de l'Homme, Paris, 1955.

New Guinea and Papua

GILL, E. R., *Catalogue of Books relating to New Guinea (but with special reference to Papua) in the Library of Evan R. Gill, Liverpool*, the author, Liverpool, 1957.

GALIS, K. W., *Bibliography of West New Guinea*, Yale Univ. Press, New Haven, 1956.

New Hebrides

O'REILLY, P., *Hébridais; répertoire biobibliographique des Nouvelles-Hébrides*, Musée de l'Homme, Paris, 1957.

English market, thanks to the industrial revolution and the falling-off in English-grown wool, provided an enormous demand for the fleeces, once their quality had been appreciated.

(Additional information on conditions in the early years of settlement will be found under ASSIGNMENT SYSTEM; CONVICTS AND TRANSPORTATION; and NEW SOUTH WALES CORPS. The explorations that led to the rapid expansion of settlement are described in the early sections of EXPLORATION BY LAND. Early visits by foreign whalers and sealers to Australian waters are mentioned in SEALS AND SEALING and WHALING INDUSTRY. Biographical entries of persons prominent in the early days should also be consulted.)

PERIOD 1820-50

Wool. For about 30 years following 1820 the economic history of Australia can be written almost exclusively in terms of wool. The graziers, always searching for more lands for their rapidly growing flocks, stimulated the exploration of the continent, or turned explorers themselves. South, west, and north from the neighbourhood of Sydney they penetrated into Victoria and reached the Murray River, Portland, and Port Phillip; they overran the Riverina district of New South Wales and reached the Darling River; they opened the Liverpool Plains, New England, the Darling Downs, and southern Queensland, always seeking "better country farther out". The British Government, viewing this disorderly advance with some apprehension, tried to check it, but "as well might it be attempted to confine the Arabs of the desert within a circle drawn on the sands", reported Governor Bourke. The pastoralists, when forbidden to settle outside the nineteen counties, or when told that they could only buy their land at £1 per acre—an impossible price for profitable grazing in the conditions of the times—simply "squatted" on it, and so laid the foundation of that "squattocracy" which has ever since played so important a part in the social and economic life of Australia. Eventually the Government had to recognize their existence, and after 1847 they were given considerable legal rights over the lands they were occupying.

Immigration and Land Sales. The first migrants to Australia were convicts and officials. By 1820 a third class was becoming important—the wealthy free settler. The emancipist farmer had been a failure, largely because he was ill-educated and lacked capital. After 1821 land was only to be granted to men of substance, who could develop it and would employ convicts. This was an attempt to keep in proportion the supply of land, of capital, and of labour.

By the early 1830s, however, it seemed that the attempt had been a failure. The Government had granted more land than could readily be cultivated with the available convict and emancipist labour. Settlement was too dispersed and there was an acute labour shortage. The remedy seemed to be to restrict land grants. In 1831 under the Ripon Regulations, land grants were prohibited and land sales were substituted. This, it was thought, would prevent settlers from taking up too much land, for they would now have to pay for it; also, if the land revenue were devoted to assisting immigration, the labour shortage would be relieved. E. G. Wakefield, who originated the theory, thought that the system would work automatically; although the Government was not so sure, it adopted some of his basic principles with, at any rate, partial success.

The land revenue made possible the first large-scale scheme of assisted immigration. The free labourers brought to the colony, together with the free native-born, effectively diluted the convict element, and helped to diversify the population and to stimulate the economy; between 1832 and 1842 nearly 70,000 immigrants arrived in New South Wales.

Nevertheless, expansion of settlement was not checked because the pastoralists, when unable to get their land by grant, did not buy it but simply squatted on it. Thus expansion continued faster than immigration, and the labour shortage remained unabated.

The Slump of 1842. Drought, a fall in wool prices, the increasing costs of squatting farther out, and the higher cost of labour after the stopping of assignment in 1840—all these causes combined to make wool-growing temporarily uneconomic and brought widespread bankruptcy to the colonies. The year of greatest panic was 1842 when pastoralists had recourse to boiling down carcasses of sheep and cattle in order to sell the hides and tallow. Recovery was not unduly long delayed, but it seemed that the limit had been put on pastoral expansion. Lack of transport made settlement in the interior expensive, and the explorations of E. J. Eyre and Charles Sturt suggested, as was true, that the interior was largely an arid and waterless desert. The slump had stopped all land sales; without a land revenue to assist migration, British migrants found it cheaper and easier to cross the Atlantic than to come to Australia. The impulse that had settled Western Australia, South Australia, and Port Phillip came from hopes of agricultural and pastoral profit—and for a time such hopes declined. Though the economy was by no means stagnant, after 1844 it lost for a time the élan of the previous decade.

(Further information on the events of the period 1820-50 will be found in articles on LAND SETTLEMENT and SQUATTERS AND SQUATTING. Attempts to restrict expansion are referered to under NINETEEN COUNTIES. The Wakefield Plan is explained more fully in the biography of Edward Gibbon Wakefield.)

Fig. 53. *The Australian Encyclopaedia.* (Copyright: Grolier Society of Australia Pty., Ltd.)

O'REILLY, P., *Bibliographie méthodique, analytique et critique des Nouvelles-Hébrides*, Musée de l'Homme, Paris, 1958.

New Zealand

Who's Who in New Zealand, Reed, Wellington, vols. 1–, 1908–, irregular.

SCHOLEFIELD, G. H. (editor), *A Dictionary of New Zealand Biography*, 2 vols., Department of Internal Affairs, Wellington, 1940.

The Modern Encyclopaedia of Australia and New Zealand, Australia House, 1965.

HOCKEN, T. M., *Bibliography of the Literature relating to New Zealand*, Mackay, Wellington, 1909. *Supplements* (by others), 1927, 1938. Includes Maori items.

WILSON, J. O., *A Finding List of British Parliamentary Papers relating to New Zealand, 1827–1900*, General Assembly Library, Wellington, 1900.

Oceania

UNITED STATES LIBRARY OF CONGRESS, *Islands of the Pacific; a Selected List of References* (comp. Helen F. Conover), the Library, Washington, 1943. *Supplement*, 1945. "Most of the material is supplementary to that contained in the Subject Catalogue of the Royal Empire Society" (above, p. 129) (foreword).

ALLIED FORCES, *An Annotated Bibliography of the Southwest Pacific and Adjacent Areas*, 3 vols., Allied Geographical Section, no place, 1944.

LEWIN, P. E., *The Pacific Region; a Bibliography of the Pacific and East Indian islands, exclusive of Japan*, Royal Empire Society, 1944.

TAYLOR, C. R. H., *A Pacific Bibliography; Printed Matter relating to the Native Peoples of Polynesia, Melanesia and Micronesia*, Polynesian Society, Wellington, 1951.

EUROPE

This continent is the home of most of the colonizing powers, so naturally has a very fully documented history as have its individual countries, through all ages, from that of classical Greece to today. Some works on Europe in English have already been listed (p. 73), as a prelude to the study of Great Britain. Charles Seignobos' *Histoire politique de l'Europe contemporaine* (Colin, Paris, 1897), and the *Europäischer Geschichtskalender* (Beck, Nördlingen, 1861–1942) are equally noteworthy French and German contributions. East Europe as a whole is covered by the *Osteuropäische bibliographie, 1920–3* (4 vols., Osteuropa Institut, Breslau, 1920–8), and L. Savadjian's *Bibliographie balkanique, 1920–38* (8 vols., Société générale d'imprimerie, Paris, 1920–38). New York Public Library, Reference Department, *Dictionary Catalog of the Slavonic Collection* (Hall, Boston, 1959) is a useful contribution in English and the *Kleine Slavische Biographie* (Harrassowitz, Wiesbaden, 1958) transcends national boundaries. The antiquities of Greek and Roman civilizations are covered by Wilhelm Engelmann's *Bibliotheca scriptorum classicorum, 1700–1878* (2 vols., the author, Leipzig, 1880–2), and its continuations by R. Klussmann covering the period to 1896 (4 vols., Leipzig, 1909–13), and S. Lambrino, 1896–1914 (Société d'Edition "Les Belles Lettres," Paris, 1951–, In progress). Current annual classical bibliographies include the French *L'Année philologique* and British *Year's Work in Classical Studies* (1906–47) which, unfortunately, has ceased publication. Among periodicals dealing with classical antiquity or mediaevalia as a whole are *Speculum* (U.S.A.—classical and mediaeval Latin), the *Classical Review* (U.K.), and the *Revue des études anciennes* (France).

Austria

Wer ist wer in Österreich, Huttern, Vienna, 1951–, In progress.

Who's Who in Austria, Intercontinental Book and Publishing Co., Montreal, 1959–, biennial.

WURZBACH, C. VON, *Biographisches Lexikon des Kaiserthums Österreich*, 60 vols., Zamarski, Vienna, 1856–1923.

Neue Österreichische Biographie ab 1815, Amalthea, Vienna, vols. 1–, 1923–, In progress. Continued by *Österreiches biograph-*

isches Lexikon, 1815–1950, Bohlaus, Graz–Köln, 1954–, In progress.

CHARMATZ, R., *Wegweiser durch die Literatur der österreichischen Geschichte*, Cotta, Stuttgart, 1912.

STRASSMAYR, E., *Bibliographie zur Geschichte, Landes und Volkskunde Österreichs*, Winkler, Linz, vols. 1–, 1929–, In progress. Covers from 1891. Continued under various titles to coverage for 1953.

Belgium

Le Livre bleu, Recueil biographique, Larcier, Brussels, vols. 1–, 1950–, Irregular.

Wie is dat in Vlaanderen?, Elsevier, Brussels, 1953.

Biographie nationale, 28 vols. and 3 supplements, Academie Royale, Brussels, 1866–1961. Main work completed but supplements in progress.

Who's Who in Belgium, including the Belgian Congo, 1957–8, International book and publishing Co., Brussels, 1959. Later editions include Luxembourg.

PIRENNE, H., *Histoire de Belgique*, 7 vols., Lamertin, Brussels, 1900–32.

PIRENNE, H., *Bibliographie de l'histoire de Belgique*, 3rd edition, Lamertin, Brussels, 1931. Covers 1598–1914; subsequently continued in periodicals.

GÉRIN, P., *Bibliographie de l'histoire de Belgique, 1789–1831*, Edited by Nauwelaerts, Louvain, 1960.

Periodical: *Revue belge de philologie et l'histoire*.

Czechoslovakia

Bibliografie československé histoire za rok 1955, Nakl. Československé Akademie Věd, Prague, 1957–, annual. Continues *Bibliografie česke Historie* (which covers 1904–41).

Denmark

Kraks blaa bog, Krak, Copenhagen, vols. 1–, 1910–, In progress.

Dansk biografisk Leksikon, 27 vols., Schultz, Copenhagen, 1933–44. Supplements in progress.

ERICHSEN, B. and KRARUP, A., *Dansk historisk bibliografi*, 3 vols., Gad, Copenhagen, 1929. This covers period to 1912 and a similarly titled work was resumed in 1956.

LIBRARY ASSOCIATION, County Libraries section. *Scandinavia*, the Association, 1958.

Historisk Tidsskrift, Luno, Copenhagen, vols. 1–, 1840–. Annual since 1896.

Eire

See under United Kingdom, Chapter 3.

Finland

Kuka Kukin on; Who's Who in Finland, Otava, Helsinki, 1960.

MALINIEMI, A. H. and KIVIKOSKI, E., *Suomen historiallinen bibliografia, 1901–25*, 2 vols. in 1, Suomalaisen kirjallisuuden seuran kirjapanon oy, Helsinki, 1940. Continued 1926–50 by Vallinkoski and Schauman, 2 vols.

OKSNEVAD, R. and THOMAS, L., *Publications sur la finlande parues dans les pays de langue française jusqu'à 1945*, Valtioneuvoston kirjapainon, Helsinki, 1959.

France

Who's Who in France, 5th edition, Lafitte, Paris (entitled 1961–2), 1961.

Dictionnaire de biographie française, Letouzey, Paris, vols. 1–, 1933–, In progress.

Dictionnaire biographique français contemporain, 2nd edition, Pharos, Paris, 1954.

(Fig. 54) LAVISSE, E. (editor), *Histoire de France depuis les origines jusqu'à la Révolution*, 18 vols., Hachette, Paris, 1900–11. Continuation by Lavisse to 1919, 10 vols., 1920–2 (*Histoire de France contemporaine*).

CHAPITRE III

LA NOBLESSE FRANÇAISE HORS DE FRANCE

I. LE MONDE FÉODAL EN MOUVEMENT. LES PÈLERINAGES. — II. LES CHE-
VALIERS FRANÇAIS EN ESPAGNE. — III. LES NORMANDS EN ITALIE. — IV. GUILLAUME LE
BATARD ET LA CONQUÊTE DE L'ANGLETERRE.

I. — LE MONDE FÉODAL EN MOUVEMENT. LES PÈLE-RINAGES [1]

MOBILITÉ DE LA SOCIÉTÉ FÉODALE. LA Féodalité semblait être, par essence, un régime d'isolement qui rivait le noble à son donjon et le paysan à sa glèbe. La rareté et le mauvais état des routes, les périls variés qui attendaient le voyageur à chaque pas, l'ignorance de ce qui dépassait l'horizon immédiat du château, du canton ou de la province, tout semblait dissuader l'homme du Moyen âge de quitter le pays natal et de s'aventurer au loin. Et pourtant, la France du XIe siècle a été le théâtre d'une circulation continue, générale, intense au delà de ce qu'on peut imaginer. Cette société, qu'on croyait figée dans ses cadres, apparaît toujours en mouvement.

LE PEUPLE. La classe populaire, elle-même, malgré le manque de ressources et la dureté de la loi féodale, ne tient pas en place. La campagne, on l'a vu, avait ses défricheurs nomades, les hôtes, et les villes avaient leurs marchands, qui sillonnaient de leurs bateaux les rivières françaises, allaient au loin, par terre ou par mer, placer ou échanger leurs produits. Bien avant le XIe siècle, les négociants de Normandie affluaient en Angleterre, ceux de Flandre et de Lorraine fréquentaient les marchés allemands, italiens et espagnols. En droit, les vilains devaient rester emprisonnés dans la seigneurie qui les exploitait. En fait, la

---

1. OUVRAGES A CONSULTER. Lalanne, *Des pèlerinages en Terre-Sainte avant les croisades,* dans Bibl. de l'École des Chartes, 1845. Roehricht, *Die Pilgerfahrten nach dem Heiligen Lande vor den Kreuzzügen,* 1875.

‹ 78 ›

Fig. 54. LAVISSE, E., *Histoire de France.* (Copyright: Hachette.)

MOLINIER, A. and others, *Les Sources de l'histoire de France*, 18 vols., Picard, Paris, 1901–35.

MONOD, G., *Bibliographie de l'histoire de France*, Hachette, Paris, 1888. Covers the period up to 1789.

Répertoire méthodique de l'histoire moderne et contemporaine de la France, 1898–1913, 11 vols., Rieder, Paris, 1899–1914. Continued for period 1920–31 as *Répertoire bibliographique de l'histoire de France*, and for 1955 onwards by the *Bibliographie annuelle de l'histoire de France*.

CARON, P., *Manuel pratique pour l'étude de la Révolution française*, 2nd edition, Picard, Paris, 1947.

PERIODICAL: *Revue historique*.

BARRAUX, M., *Le Département de la Seine et la ville de Paris; Notions générales et bibliographiques pour en étudier l'histoire*, Dumoulin, Paris, 1910. "Paris is France", it has been said, but the country has nevertheless a large number of regional works.

LASTEYRIE, R. DE and VIDIER, A., *Bibliographie générale des travaux historiques et archéologiques publiés par les sociétés savantes de la France* (6 vols., Impr. Nationale, Paris, 1888–1918) is a very comprehensive bibliography of historical material appearing in local societies' transactions. The main work covers the earliest times up to 1885, and supplements have brought it up to 1918. A similar work now in progress by R. Gandilhon aims at covering the years to 1940. There are bibliographies either separately published or given in periodicals for Alsace, Burgundy, Brittany, Champagne, Flanders, Lorraine, Normandy and Provence. The colonial period is well covered by the Compte de Favitski de Probobysz' *Répertoire bibliographique de la littérature militaire et coloniale française depuis cent ans* (Thone, Paris, 1935), and articles in the *Revue maritime*.

Germany (East and West)

Who's Who in Germany, Oldenbourg, Munich, 1956–, biennial.

Wer ist wer? Das deutsche Who's Who, Arani, Berlin, vols. 1–,
1945–, Irregular.

Wer ist wer in der SBZ?, Verlag für Internationalen Kulturaustausch,
Berlin, 1958.

Allgemeine deutsche Biographie, 56 vols., Duncker, Leipzig, 1875–
1910. Covers those deceased up to 1896. Continuation in
Deutsches biographisches Jahrbuch (1896–1913), 18 vols., Reimer,
Berlin, 1897–1917.

Neue deutsche Biographie, Duncker und Humblot, Berlin, vols.
1–, 1953–, In progress.

DAHLMANN, F. C. and WAITZ, G., *Quellenkunde der deutschen
Geschichte*, 9th edition, 2 vols., Koehler, Leipzig, 1931–2.
Continued by Franz, G., *Bücherkunde zur deutschen Geschichte*,
Oldenbourg, Munich, 1951.

Jahresberichte für deutschen Geschichte, Koehler, Leipzig, vols. 1–,
1925–, annual. This is continued under differing titles up to
the present.

WATTENBACH, W., *Deutschlands Geschichtsquellen im Mittelalter bis
zur Mitte des XIIIten Jahrhunderts*, 2 vols., 6th edition, Hertz,
Berlin, 1893–4 (7th edition of Vol. 1 only, Cotta, Stuttgart,
1904, further revision in progress); and Lorenz, O., *Deutschlands Geschichtsquellen im Mittelalter seit der Mitte des XIIIten
Jahrhunderts*, 2 vols., 3rd edition, Hertz, Berlin, 1886–7,
should be consulted for the Middle Ages.

GEBHARDT, B., *Handbuch der deutschen Geschichte*, 8th edition,
4 vols., Union Verlag, Stuttgart, 1930–60.

Ost-deutsche bibliographie, Holzne, Wurzburg, 1953–, In progress.
Covers the period 1945–52 onwards.

WJAESLAWK, J., *Serbska bibliografija, 2 rozmnozenya wuporjedzany
naklad; Sorbische (Wendische) Bibliographie*, 2nd edition,
Akademie-Verlag, Berlin, 1952.

Greece and Crete

Who's Who in Greece, 1958–9, Athens News, Athens, 1959.
Poios einai poios, eis ten Ellada, Ekloges, Athens, 1958.

CINCINNATI UNIVERSITY LIBRARY, *The modern Greek collection in the Library of the University of Cincinnati*, Hestia Press, Athens, 1960.

BAXEVANIS, JOHN E., *Modern Greece: a bibliography*, Argonaut, Inc., Chicago, 1965.

Holland

See Netherlands.

Hungary

SZINNYEI, J., *Magyar írók élete és munkái a Magyar tudományos akadémiá megbizásából*, 14 vols., Kiadja Hornyánszky, Budapest, 1891–1914. The continuation in progress is *Magyar életrajzi lexikon*.

Ungarische Fahrbucher, 23 vols., Berlin, 1921–43, contains bibliographies, and is continued as the *Ural-Altaische Fahrbucher*, Wiesbaden, vols., 24–, 1952–, In progress.

SZTARAY, Z., *Bibliography on Hungary*, Kossuth Foundation, New York, 1960.

Iceland

ÓLASON, P. E., *Íslenzkar aeviskrár frá landnámstímum til arsloka 1940*, 5 vols., Islenzka Bókmenntafélags, Reykjavik, 1948–52.

Ireland

See under United Kingdom, Chapter 3.

Italy

Who's Who in Italy, Intercontinental Book and Publishing Co., Milan, 1958.

Chi e?, 7th edition, Scarano, Rome, 1961–, Irregular.

Dizionario biografico degli italiani, Treccani, Rome, vols. 1–, 1960–, In progress.

7

La storia politica d'Italia, 3rd edition, Vallardi, Milan, vols. 1–, 1937–, In progress.

Bibliografia storica nazionale, Scalia editore, Rome, vols. 1–, 1939–, In progress.

PERIODICAL: *Nuova rivista storica.*

Bibliografia romana, Staderini Editore, Rome, vols. 1–, 1946–, annual.

CUPERTINO, E., *Regione siciliana; Bibliografia 1943–53,* Belloti & Figlio, Palermo, 1954.

Lithuania

See U.S.S.R.

Luxembourg

Biographie nationale du pays de Luxembourg, 3rd edition, Victor Buck, Luxembourg, vols. 1–, 1960–, In progress.

Monaco

HANDLEY-TAYLOR, G., *Bibliography of Monaco,* the author, London, 1961.

Netherlands

Wie is dat? Naamlijst van bekende personen, Nijhoff, the Hague, vols. 1–, 1931–, In progress.

Nieuw Nederlandsch biografisch woordenboek, 10 vols., Sijthoff, Leyden, 1911–37.

PETIT, L. D. and RUYS, H. J. A., *Repertorium der verhandelingen en bijdragen betreffende de geschiedenis des vaterlands,* 5 vols., Brill, Leyden, 1907–53. Continued as an annual bibliography since 1940.

PERIODICAL: *Tijdschrift voor geschiedenis.*

Norway

Hvem er hvem? Aschehoug, Oslo, vols. 1–, 1912–, Irregular.

Norsk biografisk leksikon, Aschehoug, Oslo, vols. 1–, 1923–, In progress.

LIBRARY ASSOCIATION, County Libraries section, *Scandinavia,* Library Association, 1958.

Bibliografi til Norges Historie, Grondahl, Oslo, Vols. 1–, 1927–, In progress. This covers the period from 1916. Ten-year cumulations are made into volumes.

Poland

AKADEMJA UMIEJETNÓSCI, KRAKÓW, *Polski slownikbiograficzny,* Akademja, Umiejetnósci, Cracow, vols. 1–, 1935–, In progress.

The Cambridge History of Poland, 2 vols., Cambridge Univ. Press, 1941–50. Vol. 3 in preparation.

RISTER, H., *Schrifttum über Polen,* Kommission für Posen, Marburg, 1953–, Irregular.

Portugal

Quem é elguém, Portugália editoria, Lisbon, 1947–, Irregular.

ACADEMIA PORTUGUESA DA HISTÓRIA, *Guia da bibliografi histórica Portuguesa,* The Academy, Lisbon, vols. 1–, 1959–, In progress.

Russia

See U.S.S.R.

Spain

Diccionario biográfico español e hispanoamericano, Instituto Español de Estudios Biográficos, Palma, vols. 1–, 1950–, In progress.

MENENDEZ PIDAL, R., *Historia d'España,* Espasa Calpe, Madrid, vols. 1–, 1935–, In progress.

SÁNCHEZ ALONSO, B., *Fuentes de la historia española e hispano-americana*, 3rd edition, 3 vols., Consejo Superior Cientificas, Madrid, 1952. Continued since 1950 by Gomez Molleda, D., *Bibliografía historica española, 1950-4*, from the same publishers, 1955.

PERIODICAL: *Hispania, Revista Española de historia.*

Sweden

Vem är dat? Svensk biografisk handbok, Norstedt, Stockholm, vols. 1–, 1912–, Irregular.

Svenskt biografiskt lexikon, Bonnier, Stockholm, vols. 1–, 1918–, In progress.

LIBRARY ASSOCIATION, County Libraries section, *Scandinavia*, Library Association, 1958.

SETTERWALL, K., *Svensk historisk bibliografi 1771–1935*, 4 vols., Appleberg, Uppsala, 1907–56, and in continuation annually since 1936 (same title).

PERIODICAL: *Historisk Tidsskrift.*

Switzerland

Who's Who in Switzerland, including the Principality of Liechtenstein, 1950–1, Central European Times, Zürich, 1952, Irregular.

GODET, M. and others, *Historisch–biographisches Lexikon der Schweiz*, 9 vols., the authors, Neuchâtel, 1921–34. (Reprint 1965).

Biographisches Lexikon verstörberren Schweizer, 5 vols., Schweiz, Zürich, 1947–61.

Neue Schweizer Biographie, 2 vols., Bruckner, Basle, 1938–42. In German, French and Italian.

BARTH, H., *Bibliographie der Schweizer-Geschichte . . . bis Ende 1912*, 3 vols., Geering, Basle, 1914–15. Continued by *Bibliographie der Schweizergeschichte*, Leeman, Zurich, vols. 1–, 1913–, annual.

PERIODICAL: *Revue suisse d'histoire.*

Turkey

Who's Who in Turkey, Cyclopedic Publications, Ankara, vols. 1–, 1958–.

KORAY, E., *Türkiy; itarih yayinlari bibliyografyasi, 1729–1950*, Millî Eğitim Basimevi, Ankara, 1952.

AKADEMIIA NAUK SSSR, *Bibliografiia Turtsii, 1917–58*, Izd-vo Vostochnoi Lit-ry, Moscow, 1959.

U.S.S.R.

Russkii biografiheskii slovar, 25 vols., Reprint by Microcard editions, Inc., Washington, 1964.

(Fig. 55) *Who's Who in the U.S.S.R.*, 1961–2, Scarecrow Press Inc., Montreal, 1962.

Porträts der UdSSR-Prominenz, Institut der Erforschung der UdSSR, Munich. No. 1–, 1960–. (Looseleaf.)

VERNADSKY, G. and KARPOVICH, M., *A History of Russia*, Yale Univ. Press, New Haven, vols. 1–, 1943–, In progress.

MORLEY, C., *Guide to Research in Russian History*, Syracuse University, Syracuse, 1951.

MEŻHOV, V. I., *Russkaja istoričeskaja bibliografija, 1800–1854*, 3 vols., Sibi-Pekov, St. Petersburg, 1892–3.

MEHNERT, K., *Die Sovet-Union, 1917–32*, Ost-Europa Verlag, Konigsberg, 1933.

BIRŽIŠKA, V., *Aleksandrynas: Biographies, Bibliographies and Bio-Bibliographies of old Lithuanian Authors to 1865*, Lithuanian-American Cultural Fund, Chicago, vols. 1–, 1960–, In progress.

BALYS, J., *Lithuanian and Lithuanians; a Selected Bibliography*, Lithuanian Research Institute of New York, 1961.

UNITED STATES LIBRARY OF CONGRESS, Slavic and Central European Division. *Estonia: a Selected Bibliography*, the Library, Washington, 1958.

Yugoslavia

Kojekou Jugoslaviji, Sedona Sile, Belgrade, 1957.

GAEVOY

1928–44 at Ukr. Zankovetskaya Drama Theater, Kiev; roles: Lyubov in Trenev's "Lyubov Yarovaya"; Natalka Kovshik in Korneychuk's "Kalinovaya roshcha" (The Guelder-Rose Grove); Ganna Zolotarenko in Dmiterko's "Naveki vmeste" (Forever Together); Kruchinina in Ostrovsky's "Bez viny vinovatye" (Guilty Without Guilt), etc.; A. USSR, Lvov, Ukr. SSR, Ukrainsky dramatichesky teatr.

GAEVOY, Anton Ivanovich, Secr. s. 1961, member and Presidium member s. 1940, CC, CP Ukr.; member, CC, CPSU, s. 1956; member, CP, s. 1930; b. 1907; Career: 1939–47 Secr., Stalino, 1947–52 Voroshilovgrad, Oblast Comt., CP Ukr.; 1952–58 First Secr., Zaporozhe, 1958–61 Dnepropetrovsk Oblast Comt., CP Ukr.; Dep., USSR Supr. Sov. of 1950, 1954 and 1958 convoc.; Dep., Ukr. Supr. Sov. of 1959 convoc.; 1959 member, Sov. deleg. to Poland; Awards: O. of Lenin, 1957; medal "For Valiant Labor", 1959; A. USSR, Kiev, Ukr. SSR, Ordzhonikidze 11, Tsentralny Komitet KP Ukrainy.

GAFEZ (real name: GAGLOEV), Fedor Zakharevich, Ossetian poet; b. 1913 Baku; Educ.: grad. Staliniri Pedag. Inst.; Publ.: poems and verse: "Chords of Harmony" (1940); "Life is Dear" (1948); "In the Forest"; "It Was"; "A Soldier's Tale"; poems: "An Appeal to Stalin" (1947); "Aminat" (1948); "One's Native Hearth" (1959), etc.; A. USSR, Staliniri, Gruz. SSR, Soyuz pisateley.

GAFUROV, Abutalib Gafurovich, Dag. folk poet; b. 1882 Shuni, Dag.; Career: fought in Civil War in Northern Caucasus on Bolshevik side; Publ.: 1934 first work published; collection "New World" (1934); "The Rivers are Sweeping to the Sea", "A Song on Stalin" (1939), "Before and Now, The Wish, Native Mountains", and "Such a Cause is to Our Liking", etc. (1939–41); "Heroes' March"; "Son of the Mountains" etc.; (1941–45) Awards: O. of Lenin; A. USSR, Makhachkala, Dagestanskaya ASSR, Soyuz pisateley.

GAFUROV, Bobodzhan Gafurovich, Historian; Orientalist; Party official; Dr. of Hist. Sci. s. 1953; full member, Tadzh. Acad. of Sci., s. 1951; corresp. member, USSR Acad. of Sci., s. 1958; Dir., Inst. of Asian Peoples (until 1960 Inst. of Oriental Studies), USSR Acad. of Sci., s. 1956; Bureau member, Dept. of Hist. Sci., USSR Acad. of Sci., s. 1957; Chief Ed., journal "Sovremenny Vostok" (The East Today), s. 1957; member, CC, CPSU, 1952–61; member, CP, s. 1932; b. 1908 vil. Ispisar, Tadzh.; Educ.: 1928 grad. Samarkand Law Sch.; 1935 grad. All-Union

Inst. of Journalists, Moscow; Pos.: 1929–32 Dept. Head, then Assist. Ed., newspaper "Krasny Tadzhikstan"; 1935 again Dep. Ed., then Ed. of above newspaper; 1936–40 instructor, then Section Head, Dep. Dept. Head, and Dept. Head, CC, CP(b) Tadzh.; 1941–44 Secr., CC, CP(b) Tadzh.; 1944–46 Second. Secr. and 1946–56 First Secr., CC, CP Tadzh.; Career: specialist in recent and contemporary hist. of peoples of the East; 1956 member, USSR Parliamentary Group at 45th Inter-Parliamentary Conference, Bangkok; 1957 headed Sov. deleg., to 24th Internat. Congress of Orientalists, Munich; s. 1958 Chm., Sov. Comt. for Implementation of the UNESCO East-West Project, and also Chm., Organ. Comt. for Convening 25th Congress of Orientalists; 1960 Pres. of this Congress, held in Moscow; Chm., Learned Counc. for the Study of the Hist. of the Nat. Liberation Struggle Against Colonialism and Hist. of the Development of the Eastern Countries, Dept. of Hist. Sci., USSR Acad. of Sci.; Dep., Tadzh. Sov. of 1938 and 1955 convoc.; Dep., USSR Supr. Sov. of 1946, 1954 and 1958 convoc.; s. 1958 member, Commission for For. Affairs, Sov. of Nationalities, USSR Supr. Sov.; Publ.: "Istoriya tadzhikskogo naroda" (History of the Tadzhik People) (1953), etc.; Awards: five O. of Lenin; World Peace Counc. Scroll of Honor, 1959; A. USSR, Moskva, Armyansky p. 2. Institut narodov azil AN SSSR.

GAGANOVA, Valentina Ivanovna, Leader of a spinning team, Vyshniy Volochek Spinning Combine, s. 1949; member, CC, CPSU, s. 1961; member, CP, s. 1959; b. 1932, vil. Tsiribushevo, Kalinin Oblast; Career: introduced new form of socialist competition by leaving a highly-efficient spinning team to take over one with a low efficiency rating, bringing it up to the standard of her original team within two months; this form of competition is known as the "Gaganova Movement" and is now widespread in the USSR; Awards: Hero of Socialist Labor, 1959; A. USSR, Vyshniy Volochek, RSFSR, Vyshnevolotsky pryadilny kombinat.

GAGARIN, Yuriy Alekseevich, Mil. pilot, Class I; first man in space, 1961; Maj.; Hon Master of Sport of USSR s. 1961; member, CP, s. 1960; b. 1934 Gzhatsk Rayon, Smolensk Oblast; Educ.: 1951 finished Trade Sch. and Sch. for Working Youth, Lyubertsy, Moscow Oblast; grad. Saratov Ind. Technicum; 1955 completed courses at Saratov Aeroclub; 1957 grad. Orenburg Aviation Sch. as fighter pilot; Career:

226

Fig. 55. *Who's Who in the U.S.S.R.* (Copyright: Scarecrow Press.)

CHAPTER 5

The Fringe of Biography and History

INTRODUCTION

In the last three chapters we have surveyed representative bibliographies of biography and history, international, national, and in some cases regional and local. These should suggest at least one starting point for almost any desired branch of historical studies; if they do not, then the reader may go back to Chapter 1, and the general bibliographies there will assuredly give a clue. Have the lists and descriptions above taught us any hard-and-fast techniques? Probably not, for if we sample and draw a blank, we must try again. Let us look at three dissimilar objectives; (a) reading about the history of Ghana, because we are taking up a post there; (b) writing the history of a British social club in celebration of its centenary, or (c) tracing details of a nineteenth-century American engineer who founded a factory in Dallas. These, let us note, are only three examples of the penetration of history into everyday life and interests, quite apart from its vocational value to prospective teachers, lawyers, historians and archivists. Ghana seems simple, and we might turn directly to Chapter 4, p. 136. But we would probably want to preface our study of Ghana with a fuller background of general African history, if we lacked this knowledge. Having acquired this, we might turn to a universal biographical dictionary for details of pioneer settlers in what was the Gold Coast, and before long we would find we were studying racial problems which are strictly no part of the study of general history.

The approach to studying a British local institution may seem generally covered by the relevant section of Chapter 3 (pp. 102–38).

Not so, because in the quest to fill out details of an organization with a definite location, we might need books on period furniture, portraiture, or we may even have to search Hansard's *Parliamentary Debates* to give substance to some official of importance in our organization, who made a shadowy appearance at Westminster. To attain any merit in our study, we must use original source materials, which we propose to discuss in Chapter 6. The American engineer might lead us to delve into patents, biographies of scientists, histories of technology, as well as histories of Texas. As there is no agreed method of approach, why plan at all? Whatever book we start with leads inevitably to others, and although we have so far studied only *general* biographies and histories, few of these fail to give information on the special trends of their subjects. Maybe they aim at being general, and their bias to the particular is unintentional. Nevertheless, there are general histories of the "drum and trumpet" school, others stressing diplomatic, social or economic history as against the democratic institutional approach of a Stubbs; local histories of landowners and manorial descents are balanced by others emphasizing the growth of industry, agriculture or trade unionism.

SOME UNCONSIDERED SPECIALITIES

Every subject has its own biography and history, and it is impossible to read or write far into an historical subject without looking at the biographies of certain classes of people, and the histories of individual disciplines. Few general biographical or historical bibliographies attempt the immense task of indicating them, though Riches (above, pp. 32–3) does to some extent for biography and Howe (above, pp. 49–51) for history. The few sample titles we append below can do no more than illustrate the enormous ramifications of biography and history, carried into special subject fields. In this book we have considered in any detail only areas and epochs, and though we have purported to study general works, many of these (even the greatest classics) have been ignored if their scope was not sufficiently wide.

Select Lives

AUBREY, J., *Brief Lives*, Secker & Warburg, 1959.

FULLER, T., *The Worthies of England*, Allen & Unwin, 1952. These are modern versions of two old classics.

DOUGLAS, D. C., *English Scholars, 1660–1730*, Eyre & Spottiswoode, 1951.

SITWELL, E., *The English Eccentrics*, Faber, 1930.

STRACHEY, L., *Eminent Victorians*, Chatto, 1918. Three modern classics. The following is a good example of the many valuable local collected biographies.

CREMER, R. W. KETTON, *A Norfolk Gallery*, Faber, 1948.

Women

BLANCH, L., *The Wilder Shores of Love*, Murray, 1954. Studies of four romantic women.

STANTON, D. M., *The English Woman in History*, Allen & Unwin, 1957.

Philosophy

PAUL, L., *The English Philosophers*, Faber, 1953.

RADHAKRISHNAN, S. and others, *History of Philosophy, Eastern and Western*, 2 vols., Allen & Unwin, 1952–3.

Religion

Crockford's Clerical Directory, Oxford Univ. Press, 1858–, In progress. Lists clergy of the Anglican Church.

LANDAU, R., *God is my Adventure*, Knopf, New York, 1936. Features pioneers in religious expression.

MOORE, G. F., *The History of Religions*, 2nd edition, 2 vols., International Theological Library, New York, 1924–5.

Political Theory and Institutions

Dod's Parliamentary Companion, Business Directories, 1832–, annual. Lists members of the English Houses of Parliament.

DUNNING, W. A., *A History of Political Theories*, 3 vols., Macmillan, New York, 1920–43.

Education

FOSTER, J., *Alumni Oxenienses*, 8 vols., Parker, Oxford, 1888–92. Covers 1500–1886, but supplements covering earlier and later periods have been issued. There is a similar work for Cambridge by J. and J. A. Venn.

The Old Public School Boys' Who's Who—Eton, St. James' Press, 1933.

GOOD, H. G., *A History of Western Education*, 2nd edition, Macmillan, New York, 1960.

Economic History

BEABLE, W. H., *Romance of Great Businesses*, Heath Cranton, 1926.

WEBER, M., *Wirtschaft und Gesellschaft*, 4th edition, Mohr, Tubingen, 1956.

Science

Directory of British Scientists, 1964–5, Benn, 1964.

Medical Register, General Medical Council, 1858–, annual.

Dentists' Register, General Dental Council, 1879–, annual.

RAVEN, C. E., *English Naturalists from Neckham to Ray*, Oxford Univ. Press, 1947.

TURNBULL, H. W., *The Great Mathematicians*, 4th edition, Methuen, 1951.

DONALDSON, J., *Agricultural Biography*, the author, 1854.

SARTON, G. A. L., *Introduction to the History of Science*, 3 vols. in 5, Wilkins, Baltimore, 1927–48.

GOTTSCHALK, A., *Histoire de l'alimentation*, 2 vols., Éditions Hippo-craté, Paris, 1948.

SHRYOCK, R. H., *The Development of Modern Medicine*, Gollancz, 1948.

SMITH, D. E., *History of Mathematics*, 2 vols., Ginn & Co., Boston, 1923–5.

Technology

SMILES, S., *Lives of the Engineers*, 5 vols., Bohn, 1874–7.

STRAUB, H., *A History of Civil Engineering*, Hill, 1952.

SINGER, C. J. (editors), *A History of Technology*, 5 vols., Clarendon Press, Oxford, 1954–8.

The Arts

Who's Who in Art, Art Trade Press, 1927–, Irregular.

GUNNIS, R., *Dictionary of British Sculptors, 1660–1851*, Odhams Press, 1953.

Who's Who in the Theatre, Pitman, 1912–, Irregular.

BÉNÉZIT, E., *Dictionnaire . . . des peintres, sculpteurs, dessinateurs et graveurs*, new edition, 8 vols., Librarie Gründ, Paris, 1948–55.

THIEME, U. and BECKER, F., *Allgemeines Lexikon der bildenden Künstler*, 37 vols., Englemann and Seemann, 1907–50. (Reprint, 1964).

The Encyclopedia of World Art, McGraw-Hill, New York, 1959–, In progress.

VASARI, G., *Lives of the Most Eminent Painters, Sculptors and Architects*, Bohn, 1850–97.

FLETCHER, *Sir* BANISTER, *A History of Architecture on the Comparative Method*, 17th edition, Athlone Press, 1961.

Music

The New Oxford History of Music, Oxford Univ. Press, 1954–, In progress.

Grove's Dictionary of Music and Musicians, 5th edition, 9 vols. and supplement, Macmillan, 1954–61.

Literature

Author's and Writer's Who's Who, Burke's Peerage, 1934–, annual.

ARNOLD, M., *Essays in Criticism*, 2 vols., Macmillan, 1888–98.
    In literature, criticism cannot be divorced from biography.

PRAMPOLINI, G., *Storia Universale della Letteratura*, 7 vols., Unione tipografico—editrice torinese, 1948–53.

Military and Naval History[1]

UNITED STATES NAVY, *Medal of Honour, 1861–1949*, U.S. Navy, Washington, 1949.

SMYTH, Sir J., *The Story of the Victoria Cross, 1856–1963*, Muller, 1963.

CLOWES, G. S. L., *Sailing Ships; their History and Development*, 2 parts, H.M.S.O., 1931–6.

OMAN, Sir C. W. C., *The Art of War in the Middle Ages, A.D. 378–1515*, revised edition, Oxford Univ. Press, 1953. The work has been continued to 1600.

The above are representative titles only, not necessarily the best, on the subjects named. They emanate largely from, or relate to, one country—the author's own. At least their inclusion may serve to point the question "would a special biography or history answer our purpose more than one claiming to be general?" To this the somewhat cynical reply may be given that however abstruse the subject, someone in some language may well have prepared a collective biographical work on it, and someone else may have written its history! In searching for material on a given biographical or historical subject we are not, of course, concerned only with books, but also with articles in periodicals (a number are listed in the appropriate sections above) and theses, dissertations, etc., which will be discussed on p. 225.

We must now try to decide which are the main ancillary studies

---

[1] As this may be regarded as history proper rather than its fringe, we may cite two bibliographies—M. J. D. Cockle, *A bibliography of Military Books up to 1642* (reissued 1965), and A. S. White, *A bibliography of Regimental Histories of the British Army*, 1965.

of the biographer and historian, leaving, however, such purely source materials as *epigraphy*, *papyrology*, *sphragistics* (*sigillography*), *palaeography*, *manuscripts* and *archives* to the next chapter. We have considered *historiography*, sometimes claimed as an ancillary to history, as a constituent part of it, and made certain references to it above (pp. 66–8, etc.). *Numismatics*—the study of coins and medals—and *iconography*—research into the illustration of a subject —we do not propose to cover, for reasons of space. Clearly, however, these sciences are pervasive of history, and it would be as well to examine one general book on each. R. A. G. Carson's *Coins: Ancient, Mediaeval and Modern* (Hutchinson, 1962), substantiates the claim that "coins provide an almost unparalleled series of historical documents. Their most immediate contribution is as illustrations of history, for in Western civilization from the end of the fourth century B.C. onwards, with the exception of a large portion of the Middle Ages, they supply contemporary portraits of many of history's leading characters" (preface). And London, National Portrait Gallery, *British Historical Portraits: a Selection from the National Portrait Gallery with Biographical Notes* (Cambridge Univ. Press, 1957), may prove in every way as adequate as a more advanced work such as the complete listing of drawings in a national museum, or one of the many admirable catalogues increasingly produced for special local exhibitions, to demonstrate the value of iconography to the historian. Plate 18 of this work depicts Queen Elizabeth I, and Plate 382 Elizabeth II; the contrast of dress, formality of expression and indeed of the setting behind the respective portraits, illustrates pictorially the changes in the character of the British monarchy in a way that no words are able to do. In iconography, the illustration is supreme; the text merely annalistic; there is a division of opinion among historians as to whether illustration aids or hampers the presentation of their subject, though the best-known short history of England, G. M. Trevelyan's *English Social History*, appeared in illustrated form as his uncle T. B. Macaulay's great work did in its day, and Churchill's *Island Race* in ours. Clearly there are many types of history—of costume, farm implements, engineering, architecture, etc., in the study of which iconography plays an essential part. The term, however, refers only to the study of illustrations *per se*, and not to those of pictures accompanying text.

Travel and topography properly accompany geography. Their study has been excluded from this book with reluctance. The descriptions of today, with great building development progressing over half the world, and rebellion's destruction over the other half, soon acquire an historical flavour. Old guide books are very valuable to the historian, because early descriptions of any country or region are normally much fuller than later ones. The published nineteenth-century explorations of Africa, the Middle West, South America or Australia are invaluable well-illustrated sources dating from a time when printing costs were no bar to authors treating their subjects as fully as they wished. At the other end of the scale, the guide books and publicity material produced by many urban and rural authorities are often the only available source of historical information about lesser known communities. E. G. Cox's *Reference Guide to the Literature of Travel* (3 vols., University of Washington, Seattle, 1935–, In progress), lists much of interest to the historian, though it unfortunately concludes at A.D. 1800.[1] One of its shortest chapters (Vol. II, Chapter XI) concerns the newest continent, Australia, but details of publications by Tasman, Cook and Governor Philip are given. We give below a select list of British published original travel and topographical works of major historical interest.

ANSON, George, *A Voyage Round the World*, Dent, 1912.

BAKER, *Sir* S. White, *The Albert N'Yanza*, 2 vols., Sidgwick & Jackson, 1962.

BECKFORD, William, *Travel Diaries*, 2 vols., Constable, 1928.

BELL, Gertrude L., *From Amurath to Amurath*, Heinemann, 1911.

BOSWELL, James, *Journal of a Tour to the Hebrides with Samuel Johnson*, Heinemann, 1963.

BROWNE, E. G., *A Year Amongst the Persians*, Cambridge Univ. Press, 1950.

---

[1] See also R. Fedden, *English Travellers in the Near East*, British Council, 1958, with a bibliography.

BULLEN, F. T., *The Cruise of the 'Cachalot' Round the World*, Murray, 1948.

BURCKHARDT, J. L., *Travels in Arabia*, 2 vols., Colburn, 1829.

BURTON, Sir R. F., *Pilgrimage to El Medinah and Mecca*, Bell, 1913.

CHERRY-GARRARD, Apsley, *The Worst Journey in the World*, Chatto, 1951.

COBBETT, William, *Rural Rides*, Macdonald, 1959.

CONWAY, W. M., *The Alps from End to End*, Nelson, 1917.

CURZON, R., *Visits to Monasteries in the Levant*, Oxford Univ. Press, 1916.

DARWIN, C. R., *The Voyage of the Beagle*, Dent, 1955.

DEFOE, Daniel, *A Tour through the Whole Island of Great Britain*, 2 vols., Davies, 1927.

DOUGHTY, C. M., *Travels in Arabia Deserta*, 2 vols., Cape, 1936.

FIENNES, Celia, *Journeys*, Cresset Press, 1949.

FORD, Richard, *Handbook for Travellers in Spain*, Murray, 1845.

GRENFELL, Sir W. T., *A Labrador Doctor*, Hodder, 1948.

HAKLUYT, Richard, *Principal Navigations*, 8 vols., Dent, 1962.

KINGLAKE, A. W., *Eothen*, Methuen, 1948.

LANE, E. W., *Manners and Customs of the Modern Egyptians*, Dent, 1954.

LAWRENCE, T. E., *Seven Pillars of Wisdom*, Cape, 1935.

LIVINGSTONE, David, *Missionary Travels and Researches in South Africa*, Dent, 1954.

PARKMAN, Francis, *The Oregon Trail*, Dent, 1954.

SHACKLETON, Sir E., *South*, Heinemann, 1951.

STANLEY, Sir H. M., *Through the Dark Continent*, 2 vols., Low, 1878.

WATERTON, Charles, *Wanderings in South America*, Dent, 1925.

WHYMPER, Edward, *Scrambles Amongst the Alps*, Murray, 1936.

These are mainly extracted from the 1963 edition of F. Seymour Smith's *An English Library* (Deutsch), a work which we did not consider quite formal enough to consider among the general bibliographies studied in Chapter 1, though it is a most fascinating listing of those readable English books which have acquired the standing of classics.

Before leaving our consideration of the effect of travel on history, we will note, as further examples, three sample descriptive works available in most British public libraries:

A Muirhead Blue Guide. The Muirhead series of guides has completed post-war coverage more rapidly than the rival productions by Fodor, Hachette or Nagel, though the general remarks about it apply in some degree to them also. Older editions of the *Baedekers* or *Cook's Travellers' Guides* are not to be despised by the historian. The former are, in their pre-war guise, the fullest of all. The present emasculated versions are further casualties of current printing costs. The *Ward Lock* guides relate only to Great Britain.

    The 2nd edition of Muirhead's *Blue Guide to Southern Spain* appeared in 1964 (Benn). Of its 419 closely printed pages, 104 are taken up with the general history of Spain, painting, architecture and sculpture, and in the main descriptive section, history and topography are inextricably mixed up.

A Pre-war Kelly's County Directory. The 1938 (last published) edition of Kelly's *Kent* ran to 1174 pages, and in its general introduction and descriptions of individual places, topographical and historical details are listed side by side.

A Modern Civic Guide Book. We may check two examples: the City of Birmingham Information Department's guide to the second city of Great Britain, and a guide to one of the smaller English counties (Bedfordshire) produced on an advertising basis by E. J. Burrow & Co. of Cheltenham, who produce a very large number of these guides. The Birmingham production, though naturally concentrating on present-day amenities (the book is aimed mainly at short-term visitors and prospective residents), contains a considerable amount of historical material. Of its forty well-illustrated pages only four dealing with industry and four giving directory information have no current value for the historian. These will, of course, acquire such value as the years pass. *The Bedfordshire County Handbook*, like all its companion volumes, concentrates more on the county area than on the towns within it, several of which issue their own separate productions. About a third of its text contains references to the historical background of the county and its constituent communities.

It is not claimed that any of the above three productions are the best sources for the history of the localities concerned. In lieu of the best, however, students are concerned with what is available; tourists with what is portable; the general public with what is convenient and assimilable. There are many small communities, not well written up, for which an analysis of the differences between successive editions of the local guidebook provides the obvious starting point for a historical study.

CHRONOLOGY AND TABULATIONS

Although history is concerned with opinion as much as with fact, it is necessary to work on as accurate a basis as is possible. For that reason, books which establish the dates of the past, the succession of events or rulers, officials, clergy, legislators, etc., are most valuable. R. L. Poole's *Medieval Reckonings of Time* (S.P.C.K., 1918), is a simple introduction to a most difficult subject. E. A. Fry, *Almanacks for Students of English History* (Phillimore, 1915), gives thirty-five different almanacs from which any date between A.D. 500 and 2000 can be calculated, if the date of Easter or certain feast days is known. The almanacs take leap-years into account and there is a supplementary table showing how to calculate dates for those countries that adopted a new style of date in 1582; this style was only adopted in England in 1752. C. R. Cheney's *Handbook of Dates for Students of English History* (Royal Historical Society, 1955), has more descriptive matter than Fry, and repeats his almanacs with corrections and additions. Both these works have tables of the regnal years of English sovereigns. Still fuller is F. M. Powicke's *Handbook of British Chronology* (1st edition, Royal Historical Society, 1939; (Fig. 56) 2nd edition, 1961, from the same publisher). The first edition includes the almanacs given in Fry and Cheyney, but these are omitted from the second edition which gives in addition much information about English and Scottish rulers and officials (and also includes some for Ireland and the Isle of Man), archbishops and bishops of the four countries of the British Isles, dukes, marquesses and earls from 1066 to 1714 and parliaments before 1832. Powicke's work has clearly developed from a mere chronological device into a fully annalistic work, of which there are several examples, J. Haydn's *Dictionary of Dates and Universal Information* (25th edition, Ward Lock, 1910), being the best known. Although arranged as an ordinary dictionary, information under each head is arranged chronologically. The heading "wrecks", for example, has a list of "remarkable cases of British vessels wrecked or burnt"; under "Würtemberg" is given a list of dukes and kings. Similar shorter works are *Everyman's Dictionary of Dates* (4th edition, Dent, 1964), and *Newnes' Dictionary of Dates and Anniversaries* (1962). Under "Battles", *Everyman's* gives a very comprehensive list alphabetically arranged, with major items in bold type, and references to the battles described in Edward Creasy's *Fifteen Decisive Battles of the World* (Oxford Univ. Press, 1915). Under "places" there is no description but merely dates of principal events, e.g.:

> Bedford, England. Burned by Danes, 1010. B. School founded, 1552. B. Modern School founded, 1566. Bunyan imprisoned, 1660–72.

Newnes' compilation is useful to supplement Haydn and Everyman with a few more modern items. "I have tried to follow the present vogue for facts and allusions, many of which relate to scientific and technological achievement, rather than wars and battles, and for cultural and sociological leaders in preference to field-marshals and admirals" (preface).

S. H. Steinberg's *Historical Tables 58 B.C.–A.D. 1963* (7th edition, Macmillan, 1964) is perhaps most useful in guarding against excessive insularity when studying history, for it gives six simul-

ST. EDMUNDSBURY AND IPSWICH

Henry Bernard Hodgson	nom. 18 Feb., cons. 24 Feb. 1914	d. 28 Feb. 1921
Albert Augustus David	nom. 21 June, cons. 25 July 1921	trs. Liverpool 18 Oct. 1923
Walter Godfrey Whittingham	nom. 22 Oct., cons. 1 Nov. 1923	res. 1940 (d. 17 June 1941)
Richard Brook	nom. 24 Sept., cons. 1 Nov. 1940	res. 1953
Arthur Harold Morris	trs. Pontefract (suff.), nom. 4 May, conf. 2 June 1954	

SALISBURY

Osmund	cons. *a.* 3 June 1078	d. 3–4 Dec. 1099
Roger	nom. 29 Sept. 1102, el. 13 Apr. 1103, cons. 11 Aug. 1107	d. 11 Dec. 1139
[Philip de Harcourt	nom. Mar. 1140	qua. *1141*]
Jocelin de Bohun	cons. 1142	res. 1184 (d. 18 Nov. 1184)
Hubert Walter	el. 15 Sept., cons. 22 Oct. 1189	trs. Canterbury *p.* 29 May 1193
Herbert Poore	el. *a.* 5 May, temp. *15 May*, cons. 5 June 1194	d. *7 Jan.* 1217
Richard Poore	trs. Chichester *a.* 27 June 1217	trs. Durham 14 May 1228
Robert Bingham	el. *a.* 25 Sept. 1228, cons. 27 May 1229	d. 2–3 Nov. 1246
William of York	el. 10 Dec. 1246, temp. 29 Jan., cons. 14 July 1247	d. *31* Jan 1256
Giles of Bridport	el. 13 Feb.–15 Apr., temp. 17 Aug. 1256, cons. 11 Mar. 1257	d. *13* Dec. 1262
Walter de la Wyle	el. 29 Jan., temp. 10 Apr., cons. 27 May 1263	d. 3–4 Jan. 1271
Robert Wickhampton	el. *a.* 6 Mar. 1271, cons. 13 May 1274, temp. 15 Aug. 1274	d. 24 Apr. 1284
Walter Scammel	el. *a.* 12 July, temp. 10 Aug., cons. 22 Oct. 1284	d. 20 Sept. 1286
Henry Brandeston	el. 2 Jan., temp. 15 Mar., cons. 1 June 1287	d. 11 Feb. 1288
William de la Corner	el. 24–25 Nov. 1288, temp. 26 Feb., cons. 8 May 1289	d. *10 Oct.* 1291
Nicholas Longespee	el. 8 Nov.–12 Dec., temp. 16 Dec. 1291, cons. 16 Mar. 1292	d. 18 May 1297
Simon of Ghent	el. 2 June, temp. 7 Aug., cons. 20 Oct. 1297	d. 2 Apr. 1315
Roger Martival	el. *a.* 11 June, temp. 18 July, cons. 28 Sept. 1315	d. 14 Mar. 1330
Robert Wyvil	prov. 16 Apr., temp. 10 June, cons. 15 July 1330	d. early Sept. 1375
Ralph Erghum	prov. 12 Oct., cons. 9 Dec., temp. 28 Dec. 1375	trs. Bath 3 Apr. 1388
John Waltham	prov. 3 Apr., temp. 13 Sept., cons. 20 Sept. 1388	d. 17 Sept. 1395
Richard Mitford	trs. Chichester, prov. 25 Oct. 1395, temp. 30 Jan. 1396	d. 29 Apr.–9 May 1407
Nicholas Bubwith	trs. London, prov. 22 June, temp. 14 Aug. 1407	trs. Bath 7 Oct. 1407
Robert Hallum	prov. 23 Oct., cons. 1407, temp. 1 Dec. 1407	d. 4 Sept. 1417
John Chaundler	el. 15 Nov., cons. 12 Dec. 1417, temp. 8 Jan. 1418	d. 16 July 1426
[Simon Sydenham	el. *p.* 23 July 1426	qua. 9 July 1427]

Fig. 56. POWICKE, F. M., *Handbook of British Chronology*. (Copyright: Royal Historical Society.)

taneous tables of events, the divisions being partly of area, and partly of activity. In 1903, for example, we learn under "Western and Southern Europe" that Edward VII visited the Continent and Pope Pius X succeeded Leo XIII. In "Central, Northern and Eastern Europe", King Alexander of Serbia's murder is reported; under "Countries Overseas" we are informed that the Alaska frontier dispute between Canada and the U.S.A. was settled whereas Russo-Japanese difficulties were not. Constitutional, economic and scientific and cultural history are given separate columns; they record the earliest flight of the Wright brothers in the U.S.A. and the posthumous publication of Samuel Butler's *Way of All Flesh*, W. L. Langer's so-called *Encyclopedia of World History* (3rd edition, revised, Harrap, 1956) is also compiled on the annalistic principle, but under individual periods, divided by continents, civilizations and countries. As might be expected "the Pacific area" is not brought in until p. 894 of 1243 pages. There are early entries under this head for Balboa (1513) and Magellan (1520), but use of the work is hampered to some extent by the non-incorporation of supplements in the main sequence. There are excellent indexes.

It is possible to do much historical study without using any of the chronological or annalistic works referred to above. For accurate dating of obscure or little-known events, however, they are invaluable. Much of the information in local newspapers is less accessible than it should be if chronologies and similar tools were available to a greater extent in local areas. One such publication is C. Mackie's *Norfolk Annals, 1801–1900* (2 vols., Norfolk Chronicle, Norwich, 1901), which had a predecessor in the *Norfolk and Norwich Remembrancer* (covering 1701–1800), and a successor 1901–50 (*Norfolk Events* by H. B. Jaffa). There are also available for some local areas chronologies such as Hamon le Strange's *Norfolk Official Lists* (Goose, Norwich, 1890). In addition to the type of person covered by Powicke (bishops, etc.), this gives lists of lord lieutenants and sheriffs for the county, and mayors, town clerks, etc., for individual boroughs.

MAPS AND HISTORICAL GEOGRAPHY

The use of maps and plans to study history is sometimes known as historical geography. Clearly, such study is indispensable, not only in looking into wars and campaigns, but in investigating the development or the non-development of social or economic movements as influenced by such factors as river valleys or mountains. There are historical maps and atlases specially designed for the use of historical students, but old maps in themselves, including modern reproductions of them, are also of very great value. Maps may be either international, national or local; they may illustrate political, economic, social or indeed any branch of history. Their definition may be taken as including plans of cities, fortifications, etc. Following are some important general historical atlases:

> *Grosser historischer Weltatlas*, 3 vols., the proprietors, Munich, 1953–, In progress. This is fuller than any work in English.
> SHEPHERD, W. R., *Historical Atlas*, 9th edition, Philip, 1965.
> *Muir's Historical Atlas, Ancient, Mediaeval and Modern*, 8th edition, Philip, 1958. A later edition of the mediaeval and modern section of this work appeared in 1965 and of the ancient section in 1964. Briefer coverage than Shepherd.
> *Rand McNally Atlas of World History*, Rand McNally, Chicago, 1957. Includes a full treatment of the Americas with modern presentation and commentary between the map pages.

The *Cambridge Histories* have accompanying volumes of maps, and there are several atlases of the classical period. It is not possible to deal here with the historical cartography of individual areas or countries. G. R. Crone's *Maps and Their Makers* (2nd edition, Hutchinson, 1962) is an excellent modern description. We may, however, refer to a few British developments. The Ordnance Survey has issued various historical maps on the 1 to a million scale (the Dark Ages, Roman Britain, Monasticism, etc.). The Royal Geographical Society has published *Early Maps of the British Isles, A.D. 1000–A.D. 1579* (R.G.S., 1961), and the British Museum has a full catalogue, the *Catalogue of the Printed Maps, Plans and*

1611

XXII.

SPEED, JOHN.

The Theatre of the Empire of Great Britaine : presenting an exact geography of the
Kingdomes of England, Scotland, Ireland, and the Isles adioyning : with The Shires,
Hundreds, Cities and Shire-townes, within y⁰ Kingdome of England, divided and de-
scribed by John Speed. Imprinted at London. Anno, cum Privilegio, 1611[—1612].
And are to be solde by John Sudbury & Georg Humble, in Popes-head alley at y⁰ signe
of y⁰ White Horse. fol. 9½ × 15 inches.

Sixty-seven maps prepared by John Speed from the surveys of John Norden, and
Christopher Saxton, except the Isle of Wight, which is by William White, and the
Isle of Man by Thomas Durham.

The maps were engraved, chiefly, by Jodocus Hondius. Richard Gough, in his
British Topography, London, 1780, in speaking of the engraving of these maps, says :
" Others were done by Abraham Goss, though his name is not to them." The plates
bear the imprint of John Sudbury and George Humble, except those of Bedford,
Bucks, Essex, the Isle of Man, Middlesex, Lancashire, Merioneth, Shropshire, Suffolk
and Westmoreland, which have the imprint of G. Humble, only.

The text on the back of the maps is chiefly abridged from *Camden's Britannia* ; but
that of Norfolk was supplied by Sir William Spelman.

This is the first atlas with the counties divided into hundreds. The work is in
four parts, being books 1—4 of Speed's *History of Great Britain*.

THE FIRST BOOK.

A pictorial title-page, the central figure at the top, a Briton ; on the left, a Roman ;
on the right, a Saxon. Below the central figure, the title, on the left, a Dane ; on
the right, a Norman. The verso of the title-page is blank.

A list, with an ornamental border, of the kingdoms of England, Scotland, Wales,
Ireland and Man. On the verso, the Royal Arms, surrounded with shields, bearing
the arms of the early British kings, engraved by Jodocus Hondius. Then follow five
leaves with the dedication, contents of the various parts, letters and verses in praise
of Speed's work, and Speed's preface " To the Well-affected and favourable Reader."
The verso of the fifth leaf is blank.

All the maps have descriptive text on the back, both recto and verso, unless otherwise stated.

Maps—

1. THE KINGDOME OF GREAT BRITAINE AND IRELAND. Graven by J. Hondius . . .
   1610. The scale of miles, 80 [=2¼ inches]. Plans : London, & Edinburgh.
2. BRITAIN as it was devided in the tyme of the Englishe-Saxons . . . performed
   by John Speede, etc. [Scale, 40 miles=1⅛ inches].
3. THE KINGDOME OF ENGLAND. Described by Christopher Saxton, augmented
   by John Speed . . . Jodocus Hondius . . . cælavit . . . 1610. The
   scale of miles, 50 [=2¼ inches].
4. KENT with her Cities and Earles described and observed. Plans : Canterbury
   and Rochester.
      Arms : Odo Bishop of Bayen, Will. Iprese E. of Flan., Hubert de Burgh,
   Edmond Woodstok, Thomas Holland, William Nevill, Edmond Graye, Canterbury, Rochester, and the Royal Arms.

Fig. 57. CHUBB, T., *Printed Maps in the Atlases of Great Britain and
Ireland.* (Copyright: Homeland Association.)

Charters in the British Museum (2 vols., 1885). However, the principal work on British historical maps and atlases is (Fig. 57) T. Chubb's *Printed Maps in the Atlases of Great Britain and Ireland*, Homeland Association, 1927. This gives full descriptions of the British atlases up to 1870, and of their constituent maps, most of which, alas, are now found mainly in separate form. The introduction to this work and the biographical notes upon the individual map-makers should be read by all students of English local history. The first British atlas was published by Christopher Saxton in 1579, but the best-known one is John Speed's *Theatre of the Empire of Great Britain* (Sudbury and Humble, 1611). There have been modern reproductions of both Saxton's and Speed's maps. Chubb's great work has prepared the way for several studies of the maps of individual English counties. Town plans—usually available only in guide books and certain encyclopaedias—were also included in *Norfolk Maps and Norwich Plans* (Jarrold, Norwich, 1928), which Chubb himself compiled in conjunction with G. A. Stephen.

HERALDRY: FLAGS

Heraldry and flags present some of the more colourful and interesting by-ways of history. There is a useful bibliography by S. T. Cope, *Heraldry, Flags and Seals . . . 1920 to 1945* (Aslib, 1958), and Manchester Public Libraries, *Subject Catalogue*, Section 929 Part 3 (Libraries Committee, Manchester, 1958) also deals with this subject. (Fig. 58), C. Boutell's *Heraldry* (revised by C. W. Scott-Giles, Warne, 1963), is probably the clearest presentation. The science of heraldry is derived from the situation in the Middle Ages, when illiteracy was rampant.

In war, opposing armies carried shields, and information was conveyed by means of pictorial diagrams on them. Heraldry is now restricted to the science of deciphering shields or similar devices, or portions appended to them—crests on the top; supporters on the side. The subject is of interest to artists as well as to students of history. We may say something about the unofficial heraldry of war, and the Scottish tartan, as it is impossible to consider

BADGES AND KNOTS

338. Knots

A badge of the Lords Dacre of Gilsland consisted of a knot gules linking a silver escallop (from the Dacre arms) with a ragged staff argent (339); the staff may allude to the barony of Greystock, united by marriage with that of Dacre.

In the badge of the Lords Hastings and Hungerford, a knot unites the Hungerford sickle with the garb of the Peverels (340).

Advocating a revival in the use of badges, Boutell said: " Unlike crests, which must necessarily be associated with helms, and the wearers of helms, and consequently have both a military and a medieval character, badges are equally appropriate for use by ladies, as well as by men of every profession, and they belong alike to every age and period." He also pointed out the unsuitability of using a crest, which should be borne on a helm, as a device on such things as livery buttons.   Since he wrote, heraldic badges have again come into use.   An armigerous

339. Badge of
LORD DACRE OF GILSLAND

340. Badge of
LORD HASTINGS AND HUNGERFORD

Fig. 58. BOUTELL, C., *Heraldry*. (Copyright: Warne.)

Scottish heraldry without doing so, but we do not intend to investigate other branches of ceremonial, e.g. civic, academic, ecclesiastical, masonic or friendly society robes—as although they have a considerable intrinsic historic interest in relation to their subject, they are less valuable for the study of general history than heraldry. Boutell's book refers briefly to hatchments, badges, knots, mottoes, modern civic and military heraldic representation, the insignia of the British orders of knighthood, dominion and foreign examples, and includes a brief treatment of flags though there are more specialized works on all these subjects. Other useful one-volume works include A. C. Fox-Davies' *Complete Guide to Heraldry* (Jack, 1909), and G. C. Rothery's *ABC of Heraldry* (Paul, 1915). A. C. Fox-Davies also completed *The Art of Heraldry* (Jack, 1904), probably the fullest work in English on the subject. Is heraldry a mere survival from the past, or has it much practical value for the biographer, historian or genealogist? A knowledge of heraldry cannot lightly be acquired, but it is undoubtedly of great value in settling the descents, relationships and habits of individuals, owing to the practice of incorporating objects on the surface of the shield which have some relationship to personal character or occupations. Such objects are still employed today when coats-of-arms are granted to individuals, firms or corporate bodies by the College of Arms. (Fig. 59), C. W. Scott-Giles, *Civic Heraldry of England and Wales* (2nd edition, Dent, 1953) is a useful comment on the value of heraldry in Britain today. Of the example described it will be seen how every feature of the arms, or achievement, as it is more properly termed, illustrates some local association. The eagle, for instance, depicts not only the Roman associations of the area, but its importance as an R.A.F. base. A. C. Fox-Davies' *Book of Public Arms* (Jack, 1915) is an older work of similar scope, still useful.

J. W. Papworth and A. W. W. Morant's *Alphabetical Dictionary of Coats of Arms* (Papworth, 1874) lists family arms alphabetically under heraldic descriptions, giving the family name at the end, whereas Sir J. B. Burke's *General Armory* (Harrison, 1884), does exactly the reverse of this. "Armory" is a term preferred by some authorities to "heraldry", and both these very valuable books,

CAINSBOROUGH R.D.C.   GLANFORD BRIGG R.D.C.   SOUTH KESTEVEN R.D.C.

oldest learned society in the kingdom. The tulips stand for the flower industry. The galley recalls the town's maritime history, and is also an emblem of St Nicholas, while the lily stands for St Mary—patron saints of the town.

The motto is usually translated, 'She nourishes the neighbouring cities.' This was adopted many years ago, probably with reference to the agricultural produce of the district.

GAINSBOROUGH Rural District Council

ARMS: Parted palewise, the dexter side barry wavy of six pieces azure and argent, and the sinister side ermine; on a gold pale a chevron vert between in chief a mitre gules charged with a gold fleur-de-lis, and in base an eagle displayed gules.

CREST: On a wreath gold and azure, a Danish dragon-ship sable, a pennon azure flying from the mast, the sail gold charged with a boar's head torn off sable with tusks and tongue gules.

MOTTO: *Trust and triumph.*

These were granted in 1952.

A note issued by the Council states:

The shield is an heraldic map of the District. The blue and white waves represent the Trent with its eagre, the ermine portion is for Ermine Street, and between these boundaries lies a rich agricultural area represented by the gold middle portion. The chevron is common to the arms of John Wycliffe, Thomas Sutton, and Admiral Lord Hawke, all having associations with the area. It is coloured green and so represents the central ridge called the Cliff. The mitre for the ancient bishopric of Lindsey, with its head at Stow, from which the present Diocese of Lincoln descends. The fleur-de-lis is the emblem of St Mary, and in gold on red gives the present diocesan colours. The eagle represents the numerous Roman associations of the district, and also its importance as a Royal Air Force base.

Fig. 59. SCOTT-GILES, C. W., *Civic Heraldry of England and Wales.*
(Copyright: Dent.)

which have never been superseded, demand some grounding in the subject before they can be used adequately. A similar work to Papworth for European arms is J. B. Rietstap's *Armorial général* (2 vols. and supplements, 2nd edition, Dupont, Paris, 1904). Another very full work by A. C. Fox-Davies is *Armorial Families* (7th edition, 2 vols., Hurst & Blackett, 1929) giving a full list with illustrations of those families whose arms are officially recorded at the College of Arms. J. Fairbairn's *Book of Crests* (2 vols., Jack, Edinburgh, 1905) is the standard work on this subject, and for Scotland, *Scots Heraldry* by Sir Thomas Innes (2nd edition, Oliver & Boyd, Edinburgh, 1956) is most illuminating. The same author has published *The Tartans of the Clans and Families of Scotland* (7th edition, Johnston & Bacon, 1964), which has a fully descriptive preface on the clan system of Scotland, with 116 coloured illustrations of tartans.

We decided earlier not to consider numismatics (the study of coins and medals), nor ceremonial uniforms, in this brief work, but it is difficult to give any consideration to the heraldry of the armed forces without saying something about uniforms and military medals, as well as cap and other badges. Two works by R. M. Barnes deal with *The Uniforms and History of the Scottish Regiments 1625 to the Present Day* (Seeley Service, 1956), and *Military Uniforms of Britain and the Empire, 1742 to the Present Time* (Seeley Service, 1960). H. T. Dorling, *Ribbons and Medals* (new edition, Philip, 1963) (British and foreign examples), and L. L. Gordon, *British Battles and Medals* (the author, Gnosall, 1962) (fuller illustrations than Dorling), are the leading works on their subject. Heraldry played a bigger part in World War II than in its predecessors, and there are numerous books on formation signs, buttons, badges on dress, etc., as well as on the historically older cap badges, worn by armed units. The standard work for Britain on the latter subject is Major T. J. Edwards' *Regimental Badges* (3rd edition, Gale & Polden, Aldershot, 1963).

Flags are more easily understood by the man in the street than other heraldic devices. H. G. Carr's *Flags of the World* (Warne, revised edition, 1961) describes not only national flags, but those of the services, house flags of shipping companies, yacht flags and flags of corporations and public bodies; the British Commonwealth and, less fully, the U.S.A. are dealt with. Much fuller though less clear is the Admiralty's *Flags of all Nations* (H.M.S.O., 1955–, In progress). The two volumes are appearing in loose-leaf form; arrangements for amendments are certainly necessary in works on flags. While this work was being prepared new national flags were being devised for several African states and also for Canada. The detail in the Admiralty work extends to the flags used by ministers, generals, etc., on cars. The later pages will deal with the flags of public bodies. A useful brief introduction to a complicated subject is the *Flag Book of the United Nations* (United Nations, New York, 1963).

GENEALOGY

Much of genealogy is vanity, but it cannot be overlooked in any treatment of history. There is a great interest in genealogy in the newer English-speaking countries. Individuals in Britain derive much satisfaction from seeking to discover whether their ancestors are on the roll of those who came over with William the Conqueror. The growing number of members of the Mormon Church (officially the Church of Jesus Christ of Latter-day Saints, which has branches now in many countries outside the U.S.A.) are compelled for religious reasons to investigate their ancestors. Reference will be made again to genealogy in the next chapter, as advanced investigations demand the use of original documents.

L. G. Pine's *Your Family Tree* (revised edition, Jenkins, 1962) is a very useful introduction to genealogy, and we may quote from its opening chapter: "Genealogy illuminates the history of the country. It is impossible to understand the wars between England and France, or the struggle for independence by the Scots in medieval times, without recourse to genealogical tables. If there had not been twelve claimants to the throne of Scotland in 1295, Edward I of England could hardly have interfered in the affairs of that country. There would have been no Wallace, no Bruce, and no doubt some dynastic marriage would have united England and Scotland as Castile and Aragon united. Similarly, the Wars of the Roses in England are completely inexplicable unless one looks at a family tree of York and Lancaster". The fullest bibliography on genealogy (also including heraldry) is G. Gatfield's *Guide to Printed Books and Manuscripts Relating to English and Foreign Heraldry and Genealogy* (Mitchell & Hughes, 1892), which is very badly arranged as well as being out of date, and it may be supplemented or substituted by parts 1 and 2 of the Manchester Public Libraries *Subject Catalogues, Section 929* (Libraries Committee, Manchester, 1956–7). Americans are particularly interested in (Fig. 60) J. C. Hotten's *Original Lists of Persons of Quality, Emigrants, Religious Exiles, Political Rebels . . . and Others who went from Great Britain to the American Plantations* (Baker, New York, 1931); this covers emigration between 1600 and 1700.

U.S. Bureau of the Census, *Heads of Families at the First Census, 1790* (12 vols., Government Printing Office, Washington, 1907–9) gives the town in which families of a given surname were living in 1790, and therefore provides a useful starting point for further research. The fullest secondary treatment of the subject is D. E. Gardner and Frank Smith's *Genealogical Research in England and Wales* (3 vols., Bookcraft Publications, Salt Lake City, 1956–64). Volume I of this work deals with such subjects as burial grounds and churchyards, civil registration of births, marriages and deaths, the census records, the Anglican parish and its administration, bishops' transcripts, the history and records of nonconformists, Jews and Roman Catholics. Volume II goes on to wills and other probate records, naval and military sources and a summary of the situation as regards original material in every English and Welsh county.

Turning now to lists of noble families, etc., the best is undoubtedly the *Almanach de Gotha* (Perthes, Gotha, 1763–1944), an annual, which gives very full information on the princely houses of Europe. This work, which was at its best some fifty years ago, is no longer published, as so many of the persons concerned have lost their titles. A similar work is the *Genealogisches Handbuch des Adels* (Starke, Glücksburg, 1951–, Irregular). Separate volumes deal with

LISTS OF CONVICTED REBELS.   329

CERTIFICATE of the disposall of CAPT. KENDALL'S Rebells.

Barbadoes.

A LIST of Ninety Rebells by the *Happy Return*, of Pool, CAPT. ROGER WADHAM, Comander, with the names of the Masters to whom they were disposed of, by the Honᵇˡᵉ· COLLOᴸᴸ· JOHN HALLETT & Company, for account of SIR WILLIAM BOOTH and CAPTAIN JAMES KENDALL. December, 1685.

Servants' names.	Masters' names.
BENJAMIN CROW	
JOHN GUY	
JOHN ALSTONE	COLLONEL JOHN HALLETT.
WILLIAM BROWN	
EDWARD WILLMOTT	PETER FLEWELLIN.
RICHARD ALLEN	WILLIAM LOWGAR, Esq.
JOHN BROWN	BENJAMIN BORD.
ELIAS STEVENS	CAPT. JOHN STEWART.
WILLIAM CLARKE	
WILLIAM WILLS	CAPT. WILLIAM MARSHALL.
JAMES POMREY	
EDWARD MORTON	
JAMES SALTER	AGNIS FENTON.
JOHN EDWARDS	CAPT. MATHEW HAVILAND.
JAMES FOWLER	
THOMAS CORNELIUS	COLLOᴸᴸ· JOHN FARMER.
ROBERT SPURNEY	
THOMAS TOWNSEND	CAPT. TOBIAS FRERE.
JOHN HUGENS	
NATHANIEL WEBBER	WILLIAM WEAVER.
JOHN LOVERIDGE	
JOHN SPEERING	MAJOR GLORGE LILLINGTON.
THOMAS HALLETT	COLL. SAMUEL TITCOMB.
JASPER DIAMOND	RICHARD HARWOOD, Esq.

42

Fig. 60. HOTTEN, J. C., *Original Lists.* (Copyright: Baker.)

European reigning and princely houses, counts, barons and other ennobled ranks. The *Handbuch* endeavours to begin where the *Almanach de Gotha* left off, but it is difficult for the English-speaking reader to use, owing to the large number of abbreviations. It does not include information about diplomatic officers, as did its predecessor. For the older individual countries, there are very full works:

France

LA CHESNAYE-DESBOIS, F. A. A. DE, *Dictionnaire de la Noblesse . . . de la France*, 19 vols., 3rd edition, Schlesinger, Paris, 1863–77.

Germany

Familiengeschichtliche Bibliographie, Degener, Schellenberg, vols. 1–, 1900–, In progress.

Italy

SPRETI, V., *marchese*. *Enciclopedia Storico-nobiliare Italiana*. Edited by Enciclopedia Storico-nobiliare Italiana, 8 vols., Milan, 1928–35, with a supplement, 1936.

Several works for Great Britain may be considered in greater detail. Dealing first with ennobled houses, the fullest is G. E. Cokayne's *Complete Peerage* (13 vols. in 14, St. Catherine Press, 1910–59), which gives immense detail, and numerous scholarly appendices on particular aspects of the peerage. Clearly this has to be supplemented by a serial publication of which there are three, all differing somewhat. Burke's *Genealogical and Heraldic History of the Peerage* (Burke, 1826–, Irregular) is the fullest, giving descents, sons and daughters (and their issue), and brothers and sisters of the peers concerned. Debrett's *Peerage*, *Baronetage*, *Knightage and Companionage* (Odhams, 1713–, Irregular) is much less full but gives more detail on female descendants, and covers the additional sections of the "upper ten" that its title implies. The companions of honour and of the Bath, etc., are, of course, not hereditary, so we should possibly have dealt with this work with the collected biographies, in Chapter 2, above. This remark applies even more to *Kelly's Handbook to the Titled, Landed and Official Classes* (Kelly, 1880–, annual). Although much more up to date, because of its frequency of publication, it is scarcely fuller than a Who's Who. Sir J. B. Burke's *Genealogical and Heraldic History of the Landed Gentry* (17th edition, Burke, 1952, with *Supplement*, 1954) is an extremely full treatment of between 4000 and 5000 families who hold or held land, but who are not ennobled. It deals simply with Great Britain, and there is a separate *Genealogical and Heraldic History of the Landed Gentry of Ireland* (4th edition, Burke, 1958). Both these works are edited by L. G. Pine. Old editions of Burke's publications never lose their value, as many of the details cannot be transferred from edition to edition. Families lower down the social scale may be traced in T. R. Thomson's *A Catalogue of British Family Histories* (2nd edition, Murray, 1935). The final genealogical work that may be mentioned, at least until we study sources, is the *Genealogist's Magazine* containing articles, lists of accessions (printed and manuscript) to the Library of the Society of Genealogists, and a readers' query section, where genealogists can exchange information with those working in similar branches of study.

The above are perhaps the main branches of study that may be properly considered as on the fringe of biography and history. Linguistics, politics, statistics, cosmography—these and other sciences might, however, have been included, for history pervades every activity of mankind.

CHAPTER 6

The Sources of History

INTRODUCTION

So far this book has dealt entirely with what are known as *secondary* materials, books about books, bibliographies, guides and similar printed materials. It is probably true to say that no one embarking on a work of history or biography can feel really satisfied with his efforts unless he makes some attempt to use original materials, or *primary* sources, e.g. letters to or from a particular individual; wills, parish registers, state papers either in their original form or reprinted for the use of scholars, perhaps even such miscellaneous material as inscriptions on tombstones, portraits, or even lantern slides. For example, W. A. Munford published *William Ewart, M.P. 1798–1869* (Grafton) in 1960, and he lists both primary and secondary source material used. The former comprises mostly unpublished family letters, Liverpool directories, Hansard's *House of Commons Debates*, *The Times* and other newspapers, reports of Select Committees of the House of Commons; the secondary sources include works by other writers— Edward Edwards' *Memoirs of Libraries*, Trevelyan's *English Social History*, etc. No work which claims to aid those who would find out about history can ignore the original source material of Great Britain and elsewhere. We may here define certain sciences, a knowledge of which is necessary to understand source materials. *Epigraphy* is concerned with inscriptions on walls, tombstones or other solid objects; *Palaeography* with the study of handwriting, which can present great difficulties. To understand it, a knowledge of languages, normally mediaeval Latin and Norman French, is essential. Fortunately, for would-be amateur historians, many modern letters and other materials can be read without a knowledge of palaeography. *Papyrology* is the science which concerns itself with the make-up and deciphering of portions of papyrus—bark on which writing was placed in ancient Egypt and other oriental countries. *Diplomatic* relates to the study of diplomas; hand-written instruments such as treaties or charters by which administrative action was taken, particularly in the Middle Ages. *Sphragistics* (sigillography) deals with one aspect of such study—the seals with which documents were authenticated. We propose to say no more about these sciences except to refer to the following:

THOMPSON, *Sir* E. M., *An Introduction to Greek and Latin Palaeography*, Clarendon Press, Oxford, 1912.

GRIEVE, H. E. P., *Examples of English Handwriting 1150–1750*, 2nd edition, Essex Record Office, Chelmsford, 1959.

PROU, M., *Manuel de paléographie Latine et française*, Picard, Paris, 1924. With volume of plates.

GIRY, A., *Manuel de Diplomatique*, Hachette, Paris, 1894.

NATIONAL SOURCES

The amateur historian is far more likely to use local rather than national sources when he first sets out to study original materials. Nevertheless, it is in accordance with the plan of this book in treating national and regional history and biography before their local applications to say something about the great national repositories of English and other archives and manuscripts before going on to local sources. The Public Record Office in Chancery Lane, London, is the national repository for the records of the British Government, though many records kept by individual statesmen in the course of their duties have been left to the greatest centre of artificially made-up manuscript collections, the British Museum. There are, of course, a great many other repositories of national manuscripts (see below, pp. 219–20). A smaller amount of such material is in the Bodleian (Oxford), and Cambridge University libraries, and indeed in local repositories. (Fig. 61) *A Guide to the Contents of the Public Record Office* (H.M.S.O.) appeared in two volumes in 1963. Volume I deals with legal records, but in practice includes all national archives from the time of Domesday Book (A.D. 1086) to 1509, because legal and administrative matters were interconnected in early times. On opening this *Guide*, it is clear that it differs completely from the many bibliographies of printed books we have already examined. Archives and manuscripts differ fundamentally from printed books, which are usually arranged according to some classification scheme. In this book we have tried to list all the recommended works by their authors' names, because usually this is the easiest way to be sure of finding them, whether we are looking for them in a large or small library, or trying to buy them from a bookseller. To help in the latter case, we have in nearly every example given the name of the publisher, though this is not a great deal of use where the book is out of print —i.e. sold out so that no more can be bought from sellers of new books (in such cases second-hand copies may still be obtained from dealers who specialize in such works. In most British towns there is usually one such dealer, though they are a dying race). If we want to find out books on some aspect of history of which we do not know the author (there are many books brought out by government departments, etc., where even trained librarians find it difficult to decide who is the author), we can usually find someone to ask, or with a little practice discover sections of library catalogues or shelves where, by some magic we don't quite understand, most of the books in which we are likely to be interested are to be found. Certainly, if we are setting out to find out about history as a science for ourselves, and not merely reading books for pleasure, time spent in learning how to use the library catalogues and shelf arrangement is well worth while. Not that we should underestimate the difficulty of such a task, particularly in a large library of printed books, or one arranged by a different plan from the one we have always been used to. To ease the difficulty, many libraries have as well as author catalogues, entries under subjects where it is possible to find either a list of all the books on the particular subject, or a

RECORDS OF THE COURT OF STAR CHAMBER

The name 'Court of Star Chamber' came to be applied in the late 15th century to the King's Council, or an informal committee of it, sitting in the *Camera Stellata* of Westminster Palace or elsewhere as a tribunal exercising summary jurisdiction to enforce law and order, particularly statute law. Its aid was at first invoked mainly against oppressive behaviour by local magnates and in other cases where the processes of the common law were too slow or too ineffectual to provide redress. Under the Stuarts the Court fell into disrepute as an arbitrarily used instrument of the royal prerogative; and it was abolished by Stat. 16 Charles I, c.10.

The records consist of bills, answers, depositions, and other proceedings; but the decrees and orders have not survived. A set of fee books for writs issuing from this court during the period 1580 to 1633 will be found in the class of *Gifts and Deposits* (P.R.O. 30/38).

PROCEEDINGS

Henry VII (Sta. Cha. 1). 2 volumes.

Henry VIII (Sta. Cha. 2). 35 volumes and bundles.

Edward VI (Sta. Cha. 3). 9 bundles.

Mary (Sta. Cha. 4). 11 bundles.

Elizabeth I (Sta. Cha. 5). 982 bundles.

Elizabeth I (*Supplementary*) (Sta. Cha. 6). 9 bundles.

Elizabeth I (*Addenda*) (Sta. Cha. 7). 31 bundles.

James I (Sta. Cha. 8). 312 bundles.

Charles I (Sta. Cha. 9). 1 bundle.

CALENDAR. 1485 to 1558. *Lists and Indexes No. XIII*, 1901. There is a typescript index of persons and places to this calendar.

TRANSCRIPTS (select cases). 1477 to 1544. *Select Cases in the Star Chamber*, Selden Soc. Vols. XVI and XXV, 1903 and 1911.

Miscellanea (Sta. Cha. 10). 21 bundles.

Undated proceedings, fragments, etc., including a treatise on the Court of Star Chamber apparently compiled *temp.* James I or Charles I (No. 21).

Fig. 61. *Guide to the Contents of the Public Record Office.* (Copyright: HMSO)

number which will be a direction post either to a second catalogue (usually called a classified or systematic catalogue), or straight to the section of the book shelves desired.

Complicated as it sometimes is for scholars to use libraries of printed books, it is far more difficult for them to use *manuscripts*, unpublished items which may be of any shape or size. Difficulties, in fact, have been accentuated by well-meaning librarians who in the past have mistakenly treated manuscripts according to principles suited to printed books, though most manuscripts (a) have no recognizable author, (b) are on no particular subject, or if they are, then this is purely incidental circumstance, (c) are not suitable, owing to their lack of volume, unsuitable shape, etc., to arrange on shelves for personal handling. Many manuscripts in the Public Record Office and greater and smaller libraries are arranged according to some topic or subject, through the whim of some scholar in the past, though fortunately in many of these cases detailed catalogues have been printed, which can be consulted before students make a special journey to ask for what they want. Most manuscripts except those which physically resemble printed books—literary or artistic manuscripts—are now in charge of professional archivists, who arrange them according to their origin or *provenance*, as it is sometimes called, in a completely objective way, without any regard as to whether they may be interesting or not. This means that the student of any particular subject, e.g. the voyages taken by one of His Majesty's ships in 1778, is directed to the whole of the ship's papers, or such as have survived for that particular period, and not merely to what some librarian or archivist may have considered interesting, and personally selected from a larger bulk. Of course, the mistakes of the past cannot be undone. Most of the letters and papers written by or relating to such eminent figures as Admiral Lord Nelson have been extracted from other supposedly less interesting material years ago. Many have been sold as individual items for high prices to libraries and other institutions all over the world. Archivists are doing what they can to rectify old mistakes—by listing the whereabouts of items missing from their collections or what they term their archive groups; by obtaining photocopies, when the originals are far away, etc. We have digressed rather extensively on this point which must be understood before any original research is even contemplated. The Public Record Office authorities frankly admit that their predecessors have made mistakes of sorting, and that there is a tremendous amount of material in their charge styled *miscellanea* which must be considered along with what has vanished before the other archival groups can be regarded as being as complete as possible. In the new guide "the arrangement is by administrative provenance throughout. The records of an individual court or department form a 'group', which is made up from a number of 'classes', each corresponding as a rule to a function or to some aspect of the work which produced the records". The prospective user, therefore, should first of all decide in what Department of State—Chancery, Exchequer, etc.—the matter he seeks is likely to fall. Difficulties are increased in the part covered by Vol. 1, because most of the documents are in Latin or Norman French. Volume 2 is devoted to the records of the former State Paper Office (records of the principal secretaries of State from the accession of Henry VIII onwards), the records of government departments, some royal commissions and similar bodies, and a collection of microfilms of the former German Foreign Ministry and German Navy. These are mainly in English or modern languages. Like Vol. 1, the second volume lists a great deal of miscellaneous material arranged years ago according to the discredited principles described above. The *Guide* does not go beyond 1960, but important later accessions to the Public Record Office are referred to in an annual H.M.S.O. publication, the *Report of the Keeper of Public Records*. Excellent as the *Guide* is, its index does no more than to refer to departments that produce documents.[1]

Before actually proceeding to the Public Record Office to search among the national archives, students should heed the warning "not to embark on the examination of original records before they have exhausted the information relevant to their enquiries which is

[1] The List and Index Society publishes from 1966 photographic copies of unpublished search room lists at the Public Record Office.

available in printed sources" (preface). Many of the public records have been published *in extenso* and these are given in the H.M.S.O. publication *List of Record Publications*, frequently reissued (see below). Series published include *State Papers Domestic*, *State Papers Foreign*, etc., over a long period, and these, available in many libraries all over the world, should be used before the originals are consulted, though it is true that the original papers have some value for the scholar that the published transcripts lack. Many records in the Public Record Office have been published by such national societies as the Selden Society, Pipe Roll Society, Navy Records Society, or by local record societies; E. L. C. Mullins' *Text and Calendars* (Royal Historical Society, 1958) should be searched in order to discover whether any particular record is likely to have been printed (see pp. 95–7 and 219).

If, after all this preliminary checking, it is found necessary to go to the Public Record Office, the means of reference to the collections there should be thoroughly understood before work is started. Working from the general to the particular, they comprise numerical lists, enumerating the items in a particular class or portion of a class; descriptive lists, giving fuller descriptions; calendars, with fairly full summaries; transcripts, giving a complete record of particular documents, and in some cases indexes of names of places, persons and subjects, and catalogues of particular types of documents. Of course all these aids do not exist for every document in the P.R.O., and it is largely a matter of chance as to what help can be given. That is why it is far more necessary in a record office than in a library of printed books for searchers to ask the staff for help. The number of manuscripts in great repositories is so large, and so many more are continually being added, that cataloguing and listing can never be as up to date or comprehensive as in a large library with millions of volumes.

Before considering British local sources, something may be said of the following three publications:

GREAT BRITAIN, PUBLIC RECORD OFFICE, *Record Publications* (*Government Publications Sectional List 24*), H.M.S.O.

Frequently reissued. As well as the state papers mentioned above, this lists what has been published from the charter rolls, patent rolls, close rolls, exchequer records, etc. Some of the works listed in this publication as having been published by the Government are not in the public records at all, such as the *Chronicles and Memorials of Great Britain and Ireland During the Middle Ages* (popularly known as the *Rolls Series*), or the extracts from the Vatican, Spanish or other foreign archives. Some are in the form of indexes to material in the Public Record Office, as the *Lists and Indexes*. Anyone embarking on original work on the official archives of Great Britain should certainly consult *List 24*, and the calendars and guides referred to. The list includes out-of-print publications, though there is hope for those libraries in the newer countries which lack these, as many are currently being reprinted by the Kraus Corporation.

> BRITISH MUSEUM, *Catalogues of the Manuscript Collections*, revised edition, the Museum, 1962.

Like *Sectional List 24*, this is not a source but a guide to *other* (mainly) printed sources. It is of little use in itself. Next to the Public Record Office, the British Museum in London contains more manuscripts than any other great repository, many of them relating to figures of national importance. The published catalogues of these manuscripts, individually available in many libraries throughout the world (and some now being reprinted for the benefit of the newer libraries which did not originally acquire them), are described in the above publication. The main series of manuscripts is known as the *additional manuscripts* (i.e. additional to the basic foundation collections, the Sloane, Harleian, etc., which are all described in the pamphlet), of which many volumes have been published, the last being of the papers of the nineteenth-century Prime Minister W. E. Gladstone (British Museum, 1953). Recent accessions that have not got into a new volume of additional manuscripts are bound up in a series of quinquennial volumes, but for the latest information on accessions there are typed lists available at the Museum. Its manuscripts are not arranged on archival principles, and therefore cannot be used without the printed catalogues or supplementary indexes, or personal inquiry from the staff.

> MULLINS, E. L. C., *Texts and Calendars; an Analytical Guide to Serial Publications*, Royal Historical Society, 1958, has already been described when dealing with printed books (p. 217 and Fig. 38).

Unlike the two previous publications referred to, Mullins does not describe catalogues of original manuscripts that may be regarded as part of Britain's national heritage of manuscripts and archives. It does, however, list in very great detail the contents of individual volumes of the national publishing historical societies such as the British Academy, British Record Society, Harleian Society, etc., many of which reprint items from the public records. As these are widespread in libraries throughout the world it would be foolish to ignore Mullins' summaries before obtaining individual volumes of these series on a trial and error basis, or before going at great expense to the original sources if they have already been extensively worked over by another scholar. The above sources do not, of course, exhaust the means of reference for British archives of a non-local character. Further catalogues of what may be regarded as national libraries' or other institutions' *manuscript* holdings are given in Chapter 3 of P. Hepworth's *Archives and Manuscripts in Libraries* (2nd edition, the Library Association, 1964). The following are of particular interest:

> *Ibid.*, pp. 27–8. Catalogues of the British Museum, British Museum (Natural History), Imperial College of Science and Technology, and India Office.
>
> Pp. 29–30. Catalogues of Kew Gardens, the Royal Army Medical College, Victoria and Albert Museum, Church of England, Dr. Williams' Library, Lambeth Palace, the Burlington Fine Arts Club, College of Arms, Gray's Inn, Inner Temple and Lincoln's Inn.
>
> Pp. 31–2. Catalogues of the Linnean Society, Lloyd's, the

Medical Society, Roxburgh Club, Royal Asiatic Society, Royal College of Music, Royal College of Physicians, Royal College of Surgeons, Royal Institute of British Architects, Royal Society, Royal United Service Institution, Society of Antiquaries, Wellcome Historical Medical Library, Historical Manuscripts Commission and House of Lords.

P. 33. Catalogues of the London County Council, National Maritime Museum and Public Record Office.

Pp. 35–8. Catalogues of the Cambridge University Library, and the separate Cambridge colleges (the Cambridge University Library is one of the British copyright libraries, entitled to demand a copy of every book published in Great Britain, like the British Museum, and has tended therefore to attract a national collection of manuscripts).

Pp. 48–50. Catalogues of the Oxford University Library, and the separate Oxford colleges. The Bodleian, as the Oxford University Library is called, is also a British copyright library. Not a bibliography but a most valuable guide to historical statistics of all kinds from the earliest times is B. R. Mitchell's *Abstract of British Historical Statistics* (Cambridge Univ. Press, 1962).

These catalogues give only an imperfect record of the nation's manuscript holdings. They are in no way complete even for the holdings of the institutions they represent, and many similar institutions of national importance have never published catalogues of their manuscripts. Other catalogues—to which the same criticisms apply—will be referred to when we go on to discuss local sources. Imperfect as they are, they are available in a large number of libraries, and it would be foolish to write to the institutions concerned, or to go to them from another town or country, without first mastering the relevant catalogues with all their imperfections and varying styles of compilation.

The following should be noted for other British national collections:

Scotland

LIVINGSTONE, M., *A Guide to the Public Records of Scotland Deposited in H.M. General Register House, Edinburgh*, the Register House, Edinburgh, 1905. There is a *Supplement* in the *Scottish Historical Review*, XXVI, 1947, pp. 26–46.

See also Hepworth, *Archives and Manuscripts in Libraries* (pp. 58–9), catalogues of Edinburgh and Glasgow University Libraries, the National Library of Scotland, the Scottish Central Library and the Royal Observatory, Edinburgh. Note *Index to the post mediaeval manuscripts in Edinburgh University*, 2 vols., Hall, Boston, 1966.

Wales

Many Welsh records are covered by the British Public Record Office *Guide*, though the various catalogues of the National Library of Wales, particularly the *Handlist* (parts 1–, 1940–, In progress) contain much material of national interest.

Ireland

IRELAND, PUBLIC RECORD OFFICE, *Guide to the Records Deposited in the Public Record Office of Ireland*, Stationery Office, Dublin, 1919.

NATIONAL LIBRARY OF IRELAND, *Manuscript Sources for the History of Irish Civilisation* (11 vols., Hall, Boston, 1965—In progress).

On Wales and Ireland, pp. 59–61 of Hepworth, *op. cit.*, are relevant; the Cardiff Public Library, National Library of Wales, Belfast Diocesan Library, Merchants' Quay Convent, Dublin, and Marsh's Library, Dublin, all contain manuscripts of national import.

A. R. Hewitt's *Guide to Resources for Commonwealth Studies* (Athlone Press, 1957) is very full and detailed on contents of libraries and record repositories, with an index of places, and information on printed catalogues, etc. It is the best general guide to printed and manuscript sources for the British Commonwealth.

A secondary work we may mention in passing is *English Historical Documents, A.D. 500–1914* (12 vols., Eyre & Spottiswoode, 1953–, In progress).

On the European continent archives are generally more systematically organized than in Great Britain. This being so, it is surprising how few published general guides to archives there are, corresponding to the Public Record Office *Guide*. There are general books such as G. Ottervick and others, *Libraries and Archives in Sweden* (Swedish Institute, Stockholm, 1954), and accounts of individual countries' archives by such distinguished archivists as T. R. Schellenberg (who visited Australia to advise on the national archives) and Dr. W. Kaye Lamb, Dominion Archivist of Canada. More cannot be mentioned in a work of this scope, nor can catalogues of individual manuscript collections in foreign libraries.

We have been able to discover very few guides to national archives as such:

France

LANGLOIS, C. V. and STEIN, H., *Les Archives de l'Histoire de France*, Picard, Paris, 1891–3.

New Zealand

Dominion Archives—A Guide to the Dominion Archives, Department of Internal Affairs, Wellington, 1953. There is a preliminary inventory in progress, 1953–.

Mexico

MILLARES CARLO, A., *Repertorio bibliográfico de los archivos mexicanos y de los europeos y norteamericanos de interés para la historia de Mexico*, Instituto Bibliográfica Mexicano, Mexico City, 1959.

Rhodesia

CENTRAL AFRICAN ARCHIVES, *A Guide to the Public Records of Southern Rhodesia*, Longmans, 1956.

U.S.A.

ANDREWS, C. M., *Guide to the Materials for American History to 1783, in the Public Record Office of Great Britain*, 2 vols., Carnegie Institute, Washington, 1912–14.

PAULLIN, C. O. and PAYSON, F. L., *Guide to the Materials in London Archives for the History of the United States since 1783*, Carnegie Institute, Washington, 1914.

ANDREWS, C. M. and DAVENPORT, F. G., *Guide to the Manuscript Materials for the History of the United States to 1783 in the British Museum, in minor London Archives and in the Libraries of Oxford and Cambridge*, Carnegie Institute, Washington, 1908.

These out-of-print volumes can all be obtained on microfilm from Micromethods Ltd., Wakefield.

BELL, H. C. and others, *Guide to British West Indian Archive Materials in London and the Islands, for the History of the United States*, Carnegie Institute, Washington, 1926.

LOCAL SOURCES

Sources of local history, which the amateur historian may use in his own town or village, are legion. John Hobbs' *Local History and the Library* (Deutsch, 1962) treats the subject thoroughly. John West's *Village Record*, Macmillan, 1962, gives many examples and facsimiles of the types of record most commonly met with in local studies. An older book is W. E. Tate's *The Parish Chest* (Cambridge Univ. Press, 1960). Dealing first with printed materials, Hobbs mentions collections of the imaginative literature of a particular area, which are complete or practically so, and which may be regarded as original rather than secondary material. Bookshops will not have these items, but most local libraries in Britain and any of the countries of the world with older civilizations will.

Some day Lord Snow, author of *The Two Cultures and the Scientific Revolution* (Cambridge Univ. Press, 1959) will find a biographer. No doubt one or more of the libraries in Leicester, Lord Snow's birthplace, will be able to produce a complete set of his publications, which the biographer may arrange in chronological order. Such a set will give him valuable information on the way Snow's mind was working at different stages of his life—as an undergraduate at the old Leicester, Leicestershire and Rutland College (now the University of Leicester), a little later when he spent a holiday on the Norfolk Broads (*Death Under Sail*, Heinemann, 1959, first published in 1932), later still when his Cambridge and scientific Civil Service background began to influence him (the Lewis Eliot series), and after he entered the British Government in 1964.

Every area in the older civilizations has publications issued by archaeological, historical, record and parish register (or similar religious) societies. Natural history societies and field clubs, as they are called in Britain, publish extensively, and unbroken sets of their transactions, often only available in the towns of publication, contain, *in toto*, a great deal of original research material. In England there are many fugitive publications of lesser societies. These include cultural, charitable and sporting organizations of all kinds. The local collection of the Birmingham Reference Library, England's second city in size, receives each year more than 500 annual reports from organizations as diverse as churches, hospitals, charitable institutions, rambling and sports clubs, dramatic, operatic, political, scientific, educational, artistic, photographic and religious societies. A good file of any of these is first-class research material for anyone writing the history of the institution or society concerned. Local authority printed material includes council minutes (there is an unfortunate tendency to duplicate these today, instead of employing print), official diaries with lists of officers, and the annual reports of the various chief officers. Irregular material such as by-laws, programmes of royal visits and civic openings, committee minutes, county and county borough development plans is just as important.

Central government publications dealing with local matters relate to such items as local boundaries, mines, trade and agriculture, public health, water supply, geology and land utilization. Local Acts of Parliament and statutory instruments; the early reports of the Charity Commissioners, reports of the former Science and Art Department which give much more detailed information on local curricula and staffs than their modern counterparts, where, indeed, such exist; minutes of evidence taken before parliamentary or at local inquiries are most valuable. The *Index to the Statutes in Force 1235 to . . . 1963* (2 vols., H.M.S.O., 1964), the *Chronological Table of the Statutes 1235 to 1963* (H.M.S.O., 1964), and the *Index to Local and Personal Acts, 1801–1947* (H.M.S.O., 1949) are useful keys to the parliamentary material.

Original source material issued by local firms includes trade catalogues, pattern books, advertising and publicity circulars, old trading cards, handbills, catalogues and bill-heads. Bus and tram tickets and local auctioneers' sale catalogues are also valuable. Collections of playbills, programmes, newspaper cuttings, photographs, etc., relating to local entertainment (theatres, concert halls, football and cricket clubs), will be found in many local libraries. Festivals of one sort or another are increasing in number all over the world; in each case the local library or in some cases the newer county record offices should be able to produce a complete record of the programmes, supplemented probably by news-cuttings. Agricultural, flower and cattle shows also produce much original material. The political history of an area is represented mainly in the squibs and cartoons, election addresses and the many pamphlets and broadsides issued by the protagonists of long ago. The poll books of the eighteenth and nineteenth centuries showing which way individuals voted are most valuable. A long file of local directories is a tremendous asset to researchers endeavouring to discover where individuals lived at particular times. J. E. Norton, *Guide to the National and Provincial Directories of England and Wales, excluding London, Published before 1856* (Royal Historical Society, 1950), is an indispensable guide to this type of material. Local newspapers and magazines in sets, and also a clippings file (subjects, biographies, etc.) based on them, local theses and dissertations, should not be overlooked. For the latter the *Bulletin of the Institute of Historical Research, University of London, Theses Supplement* (annual), and Aslib, *Index to Theses Accepted for Higher Degrees*, Aslib (annual), should be consulted. Finally, local photographs, lantern slides, museum objects and transparencies should not be disregarded particularly if these are arranged systematically.

We turn from printed to manuscript local sources. Quite often, too, these have been printed. Much therefore can be done by proper investigation of what has been recorded in print without having to possess a knowledge of palaeography, or engage the services of someone with this knowledge. Note above that the British Public Record Office distinguishes between different degrees of fullness in its means of reference; these degrees apply also to most published series of manuscripts. The fullest published series is recorded in H.M.S.O. Sectional List No. 17, *Reports of the Royal Commission on Historical Manuscripts*, frequently reissued. The Historical Manuscripts Commission was founded in 1869, and, until its Royal Warrant was changed in 1959, concentrated almost entirely upon the publication of bulky calendars and extracts from collections of manuscripts, mainly in private hands, illustrating "history, constitutional law, science and general literature". Some of the earlier reports summarize documents held by municipal corporations, bishops, etc., but these accounts are not very full. The reports have indexes to places (1914), and persons (2 vols., 1935–8), but these are somewhat out of date. The *22nd Report of the Royal Commission on Historical Manuscripts* (1946) stated where the collections of manuscripts reported on between 1869 and that time might be found (a new location list is in preparation). Many owners, during two major wars, had broken up their estates and sold their manuscripts; some had been destroyed, and some lost without trace. The printed volumes of the Commissioners' reports are full enough in many cases to enable students to do original research. In other cases where the printed text leaves queries it will be found that owners are often very reasonable in granting access to their records. A few of the manuscripts surveyed by the Commission relate to national history (e.g. the manuscripts of the House of Lords), but it is, on the whole, reasonable to regard the series as illustrating local history. The division between our two sections is however blurred, for the typical estate papers of a country gentleman are in many cases of landed families who contributed many statesmen to national affairs. In 1964 over 200 vols. had been published.

Some published volumes are even nearer to being complete

calendars of the documents they record than those of the Historical Manuscripts Commission. These are volumes put out by local record societies; collections of charters and other documents issued by municipalities; parish registers and marriage licences (invaluable in saving genealogists the trouble of going to the original parishes), etc. Many of these volumes, if published by the national and local record publishing societies, are described by Mullins (above, pp. 95–7 and 219). More of them, however, relate to local rather than to national history. The Harleian Society (registers and heraldic visitations) and Index Library (wills and administrations) are notable examples. Other volumes not published in series are listed in an invaluable guide by Sir Robert Somerville, *Handlist of Record Publications* (British Records Association, 1951). Although difficult to use, because of the large number of abbreviations used, this guide answers such important historians' questions as "Has anyone worked over the hearth tax returns or feet of fines for Suffolk?", the answer to both these questions being yes; hearth tax returns for Suffolk in 1674 were published in the *Suffolk Green Books* (No. 11, Vol. 13), and feet of fines for 1189–1480 in the *Proceedings of the Suffolk Institute of Archaeology and Natural History* for 1900. There is a similar *Handlist of Scottish and Welsh Record Publications* (British Records Association, 1954) by Peter Gouldesbrough, and A. P. Kup. Of course, many of the works of this type not covered by Mullins and Somerville are traceable in the ordinary bibliographies described in the earlier chapters of this work (e.g. Sonnenschein, Howe, etc.). Emmison and Gray, *County Records* (described more fully below) gives a list of county records in print.

If a manuscript—real or suspected—wanted for a particular purpose has not been published either in summary or in full, there is no help but to try other methods of seeing whether it exists. Local historians often write to local record offices or libraries to find out; if it is a short manuscript they can often buy a photocopy of the item they are seeking and save making a special journey. But if they are seeking many items of the same kind, or do not know approximately the location of what they are tracing, they will find *guides to locations* extremely valuable.

Although it was not designed as a finding list, many individual books may be traced in N. R. Ker (editor), *Medieval Libraries of Great Britain: a List of Surviving Books* (2nd edition, Royal Historical Society, 1964). The Historical Manuscripts Commission has issued jointly with the British Records Association *Record Repositories in Great Britain* (2nd edition, 1964), a most valuable list with a useful introduction on ecclesiastical, school and other records not covered in the main directory, and a note on general services of value to users of records. Laborious to use, but detailed and reliable, are the lists of accessions to historical manuscripts printed in the *Bulletin of the Institute of Historical Research* from 1930. In 1955 the listing was taken over by the Historical Manuscripts Commission under the title *Lists of Accessions to Repositories* (H.M.S.O.) (annual). Since its new Warrant was issued in 1959 the Commission has concerned itself more with recording the whereabouts of manuscripts than with printing extracts from them, though this latter activity still continues. A general index to the first five of the H.M.C. series of the lists of accessions is pending. The *Bulletin of the National Register of Archives* (1948 to date) is another valuable publication of the H.M.C.; it now consists mainly of descriptions of particular collections of manuscripts.

Other information on location of collections can be deduced from the *Local Archives of Great Britain* series appearing in *Archives*. The reviews of publications in this periodical; 1948–, In progress, and in the *Journal of the Society of Archivists*; 1954–, In progress, are indispensable. The *Year's Work in Archives* (1933—now brought out as *Five Years' Work in Archives*; 1956–60 edition, latest), the Library Association, is also useful. Some references to manuscript holdings in Dean and Chapters' and Bishops' archives are made in Pilgrim Trust, *Survey of Ecclesiastical Archives* (the Trust, 1952), (Anglican). Unfortunately this work is only available at certain centres. It does not deal with parochial archives but some rare church manuscript books (such as the Ranworth antiphoner, since moved elsewhere) are listed in Central Council for the Care of Churches, *Parochial Libraries* (the Council, 1959). The British Records Association's *Archives in Religious and Ecclesiastical Bodies and Organisations Other Than the Church of England* (1936).[1] and for parish registers A. M. Burke, *Key to the Ancient Parish Registers of England and Wales* (Sackville Press, 1908), and the two indexes; of parish register copies held by itself (1963) and of copies held elsewhere published by the Society of Genealogists (under revision), should be consulted. Historical sources are indicated in G. Kitson Clark and G. R. Elton, *Guide to Research Facilities in History* (2nd edition, Cambridge Univ. Press, 1965). Two general lists, the *Libraries, Museums and Art Galleries Year Book* (new edition, Clarke, 1964) and the *Aslib Directory* (1957–, periodical supplements) are not detailed enough to do more than confirm the presence of manuscripts at a known centre.

Other important works giving locations are L. K. Born (comp.), *British Manuscripts Project; a Checklist of the Microfilms Prepared in England and Wales for the American Council of Learned Societies, 1941–5* (Library of Congress, Washington, 1955); B. R. Crick and M. Alman, *A Guide to Manuscripts Relating to America in Great Britain and Ireland* (Oxford Univ. Press, 1961); W. Matthews (comp.), *British Diaries* (1950); and *British Autobiographies* (1955) (see pp. 81–3), and for material in America, S. De Ricci and W. J. Wilson, *Census of Mediaeval and Renaissance Manuscripts* (4 vols., Kraus & H. W. Wilson, New York, 1935–62). Locations of wills are given in B. G. Bouwens *Wills and their Whereabouts* (2nd edition by A. J. Camp, Society of Genealogists, 1963). See the section on Genealogy above, pp. 206–10. The sale catalogues of microfilms issued by Micromethods Ltd., East Ardsley, Wakefield, Yorks, include films of many manuscripts, ranging from the *cartae antiquae* in Lambeth Palace Library to original Eichmann documents in the Wiener Library. We may also mention the Standing Conference of National and University Libraries' projects for the recording of literary and scientific manuscripts and the Library Association's survey of personal manuscripts.

In his *Manuscript Cataloguing* (*Traditio*, XII, 1956, pp. 457–555), W. J. Wilson discusses the "perennial dream of manuscript enthusi-

[1] See also Welch, C. E., "Archives and Manuscripts in Nonconformist Libraries" in *Archives* **6** (1964), pp. 235–8.

asts, a consolidated catalogue of all the hand-written books in the world". A pioneer British work in this field was Edward Bernard's *Catalogi librorum manuscriptorum Angliae et Hiberniae* (Oxford Univ. Press, 1697), which is still very valuable, as is H. Shenkl's *Bibliotheca patrum latinorum Britannica* (1890–1908). Another interesting early work is Sir Thomas Phillips' *Attempt at a Union Catalogue of Great Britain* (1850). In the thirties of this century E. C. Richardson endeavoured once more, unsuccessfully, to launch such a project, including manuscript books, but, like his predecessors, boggling at including single documents or archives, though like Kristeller (below) he did try to make his scope world-wide. He published a *List of Printed Catalogues of Manuscript Books* (H. W. Wilson, New York, 1935), and four other "preliminary studies in method" relating to his unrealized project. In 1956 L. K. Born, whose work in connection with the British manuscripts project has been noted above, published his "Universal Guide to Catalogues of Manuscripts and Inventories of Archival Collections: a Proposal for Co-operative Listing" (*College and Research Libraries* **17**, 1956, pp. 322–9).

Among special catalogues covering manuscripts should be noted E. A. Lowe's *Codices latini antiquiores; a Palaeographical Guide to Latin Manuscripts prior to the Ninth Century* (11 vols., Oxford Univ. Press, 1934–, In progress), and P. O. Kristeller's *Latin Manuscript Books before 1600* (Ford University, New York, 1960). Works more generally available containing useful information include T. Besterman's *World Bibliography of Bibliographies* (3rd edition, Scarecrow Press, New York, 1965–6) (entries under "illustrated books" and "palaeography: bibliographies"); G. C. R. Davis' *Medieval Cartularies of Great Britain* (Longmans, 1958); J. D. Pearson's *Oriental Manuscript Collections in the Libraries of Great Britain and Ireland* (Royal Historical Society, 1954); N. R. Ker's *Catalogue of Manuscripts containing Anglo-Saxon* (Oxford Univ. Press, 1957); and the *Catalogue* of the Library Association Library (1957) (list at 016,091; supplements in *Library Association Record*).

The average local history researcher will want nothing as imposing as most of the works listed above, but he will have some idea of the area of Great Britain in which he wants to work and will be able to seek out the printed guides relating to various counties in F. G. Emmison and Irvine Gray's *County Records* (2nd edition, Historical Association, 1961). This gives useful information on the type of archives to be found in most counties, together with examples. Also included is a complete list of addresses of English (not Scottish nor Welsh) county record offices, with their hours of opening and facilities. There is nothing in print comparable with this covering the other great branches of local English archives, but the following should be noted:

PURVIS, J. S., *An Introduction to Ecclesiastical Records*, St. Anthony's Press, 1953.

HEARNSHAW, F. J. C., *Municipal Records*, S.P.C.K., 1918.

SOCIETY OF LOCAL ARCHIVISTS, *Local Records: their Nature and Care*, Bell, 1953. This has chapters on all types of archives.

Archives have been defined as "documents drawn up for the purpose of, or used during the conduct of, affairs of any kind of which they themselves formed a part, and subsequently preserved by the persons responsible for the transactions in question, or their successors in their own custody for their own reference" (Sir Hilary Jenkinson). Usually they are the type of manuscript used by researchers, but P. Hepworth's *Archives and Manuscripts in Libraries* (2nd edition, Library Association, 1964) gives a short account of non-archival manuscripts (pp. 9–12), such as illuminated and literary manuscripts, which are also often used, particularly in biographical or critical studies. The same work has a comprehensive list of guides and catalogues of all kinds to archives and manuscripts that have been published and which relate to British depositories (pp. 25–61). The work complements Emmison and Gray, which includes calendars of county documents only, and has many more titles. Those of national or quasi-national importance have been mentioned above (pp. 219–21). The difference between the two works may be illustrated from the entries for the English county of Wiltshire. Emmison and Gray record only one volume of *extracts* from the county records omitted by Hepworth, but the latter includes two guides to the County Record Office, a schedule of Trowbridge borough records, a catalogue of a Swindon collection and one of the Salisbury Cathedral Library. Figure 62 illustrates a page from one of the best-known guides to British record offices, that for Essex (2 vols., Essex Record Office, Chelmsford, 1946–8). An article by P. Hepworth ("Archives and Manuscripts in Libraries, 1961" in *Library Association Record* **64** (1962), pp. 269–83) lists the manuscript holdings of 214 libraries of various types, showing their nature (official records, dean and chapter, probate, etc.), though the items listed under Hepworth's groups are not always the main collections of a particular type in a given area. C. E. Welch has located forty-nine official diocesan record offices (C. E. Welch, "The Preservation of Ecclesiastical Records" in *Archives* **4** (1959–60), pp. 75–80).

Despite all these aids and descriptions of various British repositories, it must be remembered that many important collections of manuscripts and archives are not recorded at all outside the offices where they are deposited; that all the guides, catalogues, etc., referred to above are necessarily out of date, that many archives and manuscripts in all repositories are uncatalogued and known only to their skilled keepers, so that correspondence or a personal visit is the only answer to any inquiries. But useful information regarding manuscript holdings can be obtained from other sources to supplement a guide or catalogue. For example, articles dealing with the Guildhall Library in London can be found in *Archives*, the *Journal of Documentation*, and several monographs, as well as in the formal *Guide* (Corporation of London) issued in 1951. Similarly, although no guide to the manuscripts at Nottingham University has been published, the very full reports of the Keeper of Manuscripts from 1958 provide an adequate substitute for the collections covered. There are also catalogues (a) relating to a number of repositories as Skulund's *Catalogue of Norse Manuscripts in Edinburgh, Dublin and Manchester* (1919); (b) listing the former contents of a library now mainly dispersed; or (c) giving the present dispersed locations of books formerly in a library still in existence. Sears Jayne's *Library Catalogues of the English Renaissance* (University of

ESTATE AND FAMILY ARCHIVES

Ingatestone Hall Estate (Petre Family)

The Petre estates in Essex were mainly accumulated in the 16th century by (Sir) William Petre, one of the commissioners appointed by Henry VIII in connection with the dissolution of religious houses. Large properties of a number of Essex houses were purchased by him from the Crown, including Ingatestone (Barking Abbey), Great Burstead and Mountnessing (Stratford Abbey and Thoby Priory), East and West Horndon (Waltham Abbey) and Childerditch (Coggeshall Abbey). The pre-dissolution muniments of these houses can, therefore, be reconstituted to some extent.[1] Other considerable estates were acquired by grant or purchase from the Crown and from lay owners by Sir William and his son. The more important were Margaretting and Writtle (from the Crown), the Mordaunt family estates in Horndon and Ingrave, the properties of the Barlee family in Clavering, and those formerly of the Bayeuse, Corby and Wotton families in West Thurrock. · Writtle had belonged to the de Bohun family, and among the records from this source are some relating to the former vast estates of the Earls of Hereford.

MANORIAL. Court rolls, etc.[2] Ingatestone, 1279-1895, with estreats, 1577-1651, rentals and surveys,[3] 1521-1817, and bailiffs' accounts, c.1450, 1581. Fryerning, 1582-1636. Writtle, 1379-1886, with aveage rolls, 1377, 1593-1626, estreats, 1447-1713, rentals and surveys, 1328-1842, bailiffs' accounts, 1360-1538,[4] lists of constables, headboroughs and 'deciners', 1614-28; and coroners' inquisitions, 1596-1841, and original papers of pleas, 1615-1852, at Writtle manor court. Fithlers, 1654-1793, with rentals, 1654, 1700; Wades and Wallexstons, rentals, 1458-1578; all in Writtle. Roxwell and Tye Hall in Roxwell,

---

[1] See J. L. Fisher, 'The Petre Documents' in *Trans. E.A.S.*, N.S.; vol. xxiii, pp. 66-97, and the E.R.O. summary catalogue.

[2] See explanatory note on form of entry, p. 15.

[3] To the earliest rental is attached a 'domesdaye', c.1275.

[4] Included physically in these rolls are accounts for other Bohun manors :— Chignall, 1404-23; Mashbury, 1404; Boyton Hall in Roxwell, 1417-1533; (Cold) Norton, 1422; Hatfield Regis cum Broomshawbury in Hatfield Broad Oak, 1427-1522; Heydon, 1440-1522; Chipping Ongar, 1439-1522; Fobbing, 1446-1522; Stanford Rivers and Tracies in Stanford Rivers, 1447; Suttons in Stapleford Tawney, 1447; hundreds of Ongar and Harlow, 1427-1522; Forest of Writtle, 1469.

19

Fig. 62. *Guide to the Essex Record Office*. (Copyright: Essex County Records Committee.)

California, Los Angeles, 1956) is an interesting study of many of these catalogues between 1500 and 1640. Some of these lists are invaluable aids to the study of the manuscripts still existing:

KER, N. R., *Medieval Manuscripts from Norwich Cathedral Priory*, Cambridge Bibliographical Society, 1949.

JAMES, M. R., *Ancient Libraries of Canterbury and Dover; the Catalogues of the Libraries*, Cambridge Univ. Press, 1903.

MYNORS, *Sir* R. A. B., *Durham Cathedral Manuscripts to the end of the Twelfth Century*, Oxford Univ. Press, 1939.

Britain's leading inquiry bureau relating to the whereabouts of given manuscripts is the National Register of Archives, Quality Court, London, not far from the Public Record Office. This office receives a great many calendars from a large number of archive repositories of all kinds, itself supplying the duplicating material to facilitate this valuable form of co-operation. If the Registrar of the N.R.A. cannot himself provide information, he can often direct inquirers to a particular repository, on knowing their requirements. Reports received during 1957–61 are summarized in the *Twenty-third* and *Twenty-fourth Reports of the Royal Commission on Historical Manuscripts* (1961–2). Those received later will be listed in subsequent reports of the Commission. Unfortunately, the many earlier lists received by the National Register of Archives have not been summarized in their entirety so far. A few similar lists are given in University of London School of Librarianship and Archives, *Bibliographies, Calendars and Theses Accepted for Part II of the University of London Diplomas in Librarianship*, Occasional Publications Nos. 10 (1960) and 12 (1963). Many of the works referred to in the last few pages may contain information on printed as well as manuscript sources. Above (pp. 223–5) we have laid John Hobbs' *Local History and the Library* under contribution for its description of the printed sources of local history; on pp. 55–77 he deals just as thoroughly with manuscript records which include manorial records of the local lords of the manors (court rolls and presentments), accounts, custumals dealing with the customs of the manor, maps, surveys and terriers, and books and documents relating to its bounds, wastes, franchises and courts. Title deeds, leases, indentures and agreements; estate surveys, rentals and terriers; personal material such as diaries, letters, wills and autographs are often retained by landowning families, and may have found their way into official repositories. Other records connected with great estates include minutes, accounts and vouchers of the estate; ledgers, journals and other books with related correspondence. There may also be literary manuscripts including poetry, notes on local history, etc. County records include not only the modern records since county councils were set up in 1888, but older records which have passed to the custody of the county clerk as clerk of the peace. These include quarter sessions records, hearth tax returns, documents concerning vagrants, land tax assessments, enclosure awards, etc. Borough records comprise both legal and administrative groups. Many boroughs have records of a mayor's court or quarter sessions records held independently of the county. Rolls of the gild merchant, freeman's rolls and records of trading guilds and companies are also widely available. There are assembly books of the common council and minute books recording the actions it took. Financial records include subsidy rolls, poll tax records and house and window tax records. The steward or chamberlain kept yearly accounts, and other financial records which may be discovered include coroners' accounts, constables' accounts, etc. Military papers (muster rolls), records of schools for which the corporation may have acted as trustee, local charities, election records, prison records, minutes of street commissioners and turnpike trusts, are other examples of the miscellaneous material which may be discovered in a borough repository.

Parochial ecclesiastical records include the registers, churchwardens' accounts, and vestry minutes. Many of these remain in the parish churches, particularly the registers, but there are many printed editions of registers, and numerous transcripts have been made (see above for the *National Index of Parish Register Copies*, p. 229). Wills, inventories and letters of administration are gradually coming into public custody; bishops and archdeacons have their own records (registers, visitation books, bishops' transcripts of returns of baptisms and deaths from parishes). Dean's records usually remain in the cathedrals, and are not always accessible.

Minute books of local societies form an easily comprehensible source of material for the amateur historian; those of trade unions, hospitals, local branches of political parties, or of family businesses, are harder to come by, though the Business Archives Council is endeavouring to trace business records.

We may conclude the British section of this treatment of local sources by referring to the National Council of Social Services' *How to Write a Parish Guide*, the Council, 1951, which illustrates how to combine printed and manuscript sources before embarking on what in Britain is one of the commonest forms of amateur history.

There are not many comprehensive foreign guides to local archives and manuscripts, but the following American examples are important:

> (Fig. 63) HAMER, P. M. (editor) *Guide to Archives and Manuscripts in the United States*, Yale Univ. Press, New Haven, 1961. This is an excellent comprehensive guide, arranged under states. There are no official United States archives, but probably the bulk of the material for national history is held at the Library of Congress, shown on the specimen page illustrated.
>
> LIBRARY OF CONGRESS, *The National Union Catalogue of Manuscript Collections, 1959–1961*, Edwards, Ann Arbor, 1962. Describes 7300 collections in 400 repositories but differs from Hamer in that no archives are given if they are in the correct location from which they emanate. An *Index, 1959–62*, 2 vols., Shoe String Press, Hamden, appeared in 1964.
>
> MODERN LANGUAGE ASSOCIATION OF AMERICA, *American Literary Manuscripts: a Check-list of Holdings in Academic, Historical and Public Libraries in the United States*, Texas Univ. Press, Austin, 1960.

WASHINGTON 25

Historical Branch, Headquarters, U.S.
Marine Corps.

   Holdings: A substantial quantity, in
the Marine Corps Historical Archives,
consisting of selected official documents, 1920 to date, relating to the
history of the Marine Corps, personal
papers of a number of Marine officers,
and compiled biographical information
about members of the Corps.

WASHINGTON 17

Holy Name College. 14th and Shepherd
Sts. NE. Rev. Fr. Guardian.

   Holdings: Medieval and Renaissance
manuscripts (94 vols.); and 17th- and
18th-century manuscripts (9 vols.),
some from the California area of Mexico.
   See De Ricci, Census, pp. 470-484,
which describes 85 of the manuscripts.

WASHINGTON 1

Howard University Library. 2401 6th
St. NW. Joseph H. Reason, Director
of University Libraries.

   Holdings: Several thousand manuscripts, 1798-1959, relating chiefly to
Negro life and history. In the general
library are some papers of and concerning Richard Le Gallienne (England; poet, critic). Papers in the
Moorland Foundation include those of
Blanche K. Bruce (Miss., D.C.; U.S.
Sen.), 1840-1900 (10 boxes); Thomas
Clarkson (England; philanthropist, antislavery advocate), 1791-1837 (50
letters); James A. Cobb (D.C.: municipal court judge), 1917-36 (363 items);
Francis Grimke (D.C.; Presbyterian
clergyman), 1893-1915 (3 shelves of
sermons); Oliver Otis Howard (D.C.,

Vt.; U.S. Army officer, Commissioner of Freedmen's Bureau, pres. of
Howard Univ.), 1853-1907 (4 boxes);
Alain Leroy Locke (D.C.; critic, Howard Univ. philosophy prof.), 1870-1956
(200 boxes); Jesse Edward Moorland
(N.Y.; Congregational clergyman),
1800-1940 (6,000 items); Pinckney Benton Stewart Pinchback (La.; Civil War
officer, Gov.), 1867-1901 (2 boxes);
James T. Rapier (Ala.; newspaper
correspondent, U.S. Rep.), 1856-65
(75 letters); Arthur B. Spingarn (N.Y.;
lawyer), 1900-59 (500 pieces); Joel E.
Spingarn (N.Y.; author, pres. of National Association for the Advancement
of Colored People), 1915-20 (800 pieces); Mary Church Terrell (D.C.; Negro reformer, suffrage leader), 203
items; J. Waties Waring (S.C.; U.S.
dist. court judge), 1947-59 (84 al-
bums and 30 boxes); Daniel Hale Williams (Ill.; surgeon), 1900-40 (5 drawers); and Louis T. Wright (N.Y.; surgeon), 1898-1950 (8 drawers). Also
included are records of Negro troops
in the Civil War (430 vols., formerly
in the National Archives); a collection
of letters and documents relating to
slavery and abolition, 1792-1865 (500
pieces); and music manuscripts by
Negro composers, 1915-35 (200 pieces).

WASHINGTON 25

Library of Congress. L. Quincy
Mumford, Librarian of Congress.

   Holdings: 15,700,000 items, 7th-
20th centuries, relating to many aspects of world history but especially
to the history of the United States.
These manuscripts are in the custody
of the following divisions of the Library: (1) Manuscript, (2) Map, (3)
Music, (4) Orientalia, (5) Prints and
Photographs, and (6) Rare Book. In
addition to original manuscripts the
Library has a very large collection

Fig. 63. *Guide to Archives and Manuscripts in the United States.*
(Copyright: Yale Univ. Press.)

CONCLUSION

And so we reach the end of our quest for history. If we are students of the history of a particular country, we may find what we want in Chapter 4, always remembering that if it is not there a guide to a wider area (Chapter 2), or even one of the general guides (Chapter 1), is almost certain to give some help, and surely will be available, however remote we may be from large centres of population. If what we really want is not general history at all, but the history or biography of architecture or science, then Chapter 5 will give us some useful clues. If we are a prospective or even an active librarian or bookseller, then all the more formal chapters (the first four) will be of interest, though as new editions come racing from the presses we must be sure to correct our copy of this work if we use it as a textbook. We may derive a lot of help from studying the appearance of the page of the very famous bibliographies and other books reproduced in the sixty-three plates. If we simply want to read history as an art form, we need not go beyond the first half of Chapter 1. But if we really want to embark on producing some real history of our own, on however localized or obscure a subject, then assuredly Chapter 6, and the references there given, will interest us most. If this book has done no more than prove that history is not merely a list of kings, queens and presidents, but a very varied study, made up of innumerable facets, it will have achieved its purpose.

Index

Individual book titles, and subjects occurring very frequently (history, biography, bibliography, Great Britain, and their subdivisions, etc.), are omitted.